W9-BVX-678

"Sean Kelly is one of the great minds in this marketplace. What makes him unique, and what makes him what we consider to be one of the top industry resources, is his broad sense of understanding both the information technology issues as well as the business issues facing the corporate world. And his business model at the Data Warehouse Network much like ours at the Data Warehouse Institute, puts him in close contact with his Network associates — the real practitioners and implementors of data warehousing technologies and concepts. That interaction makes his understanding of data warehousing practical and real-world in nature."

Steven Crofts
Data Warehouse Institute

"An authoritative voice in the field of data warehousing."

David Heap
Director of Consulting Services, IBM

"Sean Kelly's experience shines through in his thorough analysis of data warehousing and provides the thought leadership necessary in understanding the need for the enterprise data warehouse strategy advocated by NR and enabled by the Teradata database solution."

Dan Harrington
Vice President, Data Warehouse Marketing,
NCR Corp

"A pioneering voice in the data warehouse market."

Jack Sweeney
President & CEO Intellidex Systems and
Co-chairperson of the Metadata Council

"Having worked closely with Sean in the development of a new methodological framework for data warehousing, he has demonstrated a rare appreciation of both the business-oriented and technology-oriented issues which impact on data warehouse design and development.

Earl Hadden
President & CEO
Hadden & Associates

"A thinker and communicator par excellence."

George Chapman
NCR Europe

"Sean Kelly clearly articulates the significant organizational and technical challenges faced in constructing successful data warehouse systems, including the significant dangers of data mart fragmentation. He strongly advocates the need for operationally robust large-scale server platforms, such as the IBM S/390, as the durable foundation of the next generation of enterprise data warehouse solutions."

Arthur Parker
S/390 General Manager
IBM Europe

"Turning corporate data into business information is a vital issue for any organisation wanting to maintain a competitive advantage. Sean Kelly is one of the industry's leading lights. This book is exactly what's needed to develop a business information strategy, with clear explanations of all the issues relating to the data warehousing process."

Alastair Sim
SAS Institute

Data Warehousing in Action

Sean Kelly

JOHN WILEY & SONS

Chichester • New York • Weinheim • Brisbane • Singapore • Toronto

Copyright © 1997 by John Wiley & Sons Ltd,
Baffins Lane, Chichester,
West Sussex PO19 1UD, England

National   01243 779777
International (+44) 1243 779777
e-mail (for orders and customer service enquiries): cs-books@wiley.co.uk
Visit our Home Page on http://www.wiley.co.uk
        or http://www.wiley.com

All rights reserved. No part of this publication may be reproduced, stored in a retrieval system, or transmitted, in any form or by any means, electronic, mechanical, photocopying, recording, scanning or otherwise, except under the terms of the Copyright, Designs and Patents Act 1988 or under the terms of a licence issued by the Copyright Licensing Agency, 90 Tottenham Court Road, London, UK W1P 9HE, without the permission in writing of the Publisher.

Other Wiley Editorial Offices

John Wiley & Sons, Inc., 605 Third Avenue,
New York, NY 10158-0012, USA

Wiley-VCH, Pappelallee 3,
D-69469 Weinheim, Germany

Jacaranda Wiley Ltd, 33 Park Road, Milton,
Queensland 4064, Australia

John Wiley & Sons (Asia) Pte Ltd, 2 Clementi Loop #02-01,
Jin Xing Distripark, Singapore 129809

John Wiley & Sons (Canada) Ltd, 22 Worcester Road,
Rexdale, Ontario M9W 1L1, Canada

Library of Congress Cataloging-in-Publication Data

Kelly, Sean, 1960–
    Data Warehousing in action / Sean Kelly.
        p. cm.
    Includes index.
    ISBN 0-471-96640-1 (paper)
    1. Industrial management—Data processing. 2. Decision support systems.
    3. Database management. 4. Business planning—Data Processing.
    I. Title.
    HD30.2.K456 1997
    658.4'03'00285—dc21   97-7326
                                                                              CIP

British Library Cataloguing in Publication Data

A catalogue record for this book is available from the British Library

ISBN 0-471-96640-1

Typeset in 12/14pt Times from authors' disks by Mayhew Typesetting, Rhayader, Powys
Printed and bound in Great Britain by Bookcraft Ltd, Midsomer Norton, Somerset

This book is printed on acid-free paper responsibly manufactured from sustainable forestation, for which at least two trees are planted for each one used for paper production.

Contents

CHAPTER 1
The Fundamentals of Data Warehousing   3

The impetus towards data warehousing — the inherent risks
of the data warehouse project — Converting data into
information — the data warehouse phenomenon — A potted
history of data warehousing — Definition of a data
warehouse — building the data warehouse — data
warehouse users — a data warehouse framework

CHAPTER 2
Achieving Competitive Advantage: A Review of Typical
Applications   32

Data warehouse applications — the marketing data
warehouse — the finance data warehouse — examples of
data warehouses in vertical industry sectors — conclusions

CHAPTER 3
Managing the Data Warehouse Project   61

Preparing for the data warehouse project — data
warehousing and the IT organisation — critical success

factors — a data warehouse methodology — causes of
failure — project principles — project sponsorship — project
team — the project charter

CHAPTER 4
The Data Warehouse Architecture   95

Data warehousing: an architectural challenge — essential
components of a data warehouse architecture — scoping the
data warehouse — assessing architectural risk — technical
architecture complexity — top-down strategy-driven
architectures — bottom-up opportunity-driven architectures
— the burden of infrastructure — stratification of data —
database design — the star schema — point solution data
marts

CHAPTER 5
Data Warehouse Technology   131

Parallel processing — massively parallel processing (MPP)
and symmetric multi-processing (SMP) contrasted —
parallel database engines — massively parallel processing
(MPP) and S/390 contrasted — selecting a relational
database management system — copy management
technology

CHAPTER 6
Metadata Management   157

Internal and external metadata — the challenge of metadata
management — sources of metadata — data stewardship —
data warehouse administration and maintenance — types of
metadata user — the metadata coalition and the metadata
interchange initiative

CHAPTER 7
Data Quality 177

The concept of data quality — business rules — customer
integration — discovering the extent of data pollution —
data quality roles and responsibilities — the data quality
project

**PART 3 — EXPLOITING THE DATA — THE DATA
WAREHOUSE APPLICATIONS** 197

CHAPTER 8
Data Access and Exploitation 199

Modeling the query domain — adding value to data —
accessing operational data — the successful query: an eight
stage process — Structured Query Language (SQL) — On-
line Analytical Processing (OLAP) — database abstraction
— query optimisation — query tool checklist — conclusions

CHAPTER 9
Data Mining 228

Data mining in context — an introduction to data mining —
statistical analysis — artificial intelligence — the business
case — approaching a data mining project — tool
capabilities

**PART 4 — LOOKING TO THE FUTURE — NEXT
GENERATION DATA WAREHOUSE** 245

CHAPTER 10
**Future Directions in the First Generation of Data
Warehousing** 247

Syndicated data — data visualization — Internet/intranets
— architecture — software agents — storage technology —

security — metadata management — multi-media — privacy and data protection — processing technology

Preface

Three years have now elapsed since writing *Data Warehousing —
the Route to Mass Customisation* (John Wiley & Sons, 1994).
During the course of that time the data warehousing concept has
been adopted by almost every major corporation globally. The
concept is now penetrating even medium and small-scale enterprises
and data warehousing has entered the mainstream of information
technology.

Now it is time to address two separate issues. The first is to
present to the reader a fully comprehensive account of how to
proceed with the data warehouse project in a clear step-by-step
fashion. This is a necessary endeavor because the data warehouse
project is unlike a conventional operational systems project and
because, as the concept grows in popularity, so too does the
confusion. The second objective of this book is to explore the shape
of the next generation of data warehousing. Trends are now
becoming visible in the mature data warehouse sites which indicate
that a new generation data warehouse architecture is being formed.

It has been inestimably easier to amass the material for this book
than for the first because so much more is now known about data
warehousing. In this regard I have to thank many colleagues,
clients, collaborators and friends internationally who continue to
maintain close contact with me. My knowledge of data warehousing has been enriched by their contribution. During the past
two years I have been deeply engrossed in research and publishing
activities in this field of information technology. These activities
have included regular contributions to *Data Warehouse Report* (a
journal I co-founded in 1995 which has provided a forum for
thought leadership in this field of information technology);

production of the monthly *Data Warehouse Technology Watch* on behalf of Cambridge Market Intelligence; facilitation of the very successful Think-Tanks for Data Warehouse Network subscribers; chairing international conferences on the topic of data warehousing and research projects for various vendor organizations. In addition, I have devoted a good deal of time, in the company of Tony Butler, to the origination of the Metis methodology for data warehouse planning, design, construction and operations. This book is informed by all of these activities and is, in a way, a consolidated compendium of all this effort.

I have a special vote of thanks to give to my close colleagues in the 'inner circle' of the Data Warehouse Network who have been instrumental in furthering the concept of information delivery through data warehousing. And so, I would like to apologize now to Chris Boon, Tony Butler, Rob Collins and Tony Sach for any blatant plagiarisms which I may be guilty of perpetrating. In addition I would like to reserve a special word of thanks, particularly with regard to the futures section, for the inspirational discussions with Professor Martin Healey of Technology Concepts, Dr Ciaran Murphy of University College Cork, Jack Sweeney of Bank of Boston and now President and CEO of Intellidex Systems, Geoff Horn of Barclays Bank and Earl Hadden of Hadden & Associates. Within the vendor community I wish to acknowledge the assistance of Alastair Sim and his colleagues at SAS Institute, David Heap and his colleagues at IBM and Dennison Chapman and his colleagues at NCR.

This book is organized into four separate sections in order to explore different aspects of data warehousing and in order to address the four distinctly different constituencies involved in the data warehouse project.

Part 1 of the book examines the motivations for data warehousing and is specifically tailored to the project sponsor and project manager of a data warehouse project. Part 2 explains the different infrastructural issues that need tackling in the data warehouse project and is addressed to the system architects and designers. Part 3 addresses the different technologies that may be employed to access and exploit the data in the data warehouse and is intended primarily for end-users of the data warehouse and for those tasked with constructing the applications. Part 4 is intended for information technology planners and strategists and is an attempt to put some shape and substance on the further evolution of the data warehouse concept.

Data warehousing is an idea rather than a system. The essence of the concept is that data is an as yet untapped and under-exploited resource and has boundless potential to transform the way that we transact business. But the manner in which the idea is implemented is continuing to change as the technological means of delivering the vision improves. In addition, the business vision of an information-intensive adaptable enterprise is constantly changing as the possibilities for data exploitation expand. Thus, while there is broad consensus about the value of the concept, the extent to which the concept is being subjected to continuous innovation brings with it a degree of risk. This book is intended to contribute to managing the inherent risk of a data warehouse project with practical advice on the common obstacles that are encountered.

Because data warehousing is, more than any other information systems initiative, a joint effort by business users and IT practitioners, this book has ranged freely across both the business and technology issues. While most of the material has been written with IT practitioners in mind, the message that data warehousing will fail unless there is a coherent business vision for data exploitation is constantly reinforced throughout the book.

Sean G. Kelly
Dublin, January 1997

Introduction

In the beginning, data warehousing was an idea which was firmly rooted in technology and which, for the most part, was of interest only to information technology professionals. Gradually it came to be of interest to the business users of information technology who began to see the possibilities for exploiting information as a competitive weapon. Now every citizen and consumer has been touched by the concept of data warehousing as organizations have moved rapidly to use the power of this concept to change the way that people interact with organizations. Retail customers are now armed with loyalty cards that capture huge volumes of data about their transactions, which is used to improve the quality, the value and, most crucially, the individual care that they are offered. Large anonymous utility companies have used this concept to segment their markets and offer customized services. Financial services organizations have integrated the data that they hold about their customers in order to devise new products. In short, the data warehouse has made the interaction between the service provider and the service user more intimate. The scope of applications that have been discovered has not been confined to marketing as every sphere of activity is enriched through the use of information. Information has become the fuel of a new industrial revolution that is moving us firmly away from the era of mass production to an era of mass customization.

The purpose of this book is not to explain why organizations should build data warehouses. It is assumed that the reader is already committed to the idea. It is, instead, directed at explaining how to build a data warehouse. For this purpose the book is divided into four parts. The first three parts are intended to offer a detailed guide to building a data warehouse with extensive use of checklists of definitions, guidelines, principles, activities and tasks. The fourth part of the book is primarily intended for the reader who is already reasonably familiar with data warehousing and is concerned with anticipating the next stages in the development of this concept. Therefore parts 1 to 3 may be said to be prescriptive. Part 4 is speculative, but it is submitted by the author as a reflection of his experience, practice, research and analysis.

This is undeniably a book about technology but it written for managers who are tasked with taking a strategic perspective of that technology. It used to be the case that information technology strategy was only a matter for technologists. That is no longer the case. Data warehousing is not essentially about technology but about the application of technology to business. Technology-enabled decision making, information delivery to the business and transforming business processes by exploiting technology opportunities are all matters that should equally concern business managers at all levels.

PART 1

PLANNING THE DATA WAREHOUSE

1

The Fundamentals of Data Warehousing

'There is one thing more powerful than all of the armies in the world, and that is an idea whose time has come.'
— Victor Hugo

THE IMPETUS TOWARDS DATA WAREHOUSING

In the modern era of increasingly intense competition, globalization and business complexity there is an ever increasing appetite by enterprises for information. Information is the fuel of the new industrial revolution in service industries and is transforming the way in which consumers interact with suppliers. The pervasive use of credit cards, loyalty cards and smart cards, allied to a phenomenal increase in the diversification and customisation of products, has led to an exponential increase in data. But this has not been matched, in anything like the same measure, by a concomitant increase in use-able information. The real problem being encountered by business leaders is not a shortage of data but an abundance of it. Estimates vary, but a conservative assessment of the growth of data being stored electronically suggests that it is doubling every two years.

At this early stage in the book it is useful to elaborate on the distinction between data and information. *Data* is a term that is

Table 1.1   Data, information and knowledge defined

Concept	Definition
Knowledge	Knowledge is represented by information which is known and verified and which is institutionalized in any business process which can benefit from that knowledge. Knowledge is measured with reference to the extent to which it may be incorporated into an activity or process.
Information	Information is represented by facts that have a meaningful context (i.e. where the relationship between the facts can be understood) and which may be analyzed to support decision making. Information is measured with reference to its relevance and usefulness in any given situation where that information might to employed to inform an action or event.
Data	Data is represented by isolated facts concerning a subject or groups of subjects that are stored on fragmented systems and which are measured with reference to the accuracy and integrity of each individual item of data.

used to refer to facts that are captured and stored, but which are not necessarily useful because they usually lack any context. By contrast, *information* is useful because it has a context which allows the analyst to draw some conclusions. At a higher level than information there is *knowledge* which implies that the trends observed in the information are known and institutionalized by the enterprise and are embedded in the business processes of the enterprise.

Most organizations are still languishing at a primitive stage in this continuum and are grappling with the large volumes of data that are trapped in operational systems and which cannot easily be accessed or integrated to provide the context that would transform the data into useable information. For many organizations this is a frustrating problem and many tactical efforts have been made unsuccessfully during the past decade to address the problem. These have included attempts to standardise the data definitions using CASE (Computer Aided Software Engineering) tools, construct reports from individual legacy operational systems, extract data

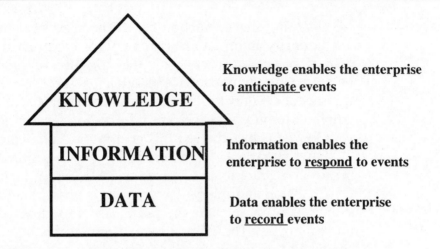

Figure 1.1 The value chain of data, information and knowledge

into EIS (Executive Information System) applications, duplicate the data in multiple business intelligence systems and the deployment of local data servers in the user community. Data warehousing is a strategic attempt to tackle the problem and is the only effort, thus far, that has resulted in any real benefits.

Only a very few organizations have developed their data warehouse infrastructure to such an extent that they are heading for the second transition — that from information to knowledge. But examples now exist where companies are using the information that has been processed in their data warehouses to enhance the functionality of their operational processes or to construct totally new processes based on knowledge. In effect, there is a value chain leading from data to information to knowledge and it is a journey which all enterprises are now embarked upon. This is illustrated in Figure 1.1.

Automation and Information

A well established distinction has now been firmly imprinted in the minds of information technology architects and strategists between systems dedicated to automation and systems dedicated to information. This distinction lies at the heart of data warehousing. Traditionally information systems were constructed to support a defined business process with the objective of reducing the cost of managing transactions and reducing the cycle times of those transactions. Many transaction-oriented systems had, admittedly, an ambition to offer management information for decision making but very few actually achieved this goal in any comprehensive fashion.

Many mainframe computers in the pre-data warehouse environment have traditionally mixed workloads of high performance OLTP, batch and query. However, it is unsatisfactory and fails to support any more than the most basic reporting requirements of the enterprise. The computer platform technology and database technology are not up to the challenge of a co-existence environment and will not be for the foreseeable future. Indeed, enterprises have become less and less enthusiastic about allowing access to operational transaction systems at all. Fears of runaway queries dominate the thoughts of system administrators of operational systems and the systems effect of a 50GB full table scan in an operational OLTP environment is guaranteed to be disastrous. Because of the very substantial system resources consumed by queries (a 50GB full-table scan is approximately 100,000 greater in terms of system resource consumption than one typical OLTP transaction), the prospect of having a co-existence of transaction-intensive and query-intensive processing is remote. A bank running an ATM network, a retail company running a POS network or a utility running a billing enquiry and payment system will always insist on the highest priority being awarded to the transaction processing.

In addition, the data structures that are constructed to optimize the performance of transaction processing are completely inconsistent with the optimum data schemas that would be implemented to optimize query processing. And there is always the insurmountable problem of data fragmentation, which will always fail to satisfy the demands of users for answers to simple business enquiries where the data that is required is spread across dozens of corporate operational systems. Therefore, there are three well established reasons why legacy transaction systems cannot offer any level of sophisticated support to decision makers.

Table 1.2 Deficincies of OLTP systems for query-processing

Lack of integration	Useful data and metadata is fragmented across multiple operational transaction systems, on PCs and available from external data providers.
Lack of efficiency	Data that is held on operational systems is stored according to physical structures that have been optimized for transaction performance rather than for query performance.
Lack of access	Because of technological constraints that apply to hardware and database products it is not possible tointroduce complex queries without severely impairing the performance of transactions.Because the query load is unpredictable there is no reliable mechanism to balance the processing load in a manner that allows reasonable access and accuracy for transaction and query users.

Operational systems are those systems which support the day-to-day running of the business and include such mission-critical systems as order-entry, payroll, billing, manufacturing, inventory, accounting and customer service. These systems have, for most enterprises, been developed over a long period and are concerned with supporting clearly defined business processes. Over time these systems have been subjected to redesign, amendment, enhancement and re-engineering. It would be a mistake to assume that these systems are tightly coupled with business processes, since most complete business processes traverse the rigid structural hierarchy of the organization while most operational systems are closely mapped on to the existing organizational structure.

It would also be a mistake to assume that all business processes have been automated — the only processes that have been auto-mated have been the 'hard' processes that are capable of being described in detail and where the tasks and activities are routine and repeatable. Business processes such as market analysis and corporate planning have never been adequately automated precisely because they are not amenable to being fully described in a tradi-tional requirements specification. What the data warehouse is intended to support is the many business processes that are based on analysis and decision-making rather than those processes that are based on transactions and events.

Historical divisions of labour between different management specialisms (e.g. engineering, accounting, sales, production) have contributed to this problem since the architectures of most corporate information systems look like multiple separate silos with no connection between them. Therefore data that is concerned with a subject such as 'customer' is hopelessly fragmented across these operational systems. An analyst can mine for data in one silo without having any idea what might exist in another silo of data that contains data that is equally valuable to the analysis. Attempting to take copies of data from multiple silos is a painstaking task and the integration of such data is rarely successful due to the many inconsistencies that are encountered.

There are many significant differences between traditional transaction-intensive operational systems and query-intensive data warehouse systems. Table 1.3 outlines the most obvious differences.

The Maturity of Data Warehousing

It is appropriate to take stock of how the data warehouse market has matured and changed in that period. Early writing on the topic of data warehousing focused a good deal on the changing culture of corporate decision making which reflected the need, that then existed, to justify the concept of data warehousing. As we reach the turn of the century the need for such justifications seem superfluous and quaintly out-of-date — the debate has shifted perceptibly from the Why? to the How?

Back in 1995 there were no adequate benchmark results to evaluate competing products. There was very little knowledge about the methods and techniques required to build a data warehouse. Terms like 'metadata', 'OLAP', 'star schemas', 'neural networks' and 'information catalogues' were only beginning to enter the lexicon of information technology. And there were only a very few vendors with a vision and strategy for data warehousing. All that has changed.

Table 1.3 The differences between operational systems and the data warehouse

	Data warehouse	Operational system
1 Usage	Query-intensive	Transaction-intensive
2 Users	Relatively small number	Relatively large number
3 Coverage	Current & historical data	Current data only
4 Integration	Data is integrated according to subject	Data is integrated according to narrow activity or business process
5 Data quality	Quality is defined in terms of consistency	Quality is normally defined in terms of integrity
6 Database	Data is refreshed or updated at intervals and is therefore non-volatile	Data is updated continuously and is therefore volatile
7 Model	Data is normally de-normalised and is modeled according to dimensions of a subject	Data is normally normalized and is modeled according to the needs of the transaction being supported
8 Scope	The data warehouse project is concerned with providing a decision-support infrastructure that is scaleable, extensible and flexible	Operational transaction systems are defined by the scope of the application which is fixed
9 Development	Data warehouses are constructed according to the principles of evolutionary and iterative development	OLTP systems are constructed rigorously having first captured a full set of requirements and then follows the well established waterfall development method
10 Sponsorship	The data warehouse requires a more complex sponsorship model because of the organizational breadth of the project	Operational systems tend to be sponsored by a clear process owner who has responsibilities which clearly map onto the organizational hierarchy

Every corporation of note has, by now, a data warehouse strategy; but the strategies are not all the same. Data warehouse aficionados have, in common with the adherents of all great concepts, fractured into different camps — the enterprise warehouse school of thought, the data marters, the data miners, the OLAP school and new modernizers who advocate an early re-integration of decision-support computing and operational processing. This is all healthy and a sign of vigorous and innovative progress in the marketplace. It is also, of necessity, confusing for users. But, as the market expands, and the services to support data warehousing matures, the level of clarity concerning which architectural and technological solution is suitable in each case is becoming clearer.

Another key indication of maturity in the data warehouse market has been the progress made in developing standards, especially in the work being done by the Metadata Coalition. The ability to exchange metadata easily between different software tools will immeasurably improve the ability of users to design and manage their data warehouse environments and will offer a degree of 'openness' that will serve to reduce the risk of failure. Whether the Metadata Coalition can go beyond their initial goal of agreeing a metadata exchange mechanism to define a standard metadata metamodel remains to be seen, but the early signs are reasonably encouraging. The development of the TPC-D benchmark test for queries also offers a baseline standard for database benchmarks, and it is considerably easier to evaluate platform and database performance for a query-intensive environment than it was two years ago.

New methodologies for designing query-intensive database application environments have also contributed to advancing the data warehouse concept along the maturity curve. There is a growing realization that traditional waterfall development techniques are inappropriate to building data warehouses, and advances in evolutionary methods has contributed significantly to managing the inherent risk involved in data warehousing.

But perhaps the most encouraging sign that data warehousing is a permanent part of the information technology landscape is the increasing awareness of applications and the profound changes being wrought on businesses because of the latent potential of data exploitation. In retailing, airlines, telecommunications and financial services the data warehouse is now at the centre of mission-critical applications on which the enterprise is dependent for its day-to-day operations.

1996 marked the year that data warehousing entered the mainstream as an undisputed part of the technological armory of the modern corporation. 1997 marks the beginnings of the second generation of data warehousing strategies which are beginning to be shaped by both the vendor community and by early adopters in the user community.

So by now it should be abundantly clear that data warehousing is not a fad or fashion. To be sure, the technologies employed to exploit data will change and it is quite possible that a new generation of data exploitation architectures may be called something different before long. But the essence — that data needs to be integrated and exploited for competitive advantage — is now a given.

THE INHERENT RISKS OF THE DATA WAREHOUSE PROJECT

Data warehousing has now moved out of the domain of large corporations to sweep the entire market as the key corporate information technology initiative of the decade. For most businesses, under pressure to provide decision makers with more and better information, the data warehouse has become a business imperative. Because of the success of the concept of data integration, the rapid wave of adoption by enterprises globally presents its own dangers — data warehousing is being presented as a 'cure-all' for the woes of end users who have been denied access to data. This will inevitably lead to confusion, misunderstanding, disappointment and frustration. As the number of data warehouse implementations grow, so too will the number of failures, with the attendant risk that the concept will be discredited. In the same way that previously hyped innovations like CASE, distributed computing and client-server failed to live up to expectations, data warehousing runs the risk of promising more than it can deliver. The message of this

Table 1.4   Common risks identified in data warehousing

	RISK	DESCRIPTION
1	Project management	Because of the complex political sensitivities involved in a pan-corporate data warehouse, the most common causesof failure relate to scoping the system and project sponsorship and management.
2	Infrastructure & operations	Because the data warehouse project is primarily about building a scalable, flexible, extensible architecture that the enterprise can leverage to build robust decision-support applications quickly, this aspect of the project is often underestimated.After the task of designing and constructing the data warehouse is completed, an additional risk is encountered in the form of administering the warehouse environment.The key to meeting this challenge lies in effective metadata replication and management throughout the entire architecture.
3	Applications	Because the real business benefits are delivered in the applications, and because user acceptance of the warehouse is determined by user reaction to the applications, this layer of the architecture should be defined and understood at the outset of the project.
4	Technology	The technology used to design, construct, use and maintain the data warehouse is evolving rapidly and the concept of the data warehouse architecture is also undergoing change. Data warehouse architects need to ensure that they are not 'blindsided' to these ongoing developments.

book is that the data warehouse has the potential to alter radically the way that business is conducted as we enter the next millenium — but it is a complex and challenging project for most enterprises and, at the time of writing, data warehouse skills and competencies are in short supply.

The inherent risk that attaches to the data warehouse project can be divided into four categories, as illustrated in Table 1.4. The task of managing these risks is explored in detail in later chapters.

CONVERTING DATA INTO INFORMATION

The phenomenon of data warehousing needs to be understood in terms of the dynamic of data exploitation. Businesses exploit data because they know that they can derive a competitive advantage from an increased awareness of trends and patterns in the data. Because everyone is doing the same thing there is a demand for more and more data to be made available in order to improve the richness of decision making.

Because the volume of data that is available is increasing and the opportunities for businesses to exploit data is becoming more visible, there has been an increasing demand from business users for access to more and more data. A natural tendency is for enterprises to unlock the data that is being made available to users without doing the necessary work to translate that data into information.

The more data that is provided increases the complexity of data analysis and increases the demands being made on the business analysts who exploit the data. Because data is being converted into information at a slower rate than the data is being made available, users are tending to have to become more and more expert about the data. This is creating a shortage of analysts sufficiently experienced to evaluate and exploit the data. In many instances the enterprise becomes dysfunctional in the face of data overload. With or without a data warehouse there is a danger of this dynamic becoming a vicious circle. The key to breaking this vicious circle lies in increasing the conversion rate of data to information in order to improve the productivity of knowledge workers in the enterprise.

Achieving this conversion can be a simple matter for some enterprises: all that is required is to transfer the existing operational data to an environment that is appropriate to query-intensive processing. For such enterprises the challenge is largely a technology one. But for most enterprises, the task of converting data into information will involve elaborate data transformations and the extensive use of external data sources.

The problem is not one of data scarcity. Data is available in abundance, but it is not always capable of being captured easily by the enterprise in a manner that makes it usable to the user. And the

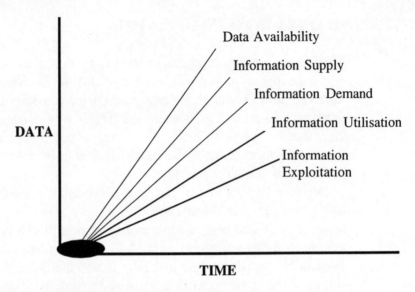

DATA

Data Availability

Information Supply

Information Demand

Information Utilisation

Information Exploitation

TIME

Figure 1.2 The data explosion

capacity of users to absorb data is limited. The time and intellectual resources of knowledgeworkers are limited and and the amount of data that they require and that they can effectively exploit is a sub-set of the data that is potentially available. The key question is, which sub-set? Even when a full enterprise data warehouse is implemented, there is a need to create sub-sets of information packaged for individual groups of users. An illustration of this general tendency — the explosion of data — is outlined in Figure 1.2.

Data is converted into information in a number of different ways. A selection of the more common means of conversion are listed in Table 1.5.

Delivering a data warehouse without any thought for the use of the data is a common cause of project failure and, for a project to be successful, the balance of concern must rest with what information is required rather than what data is available. Attempting to use a data warehouse which contains raw data but no information is analogous to steering a boat without a paddle. With some luck it is possible to reach your destination, but the outcome is uncertain and involves a lot of hard work. Certainly, there are many examples from various data warehouse projects of real

Table 1.5 Converting data into information

	Conversion Mechanism	Description
1	Summarization/ Aggregation	Data is pre-processed in order to build summarizations and aggregations of the data which can be associated with calendar periods, regions, departments or projects.
2	Derivation	Data elements can be can be combined and subject to calculations or other processing to derive new data or information.
3	Reports	Reports can be specified in respect of known requirements and produced at prescribed intervals.
4	Applications	Applications can be constructed to solve specific business problems, to identify specific trends or to calculate certain outcomes.
5	Artificial intelligence	Data mining with artificial intelligence tools has become a common means of converting datainto useable information by using data mining tools to effectively automate some of the data analysis activity.
6	Agents	Software agents are becoming increasingly common as a meansof highlighting certain significant trends or events and triggering alerts or other programs.

business benefits being derived from ad hoc queries being applied to large volumes of raw data. But reaping the rewards of data exploitation should not be based on an act of faith or on the serendipity of users.

The test of usefulness that is applied to information for the purposes of corporate decision-support is determined by the extent to which the information can be assimilated, understood and applied to a business problem. For most end-users the test of whether data is truly converted into information is determined by the following criteria:

1. Information should be available to end users who are enabled to quickly assimilate the semantics of the information (e.g. what the information means, what underlying business rules

inform the meaning, what source data were used to produce the information).

2. Comprehension of the data should be intuitive and should not require any special knowledge of the data structures or underlying database schema.

3. The information should, where appropriate, be oriented to teams and workgroups who share responsibility for a decision-making process.

4. Information should be capable of being accessed and analyzed from different perspectives and in association with different dimensions.

5. It should be possible to deconstruct the information easily into its constituent parts in order to drill down from the macro level of information to the micro level of detailed data.

THE DATA WAREHOUSE PHENOMENON

Data warehousing has become the key trend in corporate computing in the 1990s. That much is now unmistakable. But it would be a mistake to compare data warehousing to other recent trends like client-server computing, executive information systems, decision support systems, expert systems, personal computing or artificial intelligence. The difference is that all of these trends are IT innovations which have to do with the application of new technologies. Data warehousing is not a technology trend per se, and is primarily driven by the business environment. Data warehousing represents a response to the urgent demands of the business users who have, not for the first time, been stridently articulating an inchoate and poorly defined vision for an integrated corporate database. Data warehousing is a response to the frustration of decision makers and knowledge workers who know that the data that they are seeking to analyze is captured and stored somewhere in the organization but they are unable to access that data. For many non-technical managers it is an incomprehensible situation.

There are a variety of different business drivers for data warehousing, all of which have to do with the need to respond more and more quickly and flexibly to an increasingly turbulent and competitive business environment. These include a need to manage complex multinational organizations whose data is fragmented and dispersed. There is also the need to consolidate data from different organizations that have been amalgamated through merger or takeover. Strategic and financial management also want to integrate data because traditional financial control systems have proved wholly inadequate to meeting the needs of the business, especially in supporting the short-term responsiveness of the business.

But perhaps most of all, corporations are demanding access to integrated and enriched data because of the business tendency towards micro-segmentation in the marketplace that requires a massive database engine to be used as the means of defining and monitoring those segments. And now that data warehousing has been identified as a mainstream tendency in corporate computing, more and more industries (including government agencies, the healthcare industry, policing and scientific institutions) are perceiving the tremendous possibilities that are being presented by data warehousing.

Max D. Hopper, the senior vice-president for information systems at American Airlines, made the following prescient observation in 1986.

'For thirty years, much of our money and energy has focused on the process of building hardware, software, and networks powerful enough to generate useful data. That challenge is close to being solved; we have got our arms around the data gathering conundrum. The next stage, and the next arena for competitive differentiation, revolves around the intensification of analysis. Astute managers will shift their attention from *systems* to *information*.'

Data warehousing is, however, a costly project with extensive data storage and processing costs, development costs and user query tool and training costs. It is not likely to be cost-effective to duplicate all of the corporate data on the data warehouse and, therefore, it is necessary to incorporate gateways to the operational systems as well as providing a platform for the data that is populated from the operational systems. And because the task of integrating the data can, theoretically, be achieved fairly quickly, there is a pressure from the business to deliver some functionality within short timescales. The data warehouse project also suffers from the problem of scoping the extent to which it integrates the corporate data, and the boundaries placed on the project in the early stages will effectively define the architectural environment within which the data warehouse will be located.

One of the reasons why data warehousing has progressed so rapidly as a concept is that it meets the needs of both the business and the IT constituencies in the enterprise. The business need data that is integrated and available. They want a system that presents them with the big picture but one that can also reveal the details of the big picture. They want a system that can be used intuitively and that leverages the investment that has already been made in desktop tools and systems. For IT departments the data warehouse also makes sense because they are acutely aware of the extent of data inconsistency and fragmentation in the enterprise. And IT departments have also viewed with some unease the emergence of the departmental database server that is controlled by the end users and that is making increasing demands on the IT department for extract processing that tends to occur in an unco-ordinated manner across the enterprise.

The data warehouse provides an antidote to this perceived chaos. It provides a corporate filter for the enterprise data and can, therefore, be a single repository of a standard set of the corporate data. This is not to suggest that the data warehouse is a monolithic system that impedes the empowerment of end users in the sponsorship of decision-support systems. Experience demonstrates that most data warehouses spawn multiple data marts which are usually user controlled and are physically located on local area networks in the user environment. What is different is that these data marts all receive their data from a single source — the data warehouse — instead of receiving their data from a multiplicity of operational systems.

Another tendency that has driven the data warehousing phenomenon is the sheer volume of data that is now being captured and stored within companies. It is instructive to note that a single EPOS (electronic point of sale) terminal in a shop generates, on average, 1GB of data per annum. A few short years ago it was considered that the outer limits of relational database management technology was 30–40GB. Now retail companies talk confidently about building terabyte (1000 GB) data warehouses.

Once the initial business drivers became apparent, the technology market began to respond to the perceived need with a range of tools to assist in constructing a data warehouse architecture. This support from the vendor community became a secondary driver by making the task of constructing the data warehouse easier and more automated. A fully automated 'shrink-wrapped' data warehouse is still a few years away but the functional richness of data warehouse tools continues to improve steadily.

Most organizations will also have experienced the 'runaway query', where a user introduced a complex query onto a transaction systems during the course of the on-line day. As the query consumes more and more of the system resource the response times being experienced by the hundreds (or thousands) of on-line users steadily degrades. Eventually the query is aborted or the system crashs. Either outcome is highly unsatisfactory for the business. And many of the end-user tools which were capable of navigating through complex database structures are resource-hungry and very often are not tolerated at all by the IT department.

A POTTED HISTORY OF DATA WAREHOUSING

The very first data warehouses were build in the USA in the mid 1980s by large corporations in the retail, banking and telecommunications industries. By and large, these early innovators were intent on integrating data that had become hopelessly fragmented across these large complex organizations and the most common applications were (and still are) in the domain of marketing and sales. It was not until the late 1980s that the term 'data warehouse' began to be used to describe these systems. It was a term that was originated by W.H. Inmon (the 'father of data warehousing'), who was the first to publish papers on this topic. The concept was also popularised by the success database machines (early parallel processing computers with in-built databases) to handle these large data volumes. Also at about this time IBM published the first vendor commentary on the concept of the data warehouse.[1]

The data warehouse was a response to a number of failures in information technology. There was the failure of the relational database to live up to the expectation that it would provide a query engine for business users. There was the frustration of end-users with the failure of executive information systems (EIS) to provide drill-down capabilities from the high-level graphics that they displayed. There was the failure of databased marketing because of the poor quality and consistency of corporate data. There was the problem of hardware resource contention as important query activities always stood in line behind urgent transaction processing activities. This latter concern had given rise to the provision of 'reporting databases', which consisted of copies of the operational databases that were held, very often, on the production system platform.

At about this time there emerged the client-server model of computing, which was an extremely logical, elegant and attractive architecture but which was then spectacularly unstable and insecure as a transaction server. Many organizations were keen to apply the client-server principle to a database server in the less volatile environment of query processing. In addition, there was, by the late 1980s, a computer-literate cadre of managers and knowledge workers who wanted their PCs to be populated with data, which led to unprecedented and inefficient levels of extract processing. All of these frustrations with the information technology environment added up to support for the idea of a data warehouse.

At the same time that user frustration with the shortcomings of information technology was mounting inside the organization, there were dramatic changes afoot outside of the organization. Markets were changing dramatically as mass markets fragmented into micro-segments with special needs. Businesses had to cope with the special needs of many segments and the mass marketing, mass

---

[1] Devlin, B. And Murphy, P.T., "An architecture for a Business and Information System", *IBM Systems Journal*, 27, No.1, (1988).

advertising, 'once size fits all' style of business was coming to an end. the era of mass customization was heralded by industry leaders and this meant that unprecedented volumes of data needed to be captured, analyzed and processed. All points converged on one theme. And that theme was the data warehouse.

In these early stages only two vendors within the IT industry had an inkling of what was happening. One was the Teradata Corporation, a brash aggressive company that originated the database machine which could (as the company name testifies) handle a terabyte of data. Other vendors scoffed at the suggestion that enterprises, no matter how large, would ever maintain a terabyte of data on magnetic disk. But Teradata became, for five years in succession, one of the fastest growing company in the IT industry. It was the first industry-hardened massively parallel computer and it enjoyed a Fortune 500 client list. The second vendor that was conscious of the trend towards data warehousing was IBM who had published a framework for data management as early as 1987. 'Information Warehouse', quickly became an IBM trademark. What both IBM and Teradata then lacked was the range of specialized tools to extract, cleanse, map and load the data as well as repository, metadata and data access tools to exploit the data. From the early 1990s a plethora of new tool vendors emerged to fill this vacuum and the data warehouse market began to reach critical mass the USA. In the next two years the market in Europe is expected to reach a similar critical mass driven by the demand of the marketplace and the opportunities of the technology.

DEFINITION OF A DATA WAREHOUSE

There are a variety of different definitions of a data warehouse. These range from the technical description used by Bill Inmon (an integrated, non-volatile store of subject-oriented data) to more business oriented definitions like that used by the *Financial Times* to describe a data warehouse (a database modeled and fine-tuned for analysis and decision making). It is important when considering the data warehouse to understand that it an architecture and not an end in itself. The data warehouse architecture will comprise the overall structure of the data management, data communications, data processing and data presentation components of the system. The data warehouse does not deliver anything in isolation — it provides the basis for the enterprise to build decision-support applications. Thus, it is the act of exploiting the data that interests the business community more than the task of integrating the data.

A definition of a data warehouse is a single data store directed at the entire enterprise or at a subject-area of an enterprise. Here data can be integrated and cleansed in such a manner that it can be analyzed, manipulated, transformed, combined to discover correlations, trends and patterns that add value to the data. In technical terms, a data warehouse may be defined in terms of six key characteristics which differentiate the data warehouse from other database systems in the enterprise. The data in the data warehouse is:

1. *Separate* from the operational systems in the enterprise and populated by data from these systems.
2. *Available* entirely for the task of making data available to be interrogated by business users.
3. *Integrated* on the basis of a standard enterprise model.
4. *Time stamped* and associated with defined periods of time, i.e. calendar periods or fiscal reporting periods.
5. *Subject oriented*, most usually on the subject 'Customer'.
6. *Non-volatile*, to the extent that updates do not occur on an individual basis.
7. *Accessible* to users who have a limited knowledge of computer systems or data structures.

BUILDING THE DATA WAREHOUSE

A rapid application development (RAD) approach to the data warehouse project is clearly preferred to the traditional life-cycle approach. The RAD variation that the project should adopt is the iterative development approach where the prototype is not disposable, but forms the first iteration of the production system. The iterative development approach makes a number of assumptions. First it is assumed that is impossible to fully specify the system requirements accurately. Iterative development assumes that change will be constant and that requirements will be refined and altered as the project progresses. It is implicit in the success of the RAD approach that key high-level components (such as the warehouse architecture and data model) are reasonably stable, standard and well defined. These will provide a solid foundation to a system that needs to be fully flexible in terms of the data it holds and the applications that evolve.

A RAD application is always complete, but never finished — this is the essence of iterative development. The key to success in data warehousing lies in small, highly-focused, incremental deployments. The benefits of this approach include managed risk, continuous delivery of functionality, learning by doing and prioritizing resources. Each increment needs to be large enough to have a visible business impact, yet small enough to manage the risk. A common standard that is emerging in the industry is the three-month cycle, i.e. that a new iteration is initiated every three months. An iteration can be (a) additional data for the existing applications; or (b) additional applications for the existing data; or (c) new applications in respect of new data.

The business value associated with the first and second iterations of the project will reflect the discovery nature of the first iteration, where ad hoc query tools are usually deployed to access the integrated data. Experience suggests that a considerable review of the project direction follows on the discovery phase. Because the enterprise discovers things that were not previously knowable, there is an immediate and significant business benefit which is a 'one-off' experience. The knowledge gained, about the business and about the further requirements of the data warehouse, provides a basis to review the Project Charter and the Project Plan.

The second iteration (i.e. the development of the data mart layer) will be much more rigorous because more precise information becomes available to devise canned applications. The availability of canned applications will considerably widen the population of data warehouse users because much less knowledge is needed about the data or the data access toolsets.

DATA WAREHOUSE USERS

The data warehouse must serve the different needs of different kinds of corporate decision maker. To satisfy this requirement requires a rich data access layer that reflects these different requirements with different kinds of software tool. In general terms, three types of data warehouse user have come to be clearly defined. These are:

- *The operational user*. This type of user has a requirement for frequent reports that can easily be pre-defined. The needs of this type of user are generally satisfied through the development of canned reports and canned applications.
- *The power user*. This is the sophisticated user who has a range of PC skills and is capable of generating his/her own ad hoc queries. The needs of this user are satisfied through the provision of query tools to access the data and a comprehensive information catalogue describing the data.
- *The executive user*. The executive user will generally not have the time or the inclination to acquire the skills necessary for the interrogation of the database. And the executive user is likely to have ad hoc requirements which are not easily defined. The solution for this kind of user is to have either a query-desk, where professional personnel generate the SQL for the queries, or to have an EIS-type interface that allows the executive user to easily drill-down into the detail.

The use of artificial intelligence techniques to 'mine' the vast volumes of data in data warehouses has become an increasing feature of more mature data warehouse implementations. This level of interest in data mining tools is driven by the tangible business benefits that can be derived from identifying hidden correlations in data that unmask business opportunities directed at offering new services for hitherto unknown segments of the market. Because the term 'artificial intelligence' always tends to arouse technological mystique, it is necessary to identify what it means in the context of data mining and data visualization tools. At a technological level, data mining may be defined as 'the application of advanced techniques of rule induction to large sets of data with a view to identifying patterns in the data'. At a business level, data mining may be defined as 'scanning large volumes of data to glean useful business information'.

A common example of the type of applications which are being found for data mining tools is databased marketing applications, which are focused on selecting suitable prospects from millions of potential customers for a specific direct marketing or telesales campaign. Because the traditional response rate to mass mailings is rarely more than 2%, even reasonably modest improvements in the quality of targeting can realize massive benefits. Data mining is also employed to study customer behavior for frequent user analysis by airlines, utilities, telephone companies and retail shopping companies. The use of neural networks, in particular, has made possible enormously complex analyses to be performed on buying patterns of individual customers and makes possible the monitoring of micro-segments of a company customer base that is simply not possible with conventional software tools.

A DATA WAREHOUSE FRAMEWORK

The extensible nature of the architecture proposed in this book will accommodate a substantial degree of change and will facilitate the growth of the system in terms of data volumes and users as well as the growth in the number of applications supported by the data marts spawned by the central warehouse. This architecture will be underpinned by a model of the data which reflects the DSS environment and which will remain stable over time. Care should be exercised at the earliest stages of the project to ensure that the initial implementation of the physical database is not skewed towards a specific early requirement which is not representative of the evolving requirements. Flexibility of design means that the system must be responsive to its environment, which is the only true measure of success.

The first wave of applications spawned by the data warehouse are overwhelmingly decision support-oriented. These are the data marts that replicate within the data warehouse architecture, each serving the needs of a defined user population. The engines of these DSS data marts are likely to be relational, multidimensional or data mining databases. Now we are beginning to see the second wave of data warehouse applications. These are overwhelmingly operational in nature and require a re-thinking of the exclusively non-volatile data environment that has come to be seen as a core principle of the data warehouse. What is happening in practice is that operational data marts are emerging which contain a copy of a sub-set of the warehouse data which is updated via transaction-oriented applications. Gradually new operational functionality is added, not by enhancing the legacy systems, but by means of these operational data stores. In this way the data warehouse paradigm is evolving and mutating. This marks the mutation of the data warehouse architecture as enterprises transition from an industrial model of production to an informational model of service.

It is the task of the data warehouse to support the strategic decision-making activity in the enterprise. Having identified the right strategy, the corporate IT architecture must accommodate the means of implementing that strategy — this is the basis of the hybrid operational/DSS concept.

It should also be noted that the data warehouse may incorporate virtual elements where the user accesses transparent gateways to the operational systems, as well as accessing the physical data warehouse as well as accessing local data marts. Usually, all of this is transparent to the user and the data warehouse should be considered in terms of a data staging strategy where data is modeled at different levels, and physically stored at different stages for different purposes, within an overall framework or architecture. It is this architecture that the concept of the data warehouse reflects rather than any specific application.

FROM INFORMATION TO KNOWLEDGE

Just as the data warehouse marks an organization's entry into the age of information, the enterprise server is the technological engine to power the organization towards the age of cybernetics i.e. the adaptive enterprise. The transition from the primitive data-oriented organization to the more progressive information-oriented organization to the fully adaptive knowledge-based organization is illustrated in Figure 1.3. All cost justification for the data warehouse will be based on the added business value that will accrue to the enterprise as it evolves through each of the stages.

The data warehouse makes possible a new category of customer-oriented operational applications. These are a new kind of operational system directed at discounting, segmentation, databased marketing, product innovation and direct sales. These systems reside alongside the traditional operational systems (such as billing, service orders, financial applications) but can be delivered quickly to provide competitive advantage at the customer interface level.

The data warehouse has provided a platform for a new generation of application that are coming to be known as 'software agents'. Software agents are the software tools that recognize the patterns that they have been trained to identify. Software agents can come in many technological forms, but all are designed to function as 'detect and alert' triggers embedded in the data warehouse database. The task of detecting a pattern in the software is proper to decision support systems (i.e. the traditional domain of data warehousing) but the tasks of altering a business process in the enterprise is proper to the operational systems (i.e. the operational domain of transaction processing).

By and large these triggers are constructed on the basis of rule-based reasoning and the rules conform to threat or opportunity conditions that are already known to the enterprise. Increasingly, through the use of neural networks, genetic algorithms and other forms of artificial intelligence, enterprises are now able to identify significant patterns in the warehouse data that achieve even more exciting results than the traditional rule induction methods. The use of software agents generally signals a re-bundling of the decision

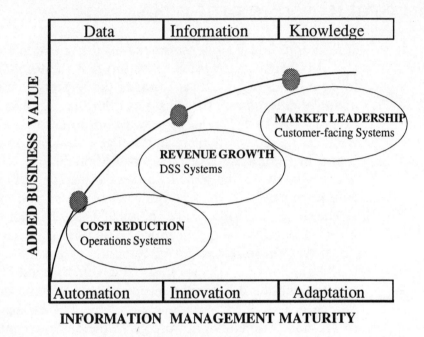

Data	Information	Knowledge

MARKET LEADERSHIP
Customer-facing Systems

REVENUE GROWTH
DSS Systems

COST REDUCTION
Operations Systems

ADDED BUSINESS VALUE

Automation	Innovation	Adaptation

INFORMATION MANAGEMENT MATURITY

Figure 1.3 The progression of the enterprise

support computing environment and the operational computing environment that were separated at the outset of the data warehousing trend.

CHARACTERISTICS OF DATA WAREHOUSING

Now that a reasonably significant amount of knowledge exists about the design, construction and implementation of data warehouses, some common lessons can be observed from this experience. The following ten characteristics of a data warehouse can be asserted from this experience.

- *Separation of operational and DSS computing*. The data warehouse assumes a high-level conceptual architecture that separates query-intensive decision support computing from transaction-intensive transaction processing. It also assumes that the data warehouse will represent a set of standard and agreed data definitions for the enterprise.

- *Extensible architecture.* There is no one data warehouse architecture that can be applied to every enterprise, but there is instead a continuum in the potential scope of the data warehouse that ranges from transparency software, to subject-area integrated data stores all the way to fully integrated pan-corporate data warehouses. As the system grows it will most likely incorporate a data mart layer with technological platforms that complement the enterprise warehouse.

- *Scaleable architecture.* The data warehouse will grow, through a number of iterations, from a relatively modest first prototype to potentially enormous volumes of data and number of users. Therefore, the ability to scale the hardware and software in small increments is important. This will usually require the adoption of multiprocessing hardware technology where processors can be added incrementally as the system grows.

- *Two-phase project planning.* The data warehouse project is divided into two separate and distinct phases. In the first phase the primary concern is with the capture of the data from the legacy systems and reaching consensus about the architectural principles ie. the infrastructure project. In the second phase, the concern shifts to the exploitation of the data using a suite of data access tools. The project manager should ensure that the separate and different skills required in the two phases are available.

- *Business-driven.* Successful data warehouses are business-driven and not technology-driven. (The most common cause of failure in the data warehouse project relates to a failure to take account of the phase two concerns in the phase one endeavour.) Under no circumstances should a project proceed beyond the pilot stage without clear business sponsorship.

- *Iterative approach.* The standard project planning methodology for the data warehouse will be based on an iterative or evolutionary approach. This will normally incorporate elements of rapid application development and the first iteration will usually result in a working prototype that is retained rather than discarded.

- *Quick delivery of benefits.* The data warehouse should deliver business benefits quickly. A 90-day standard has emerged as a outside limit to deliver the first iteration of a data warehouse implementation. This would include, at a minimum, a specified subject-area of the warehouse fully populated with integrated and cleansed data with a suite of ad hoc query tools deployed to end users.

- *80/20 Approach to design.* A struggle will usually occur in the data warehouse project between those who favor a 'bottom-up' approach and those who favour a 'top-down' approach. While best practice is not entirely clear in this area the most successful approach seems to be a top-down approach which sacrifices the usual rigor usually associated with data modeling in favour of establishing data consistency. The 80/20 rule applies to all design aspects of data warehousing and special care should be taken to avoid the analysis-paralysis trap.

- *Systems integration.* The data warehouse architecture will incorporate a wide range of components, ranging from data cleansing tools to extraction tools, metadata management tools, database management systems, hardware platforms, middleware and data access tools. On average a data warehouse solution will comprise eight different vendors. Therefore, care must be taken to ensure that all of the components work together.

- *Skills transfer.* The data warehouse is, for most organizations, a step into the unknown and the failure rate for data warehouse projects is located in the 30–50% range. Most projects will utilize specialist external assistance for architecture design and project methodology at the very least.

Responsibility for the success of the project will depend on the partnership of the vendor consortium, the user organization information systems department and the user organization business users. It is a complex systems integration project and requires the active participation of these three groups. But most of all success will depend on having a clear and agreed plan and having a formal data warehouse development process to implement that plan. The remainder of this book will address how to construct and implement such a plan.

2

Using the Data Warehouse to Achieve Competitive Advantage: A Review of Typical Applications

'Experience isn't interesting till it begins to repeat itself.'
— Elizabeth Bowen

For obvious reasons there has been a good deal of secrecy surrounding data warehouse applications and a resulting reluctance by organizations to speak openly about the applications that have been constructed to exploit the data in their data warehouses. Because the data warehouse is now perceived to be a key weapon in the corporate struggle for competitive dominance, many enterprises have implemented tight security measures to ensure that the applications that inform their corporate strategy are as confidential as the corporate strategy itself. This tendency has, to some extent, retarded the growth of data warehousing since many enterprises are well disposed to the idea of converting data into information but are at a loss to know what it is, precisely, that they are going to do with an integrated store of corporate data.

Some commentators have suggested that it is not possible at all to define the applications in advance of deploying the data warehouse and that the applications will only become visible after a period of data discovery. While it is true, in virtually every case that this author has encountered, that unexpected and innovative uses for the data warehouse do evolve from a process of ad hoc analysis of the data, proceeding on the basis that benefits will inevitably flow from having integrated data is a high risk strategy.

This chapter is devoted to examining the main business drivers of data warehousing, as well as the typical uses of a data warehouse in the different vertical industry sectors where data warehouses have been deployed, and draws on published material from a number of sources including data warehouse conferences in the USA and Europe where vendors or users have disclosed details of the projects with which they have been involved. It is clear from this analysis that some applications that are typical within a data warehouse environment are common to all types of enterprise and that others have a particular resonance within specific industries. One of the most exciting things about data warehousing is that new innovative uses for data are being discovered all the time, thus ensuring that the battle for competitive advantage is a continuous process, limited only by the creativity of talented people.

THE MARKETING DATA WAREHOUSE

Marketing is the last great frontier for information technology. Other functions in the enterprise (such as finance, logistics, billing, personnel management, sales order processing) have been rigorously defined for the purposes of automation. Until recently marketing has defied rigorous definition. It is said of marketing that, as a science, it ranks higher than astrology but considerably lower than physics! The data warehouse has become the indisputable vehicle for informating the marketing function. Surveys of data warehouse applications in Europe and in the US indicate that up to 70% of data warehouse investments are driven by the needs to exploit customer data for sales and market purposes.

Table 2.1   Moving from objects to subjects

Industry	Current process/information focus	Future process/ information focus
Retailing	Monitoring baskets	Servicing customers
Motor	Servicing cars	Servicing customers
Telecos	Provisioning subscribers	Servicing customers
Social Welfare	Paying claimants	Servicing customers
Insurance	Managing portfolios	Servicing customers
Banking	Managing accounts	Servicing customers
Airlines	Serving routes	Servicing customers
Hotels	Servicing rooms	Servicing customers
Healthcare	Maintaining patient records	Servicing customers

Focusing on the Customer

Most enterprises declare that the customer is king, but very few practice that philosophy, as a cursory examination of corporate information systems will attest. The entity 'customer' on most information systems occurs as a relation of a more dominant entity such as 'account'. Therefore most data is held about accounts, not about customers. Table 2.1 illustrates this point by selecting the key entity and processes about which the corporation keeps information.

Any evaluation of the primary business processes that have been computerized on operational systems across different industries displays an almost pathological aversion to acknowledging the existence of customers, in all of their diversity. It is for this reason that substantial data transformation has to occur in the data warehouse in order to reflect the value of the subject 'customer' from a multitude of operational systems which contain data about accounts. Because a customer can have many accounts in respect of many products and services and because customer behavior is reflected in many different systems (ranging from sales systems to payment systems) the real task is one of data integration.

In addition to transforming the data, the enterprise must also transform the culture of the organization in order to exploit customer information fully. For many corporations the data warehouse project forms part of a radical business process re-engineering effort as the corporate focus changes from products to customer. In many instances this culture change is accompanied by changes in the organizational structure which reflect this reorientation from product processes to customer processes.

In the pre-warehouse environment, marketing tends to be serviced by multiple operational systems that were never designed to support the marketing mission. Therefore, marketing analysts acquire data from sales order processing systems, billing systems, financial systems and logistics systems in an effort to glean information about customers and inventory. It is cumbersome, inefficient and, very often, simply not possible to answer simple business questions. The pre-warehouse environment tends to display the following characteristics:

1. Customer data is fragmented on multiple systems.
2. Customer data is not shared.
3. The data owners of customer data are not located in the marketing function.
4. There is no commonality of capture, storage and communication of customer data.
5. The customer does not have an individual identity or has multiple identities.
6. External (demographic or psychographic) data is normally absent.
7. Prospect data is not available.

Mass Customization

Mass customization is a concept that is rooted in the ethos of customer service. It is a direct response to the feeling of alienation felt by customers who respond to their anonymous status by behaving in a commercially promiscuous manner. After all, if the supplier exhibits ignorance of the customer's requirements how can they be aware of the customer's value. And what benefit does the customer gain from being loyal?

Mass customization is the most complete expression of a customer service ethos. Placed in juxtaposition with a culture of mass production, it represents a real business revolution in those economies of the world that are based on a consumer culture. Consumers are demanding recognition and, belatedly, commercial and government organizations are responding to that demand. Mass customization is an attempt to establish a real and informed dialogue with the customer and to demonstrate that the organization has a knowledge of the behavior of that customer over time. There is compelling evidence that companies which manage to transform their production and delivery processes to the new model of mass customization will enjoy significant competitive advantage in the marketplace. Central to the concept of mass customization is the micro-segmentation of markets down to fine levels of granularity in order to customize the product offerings to the multiple segments. Of course, this will not occur in one single stage — it is an iterative process. The process will commence with segmentation at a high-level and will progressively expand until the final objective of mass customization has been achieved — a market segment of *one* customer! The progression from mass market through niche markets to segmented markets and finally to the customized marketplace is illustrated in Figure 2.1

Traditional segmentation techniques have been based on demographic factors (e.g. age, sex, income). But demographics only indicates a customer's purchasing capacity; it offers no insight into the propensity of a customer to purchase a particular product. This requires psychographic profiling which captures lifestyle information about the customer. Therefore, the emerging basis for determining the classifications of customers will be a good deal more intangible and will focus on the behavior patterns of the customer. A customer may be observed to be compulsive (or conservative) in his/her consumption habits; may have established consumption trends based on special interests (e.g. gardening, motoring); may have displayed a particular pattern of annual income and expenditure; may have displayed a seasonal pattern of consumption; may have demonstrated a particular sequence of product consumption. Or groups of customers may have identified a pattern of consumption

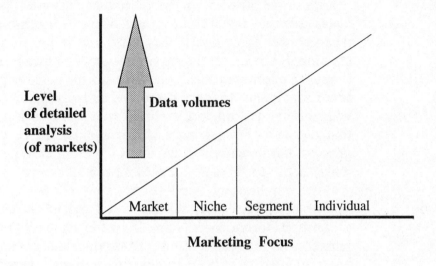

Figure 2.1 The tencency towards mass customization

which allows a new product to be designed around their needs. All of these judgments about the customer are now derived from the actual behavior of the customer rather than assumptions about how people in particular social categories might be expected to behave. The source of determining customer behavior patterns lies in integrating and observing data patterns. Current information systems are not designed to perform this function. The data warehouse is designed to specifically provide the information that allows for accurate matching of customers with products.

Customer Loyalty

Of course, once the data warehouse begins to deliver customer-oriented data to the enterprise, the first thing that is discovered is that all customers are different. Many enterprises discover that, where they thought that they were serving a mass market, they actually discover hundreds of micro-markets, each with different concerns, motivations and requirements.

Enterprises also learn more about customer behavior. It is instructive that research into the tendency for customers to 'churn' (i.e. change their allegiance from one supplier to another) is growing. Statistics on the loss of customers indicate that only 1% of losses are accounted for by the death of the customer; 99% of losses occur for reasons that are avoidable by the supplier and have to do with the nature and quality of the relationship. Studies also show that the cost of acquiring a new customer can be up to six times greater than the cost of retaining an existing customer. Therefore it makes sense to manage the customer relationship.

Data warehousing applications are used to address all of the aspects of the customer relationship, from more focused customer acquisition, to improved value from the established relationship to retention of that relationship. Traditional marketing and advertising techniques have been crude and are rarely amenable to accurate measurement. Typically, what retail chains are discovering is that approximately 30% of customers are generating value in the range 70–90%. The remaining 70% might account for a large volume of sales, but not of sales of products that are highly profitable to the enterprise. Knowing this is not enough to impact on profitability — the business needs to be able to identify which customers belong to the high-value segment. This requires that point-of-sales data is captured and transferred to a data warehouse for analysis. The mass advertising media is an expensive means of communicating a message to the 90% of customers that generate 10% of the enterprise's profit. Profit is increased far more by converting customers who are categorized as high value and promiscuous into loyal customers. In this manner information technology in general, and the data warehouse in particular, is beginning to replace mass media advertising as the key weapon of retail marketing strategies.

For many companies customer loyalty is a life-or-death issue — in the mobile telephone industry the individual churn rate can be as high as 25% per annum. There are a variety of different means of maximizing customer loyalty. Traditional methods are based on incentives based on pricing, the building of brand identity and service innovations based on social values and/or market research. None of these methods are targeted at individual customers. The data warehouse offers a new means of managing the customer relationship and strengthening customer loyalty. It is different because it builds an individual contract between the customer and the supplier and reinforces this contract through structural links with the customer (such as loyalty cards, multi-media kiosks, smart cards, segment membership or subscription membership). The quality of customer interaction with suppliers will be accelerated by the introduction of 'smart' card technology. A smart card consists of an 8-bit mucroprocessor and up to 512KB of memory embedded in a plastic body the size of a standard credit card. These cards can also incorporate a dedicated cryptography coprocessor for security. The deployment of smart card technology is more advanced in Europe than elsewhere. Card readers are expected to become a standard component of PC's and early applications will include online banking, payments transactions, electronic purses and remore access to data over the Internet.

Constructing an individual contract with the customer is a powerful means of providing recognition and reward to the customer for their loyalty. And because customers know that their behavior is being monitored by the supplier (and that the more business that they do with that supplier, the greater will be the recognition and reward) they are encouraged to alter their behavior in order to maximize the relationship to their own advantage.

A key aspect of ensuring customer loyalty relates to the servicing of the customer during the lifetime of the relationship. Financial services enterprises have learnt the rather obvious fact from data warehousing that customers' requirements change and mature as the customer matures. The services that are offered to students, to single professionals, to newly married couples, to parents and to retired people are all different. Spotting when a customer has made a transition in his/her lifestyles is crucially important to customising the service that is offered to the customer. It is particularly important since lifestyle transitions are a fragile time in the relationship between the customer and the supplier and is likely to be the moment that a customer will be tempted to change supplier. The challenge for the data warehouse architect is to decide how long to retain data about a customer in order to be able to fully model the customer's history and to be able to effectively identify a change in the pattern of a customer's consumption.

From this discovery comes the realization that the model of mass production is now defunct and that industry is entering an era of mass customization. And it is, by now, equally clear that the data warehouse is the technological means of bringing about this transition.

THE FINANCE DATA WAREHOUSE

If the marketing data warehouse is primarily concerned with strategy, the prime concern of the financial data warehouse is control. But while this is generally true it is not exclusively so. Many organizations are uncomfortable with the conventional role of accountancy as the corporate scorekeeper and are beginning to see the finance function as a player in the wider arena of corporate policy making. In a 1991 article in the *Harvard Business Review*, Robert Eccles observed the following about this tendency to redefine accounting:

> 'At the heart of this revolution lies a radical decision: to shift from treating financial figures as the foundation for performance measurement to treating them as one among a broader set of measures. The ranks of companies enlisting in this revolution are rising daily. Senior managers at one large, high tech manufacturer recently took direct responsibility for adding customer satisfaction, quality, market share and human resources to their formal measurement system. The impetus was their realization that the company's existing system, which was largely financial, undercut its strategy, which was focused on customer service.'

The core issue giving rise to the concerns being expressed in the above quotation relate to the fragmentation of corporate data in systems that satisfy only the narrow objectives of a particular function. Inevitably, this leads to inefficient and dysfunctional behavior on the part of the enterprise and gives rise to unnecessarily convoluted organizational structures.

The following list identifies the weaknesses that arise in financial systems:

Table 2.2 Deficiencies in financial accouting systems

Weaknesses in Financial Systems
1 Financial systems are designed to support only the requirements of financial reporting and not the operational requirements of the business
2 The definition and classification of financial data is inappropriate to the needs of business users
3 The time it takes to fully reconcile financial data is too long to be useful for managing the day-to-day business
4 Financial and non-financial data are not amenable to integration
5 Aggregations of data are stored at too high a level or in a manner that is not useful to the business
6 The manner in which financial data is stored bare no resemblance to business processes or business events
7 Financial data is stored in fiscal periods which are often not reconcilable with the calendar periods used by the business

Activity-based costing

Many efforts to introduce financial data warehouses are motivated by the desire to introduce activity-based costing to the enterprise. Activity-based costing involves measuring the total business process and presenting information in the context of the activities that make up that process. Traditional cost accounting measures what it costs to do a task. Activity-based costing also records the cost of not doing (e.g. the cost of machine downtime, the cost of reworking defective parts, the cost of duplicated effort or the cost of contingency).

To take a simple example, the time taken to write this book might be calculated to approximate 80 days effort — that is to say, that the cost of the writing project in mandays effort is equal to 80 days. This is the time that would be recorded on a timesheet and allocated to the project. It would, under traditional accounting practices, reflect the cost of the project. The problem with this figure is that it is only one figure of many that are involved in the production of the book and it is, in respect of the writing activity alone, misleading and inaccurate.

Common sense and experience demonstrates that the activity of researching, writing and correcting a manuscript cannot be completed within 80 days, even though that is the effort that is required. There are days that the author is idle due to computer downtime; days that interviews are cancelled or postponed; days that are unproductive because of external dependencies such as travel restrictions, the weather or Acts of God; there are days spent reworking or updating material because of technology changes that have occurred; there are days spent idle because a reviewer is late returning his or her comments; there are days engaged in research for the book that might have occurred anyway for other purposes; there are days spent in discussions with copy-editors; there are days spent in talking to typesetters and printers; there are days spent in discussion on contractual and royalty issues not directly concerned with the actual writing of the book and there are days spent in promoting and marketing the book. In addition there are days devoted by other persons (reviewers, editors, publicists) that are not recorded on the author's timesheet. And if the author was employed by the publisher to write full-time (which is not true of publishing but is more analogous to the position of workers in most commercial enterprises) he would have to be paid whether he was actually engaged on writing a book or not. So, what is the real cost associated with the activity and how do we unearth it from our conventional accounting systems?

The answer is that we don't because it is simply too complex to retrieve information which may be stored on a payroll system, an accounts payable system, an asset management system, a general ledger system and an accounts receivable system. Activity-based costing seeks to integrate the data around processes and activities in a way that these conventional financial systems cannot do.

To be successful, businesses need to have information about the total business process and measuring the total business process requires an integrated picture of the data. Activity-based costing integrates what was once several activities into one single analysis.

And, crucially, activity-based costing accepts that the cost of not doing is equal to, and sometimes exceeds, the cost of doing.

The following observation is made by the great management scientist, Peter Drucker, on the inadequacies of conventional accounting:

> 'Traditional cost accounting has not worked for service companies because it makes the wrong assumptions. Service companies must start with the assumption that there is only one cost: that of the total system. And it is a fixed cost over any given period of time'.[2]

DATA WAREHOUSING—SOME EXAMPLES

The following examples of data warehousing in different vertical industries is culled from various sources including case studies publicized by vendor organizations, material presented at conferences in Europe and the United States as well as the experience of this author in advising companies on the design and deployment of data warehouses. It is intended to provide the reader with a flavor of the applications as commonly encountered in the utilization of corporate data for competitive advantage.

Manufacturing

Hughes Aircraft Company defined their data fragmentation problem in business terms — it was difficult for their business units to negotiate discounts and leverage material requirements. The solution was to integrate data about suppliers and purchased commodities in a data warehouse. The system serves 400 key users and contained over 200 data elements. The business benefits that were cited by Hughes included strengthening supplier relationships, achieving volume discounts on material and a reduction in inventory costs.

---

[2] Peter F. Drucker, 'The Information Executives Truly Need', *Harvard Business Review*, January–February 1995.

Pripps is a Swedish drinks manufacturer and was facing increased competition from EU member states and needed to develop a decision support engine to improve the effectiveness of sales and marketing. The data warehouse comprised 28 gigabytes (GB) of data and was implemented on NonStop Himalaya systems and the Tandem NonStop SQL-MP database. The system averages 3,500 queries per month and allows the company to respond quickly to variances that arise between forecasted sales and actual sales so that the necessary decisions to increase or decrease manufacturing output can be made quickly. The system updates overnight with, on average, 100,000 order lines. One key technological factor for Pripps was the need to rebuild the database each month within a 24-hour time window.

Toyota Motor Sales in the US has embarked on a series of strategic data warehousing applications to improve auto management logistics and help reduce costs. Toyota Motor Sales handles the sale of more than one million vehicles per year.

The first major data warehouse application is designed to enable all levels of Toyota's headquarters staff to analyze the company's vehicle logistics supply chain with the aim of reducing costs and lead-time while managing a continuously changing environment. The data warehouse is expected to assist Toyota in gaining a better understanding of its geographically diverse operations and in determining key areas for adjustment. Toyota expects to be able to detect quickly whether new decision support processes are having the desired effect.

Toyota's data warehouse will draw from data stored in a variety of locations including, DB2, AS/400, and IMS databases, as well as from partner-profiled files. The data, updated nightly, consists of vehicle-related information such as processing costs, delivery costs, and lead-time data.

Using a variety of front-end tools, Toyota's business analysts can query the data warehouse to obtain information to help determine cost-saving opportunities. More than 100 users will access the data warehouse, which is expected to hold up to 27 months of data. Older data will be archived to optical storage for easy retrieval.

Glaxo Wellcome use relational OLAP technology in conjunction with their data warehouse to develop strategic analysis applications. Glaxo Wellcome has developed a strategic analysis application for its data warehouse to provide end users with analyses of sales, inventory, factory sales and prescription drugs. By analyzing the distribution cycle of pharmaceutical drugs along with historical and market data, the application aims to predict increased demand, and so enable Glaxo to respond better to consumer requirements and maximize the efficiency of the supply chain.

A principle objective of the application is to integrate multiple data sources to obtain a clear understanding of true demand versus supply chain anomalies. Glaxo hopes this will lead to elimination of the costs associated with having excess inventory or insufficient products to meet demand.

Prior to the availability of this new application, a number of key reports were being generated every month by running canned queries from different systems and pulling the results into spread-sheets. This was time-consuming and deprived users of ad hoc query analysis. Glaxo now reports that monthly reports are fully automated, have a short production time, are easy to understand, and provide users with extra analytical capabilities. A further benefit consists of Glaxo now having to maintain only one reporting system, whereas previously it had to maintain several.

Airlines

The airline industry is facing a period of industry consolidation which is characterized by growing liberalization and privatization of monopoly airline companies. Overcapacity on many international routes is leading to pressures to restructure and reduce costs. The prevailing trend is to engage in alliances and partnerships in order to survive in the intensifying competitive environment. All of these pressures amount to a need to have the capability to make strategic decisions faster, to optimize the operation of the company and to quickly identify threats and opportunities in the market-place.

The more common data warehouse applications in the airline industry have to do with achieving a better balance between supply and demand. The following list of typical applications represents the more common uses of data warehouse technology in the airline industry:

- Yield management
- Target marketing
- Customer segmentation
- Flight segmentation
- Profitability analysis (specifically route profitability)
- Fleet optimization
- Agency management
- Logistics management/spare parts analysis

Banking

Within the financial services industry the dominant theme is globalization. The ubiquitous use of credit cards and the global network of automatic bank teller (ATM) machines has presented both enormous challenges and enormous opportunities to the banking sector. There is a greater emphasis on distribution and service and the competitive pressures in banking are leading to a drastic reduction in the cost of delivering services to customers.

Many banks that have introduced data warehouses have discovered that they were losing money on up to half of their customers and that a disproportional percentage of profit was being generated by a relatively small number of customers. While the principle of Pareto analysis holds that many 80/20 rules are common to populations under investigation (e.g. 20% of stores items represent 80% of the value of inventory, 20% of suppliers supply 80% of parts) the data warehouse makes possible the discovery and ongoing monitoring of the high value customers where the attention of the enterprise should be focused. The banks are rapidly moving towards the concept of a market segment of one.

Canadian Imperial Bank of Commerce have consolidated their global transactional data in a data warehouse in order to create an aggregate financial portfolio. The goal of the data warehouse was to more effectively manage credit and market risk in their worldwide banking activities. The primary business benefit that was achieved related to improved risk management and a more secure financial position of the bank.

One bank with a successful data warehouse implementation — *Wells Fargo Bank* — developed a central data warehouse which was used as a staging area for integrated data that, in turn, populated multiple downstream data marts serving a variety of users. The system has 17 nightly feeds from transaction systems and the data warehouse applications are based, primarily, on marketing, customer management and operational reporting. Wells Fargo had acquired another bank (1st Interstate) and was committed to a programme of branch rationalization following the acquisition that the data warehouse. The warehouse applications were central to this effort and included applications focused on branch profitability analysis. These applications informed decisions on branch closures and measured how many customers would be lost as a result of a strategy of branch consolidation. They successfully managed to estimate the cost/benefit of each branch closure and implemented a much more sophisticated rationalization than would otherwise have been the case. The warehouse was also used to measure customer profitability and estimate the cost of acquisition of funds, which is a key influence on profitability. It is claimed on behalf on Wells Fargo that the data warehouse had a direct impact on the company's stock price — no higher measure of success can be imagined!

Another US bank — *Capital One* — has developed its entire strategy around data exploitation and has devoted more than 50 personnel to the data warehouse project. It is a complex data warehouse comprising 2 terabytes (TB) of stored data, relating to seven million accounts. The data warehouse targets new customers and the design of new products. Within a few weeks of launching a promotion campaign Capital One can detect whether the promotion has been successful in the markets, regions or segments where it is directed. This capability makes Capital One one of the most innovative, flexible and adaptable retail banks in North America and they have advanced the concept of mass customization to the stage where consideration is now being given to a policy of differential interest rates for different levels of risk. This kind of thinking is at the heart of the radical change in business practices that stems from data warehousing and information analysis.

Capital One, in common with many other banks at the leading edge of data warehousing, are asking fundamental questions about the business that they are in. If it is possible to offer different types of customer a different rate of interest based on the risk factor or the value factor, then it follows that the high cost of acquiring customers may be counter-productive to the enterprise if it is done crudely or done in the absence of sound intelligence about the value of those customers. Strategies that are based on optimizing customer value challenge other strategies, like the principle of critical mass and economies-of-scale where all potential customers are regarded as desirable and welcome. It is the start of a fundamental change in the business model.

First National Bank of Chicago (First Chicago) is a major US bank with over 30,000 employees and $120 billions in assets. The data warehouse project was driven by a clear vision in the finance department which focused on smart cost management which included planning for the future by the finance function as well as reporting on the past.

The system comprises 1.5TB of data on an IBM mainframe computer serving 400 users.

Four specific requirements were defined by First Chicago:

1. The need for consistent definition of terms and data.
2. The need for on-demand data availability.
3. The need for electronic delivery and accessibility.
4. The need for uniform synchronised reporting.

Eight different legacy systems were identified as sources for the data warehouse including the general ledger, the accounts payable, purchasing, fixed assets, travel and entertainment, financial reporting and management accounting. With a view to integrating the data from these different system First Chicago defined ten characteristics of the system that they required. These were:

1. Common key elements.
2. Consistent data definitions.
3. Rationalized data transformations.
4. Synchronized data capture.
5. End-user navigation using metadata.
6. Electronic information delivery.
7. Automated reconciliation of data.
8. Client-server/mainframe based system.
9. Flexible architecture.
10. Central source of financial details.

One of the impressive things about this project was the way in which the business expressed a clear vision to be implemented and the manner in which the project was tackled with a clear focus on the architecture and infrastructure that would be required.

First Chicago identified skills as an important issue for them and in the area of systems integration, client/server expertise and business subject-matter expertise were all in short supply. Therefore, considerable use was made of external experts who assisted in the project. The key enabler that was identified was the existence of a methodology and a clear process which allowed the project to stay focused on clear goals. Among the lessons learned were an acknowledgement that organizational and cultural issues need to addressed up front. In addition First Chicago offer the by now well accepted wisdom, that the project should be broken down into manageable chunks that can be completed within agreed time-frames.

The management of credit cards has become big business for many financial services institutions and data warehousing is now universally used to manage the large populations of customers. *First USA* is the third largest credit card issuer of Mastercards and Visa cards in the USA and has developed a central data warehouse with almost 2TB of data. The main business driver is to capture market-share from the competition and the strategy adopted by First USA is to identify the most profitable customers and to focus new services on these high-value segments. Because the data warehouse is central to the business mission, the operational environment of the data warehouse is based on fault tolerance and high availability.

This tendency for the data warehouse to be regarded as a mission-critical system is quickly overtaking the traditional view of the data warehouse as an ancillary system to the mission-critical operational systems in the enterprise.

Insurance

The insurance industry world-wide is facing a period when the range of insurance products is growing more complex and diverse and where the potential for cross-selling and up-selling insurance products was never so promising. Insurance companies are natural data warehouse users because one of the commonest uses of data is for risk assessment and risk management is the business of insurance companies.

One insurance company — *ITT Hartford* — with $100 billions in assets developed a data warehouse for the purpose of business profitability analysis. Interestingly, ITT Hartford eschewed the strategy of having an architected approach to data warehousing, on the grounds that the business was changing so fast that there was no time to develop and freeze an architectural design. The data warehouse is implemented via multiple subject-oriented data marts each of which uses multiple different data access tools that are chosen by the users.

The data warehouse at ITT Hartford had a significant impact on the corporate strategy pursued by the enterprise as a result of the business profitability analysis that was performed using the data. Prior to the data warehouse being implemented the enterprise was engaged in selling both annuities and health insurance and discovered, after the data warehouse was implemented, that the potential for cross-selling in both markets was insufficient to justify selling both products. In the end they decided to stay in the profitable annuity business and to withdraw from the market in health insurance. How much more strategic can a data warehouse be if it tells you what business to be in?

Another US insurance company — this time dedicated to the health insurance market — is *John Alden*, and they developed a data warehouse of 200 gigabytes of core data with 1 terabyte of disk storage. The focus of this warehouse was in risk analysis and new product design. In this case the profitability analysis persuaded them to focus on the health insurance market and the personal auto insurance market but not to expand into the annuities market.

For many insurance companies the risk that is involved in making changes to rates and products is a pressing concern and *Cornhill Insurance* in the UK wanted to establish a new rating method for the very competitive motor insurance market. The Cornhill data warehouse system uses SAS software to plan and monitor portfolios and to price products. The benefits reported by Cornhill included the business benefits of improved portfolio management and more responsive rating and pricing policies as well as the technical benefits of reducing the impact on the operational systems that was being caused by the need to generate reports.

At *General Accident Insurance*, a property and casualty insurance provider based in Philadelphia, a 100GB data warehouse has been implemented and it is expected to grow to one terabyte within three years. The warehouse will keep customer history for ten years and the main application of the systems is in household profiling, fraud detection and to satisfy the regulatory requirements of the company more accurately and quickly.

In the case of US medical insurer *BlueCross/BlueShield* the goal of their data warehouse was to establish a common information framework for measuring and managing business profitability. They consolidated data about members, medical service providers, claims and billing into a 200GB database. The benefits that were cited included a reduction in the cost of processing claims, the ability to analyze membership trends better and an improvement in their competitive positioning in the marketplace.

Utility

Southern California GAS Co. developed a databased marketing strategy, using a data warehouse, in response to the deregulation of the gas industry. Their primary concern was to reduce customer 'churn' by identifying customers who were likely to migrate to another supplier. They combined corporate data with external data from Equifax (credit data) and US Census records. The system allows them to identify customers who are more price-sensitive.

Southern California Edison is the second largest investor-owned electric utility provider in the United States and invested in an IBM S/390 Parallel Sysplex data warehouse solution to pinpoint information about its customer base of 4.3 milliom customers. More than 1,500 users access the data warehouse using a variety of decision-support tools including IBM Query Management Facility (QMF) and SAS System.For the first time customers with multiple locations can be treated as a single entity.

Distribution

McKesson Corp. is the largest US-based distributor of pharmaceuticals and other non-durable consumer goods. The data warehouse is scheduled to scale to one terabyte of data and supports over 200 users. It is implemented using Pyramid hardware and an Oracle database.

The background to this project lay in the cost control measures of the US health-care reforms that placed considerable pressure on margins. McKesson wanted to chart product-line and individual product sales, and item-by-item profit margins on a daily basis by region, by supplier and by customer. McKesson were able to make more informed supplier selections and move products more quickly — and more intelligently — to the areas of greatest demand. In addition, they were able to create a new revenue stream by selling their data analysis to both their suppliers and their retail customers.

The McKesson example is typical of the distribution and retail sectors since it leverages the improvements that are made possible in inventory management to enhance sales and profitability. In 1995 McKesson claimed that the data warehouse provided the company with a $2 million return on investment in the first year of operation.

Healthcare

HCIA was founded in 1985 and specializes exclusively in health care information and products in the US. HCIA have the largest health care database in the world, includes all Medicare patients and contains information on over 70% of all US patient discharges. HCIA have a client base of over 7,000 customers including health care providers, insurers, suppliers and employees. The database contains patient, clinical, financial, hospital and nursing home data and insurance data.

The HCIA system is implemented using Sun servers and an Informix database engine, contains 2TB of data and supports 200 users.

The main impulse to invest in a data warehouse was to increase the speed of access to data and to integrate more fully the data that was held on the legacy mainframe systems. The company felt that the cost of mainframe data storage as well as the lengthy time to access the data was an impediment to the business.

The data warehouse strategy was based on using a central data warehouse server on an Sun SMP platform with 600GB of data and four Sun server data marts each holding, on average, 100GB of data. HCIA used an Informix database to support their userbase of 200 users.

HCIA identified a number of lessons that were learned during the course of the project. These were:

1. Select a tangible business problem as a prototype.
2. Do not migrate all of the legacy data — focus on what users want.
3. Empower users to utilize the system.
4. Keep the data current.

HCIA encountered the usual hurdles, including the problem of data quality and data standardization. The surprises that HCIA discovered included the level of unanticipated growth, the level of innovation of users, the problem of tool obsolescence in the fast-changing data warehouse market and the difficulties surrounding security. But the main lesson learned by HCIA was that the main architectural issues should have been decided and defined at an earlier stage in the project and an acknowledgement that the architectural issues are more important than the tool issues.

Pharmaceuticals

In 1988 the *Bayer Corporation* surveyed their internal customers and discovered that one of the most common complaints was that it was difficult to access internal corporate data. This provided the genesis of the data warehouse project. Three teams were set up to progress the project. The Data Team was responsible for defining the data model and the data enhancement process and for creating a data warehouse directory. The Technical Infrastructure Team was responsible for RDBMS, hardware platform and middleware selection. The Customer Tools team was responsible for selecting and deploying the end-user tools that would be employed to exploit the data.

The Data Team made the following recommendations:

1. That business-area data administrators be appointed.
2. That company-wide subject-area databases be implemented.
3. That top-down divisional data architecture be implemented.
4. That bottom-up departmental data integration be implemented.
5. That data enhancement process software be acquired (Prism Solutions).
6. That a data warehouse directory be implemented (Prism Solutions).

The Technical Infrastructure Team made the following recommendations:

1. That a client/server approach be implemented.
2. That the Unix operating system be adopted.
3. That no hardware server vendor should be considered strategic.
4. That communications be based on the TCP/IP protocol.

The End-user Tools Team recommended:

1. That no access tools were determined to be strategic.
2. That a range of query and reporting tools would be supported.
3. That a range of decision-support tools would be supported.
4. That a range of EIS/OLAP tools would be supported.

The lessons learned by Bayer included the need to market the data warehouse to the corporation. Bayer produced an internal marketing brochure for the data warehouse and put in place a data warehouse roadshow which included demonstrations and presentations. They also modeled the data according to business processes in order to make the data warehouse meaningful to defined sets of users. A common dilemma experienced by data warehouse architects was reported by Bayer — demands by users to use the warehouse for operational purposes. In a way the warehouse was threatened with becoming a victim of its own success: if it is so good why can it not be used for everything!

Telecommunications

Telecommunications is one of the industries which has led the way in investment in data warehouses. At this stage virtually every large telecommunications company has deployed a data warehouse to monitor customer behavior and perform detailed traffic analysis. For most telecommunications companies the main driver has been to re-balance tariffs in line with costs and to improve asset utilization — i.e. to increase traffic throughput on the telephone network and to encourage usage of the network in the off-peak period.

Ameritech, one of the giant US telecommunications companies, with over 12 million customers and over $14 billion in revenues, selected Tandem as their data warehouse partner. The application is called 'Customer Usage Tracking Systems' and is directed at monitoring telephone call records to improve the effectiveness of marketing and the efficiency of the network. The Ameritech data warehouse is connected to the legacy systems on the corporate SNA network.

MCI Telecommunications, one of the US long-distance telephone companies, has developed a data warehouse with over 2TB of data. The main focus of MCI's warehouse is in the familiar telecommunications territory of relationship marketing. As well as standard applications, querying and reporting, MCI have employed advanced data mining techniques to analyze the data for patterns and trends.

Government

The application of data warehousing to the government sector is extremely diverse. Police forces, social services agencies, taxation authorities, census compilation boards, local authority services and planning functions all feature prominently in data warehousing. For obvious reasons, national intelligence agencies have also invested heavily in data warehousing; for equally obvious reasons, very little is known or published about these projects. The military sector have also invested heavily in data warehousing, and it has come to the attention of this author that naval services are more prominently represented in the rush to data warehousing than their colleagues in the airforces and land-based military. Both the Royal Navy in the U.K. and the US Navy have invested in sophisticated manpower and resource planning applications using data warehouse technology.

One well documented case study in government-sponsored data warehousing is the *City of Cologne* in Germany. Like all business managers, city administrators find themselves facing ever greater pressures in terms of price-performance analysis, budgeting, product orientation and quality management. The City of Cologne offers one thousand different services to 3 million customers and more than 23,000 city administrators are involved in meeting the needs of these customers. The data warehouse was conceived as the logical basis for the city's Strategic Information System, a distributed system aimed at reducing costs and enabling more flexible and accurate decision-making. Data standardization was one of the key challenges facing Cologne in their project and metadata management was central to their strategy. Like most businesses, different users required access to the same data but for very different purposes. For example, an analyst in the mayor's office has a different requirement from a city planner in the financial management department.

One of the novel features of the City of Cologne data warehouse is the aspiration to make the data available to the private sector where it could be used to inform the decision-making of commercial and other organizations in the city. The system is implemented on an Adabas database from Software AG and has EIS-type front-end functions. The overall verdict by the city administration is extremely positive. The warehouse has improved contact with citizens and businesses and provides important benefits for those living, working and visiting Cologne.

Retail

Pick 'n Pay — a South African food retail chain with 150 retail and wholesale outlets and 50,000 line items — faced the common problem that their existing system was incapable of answering simple questions about trends in the business. The first objective was to perform basket analysis using point-of-sale data in order to develop loyalty programmes. The second objective was to perform sales forecasting. With up to 200 users and a 200 GB database, linear scalability and price-performance were cited as the critical technology issues for their data warehouse architecture.

Bass Taverns is a UK chain of bars with an annual turnover of $1.5 billion at 2,700 outlets. Faced with regulatory changes by the UK Monopolies and Mergers Commission as well as increased competition and declining volumes of sales, Bass Taverns implemented an information technology strategy based on data warehousing. The traditional forms of stovepipe applications were no longer suitable to the business environment and couldn't answer simple business queries such as 'How did the sales of Caffrey Irish ale compare with the sales of Guinness on the last three Thursday nights on our city outlets?' The business found that it had a requirement to capture, integrate, transform, summarize and collate data in ways that satisfied the needs of those decision makers who were having to respond quickly to changing tastes and patterns of behavior in the marketplace.

The benefits of data warehousing enjoyed by Bass Taverns included a greatly improved understanding of customer needs; the negotiation of better deals from suppliers; a more accurate assessment of price elasticity; the optimization of profit margins and a better response to competitive threats. Because the data warehouse was central to the operation of the business, technical issues such as reliability, availability, backup and recovery were high on Bass Taverns' list of priorities.

CONCLUSIONS

The key to data warehouse success is that every company is different, has different strengths and weaknesses, has different threats and opportunities, has different organizational structures and cultures and has different core competencies. The goal of the data warehouse is to discover from the data of a particular enterprise what corporate strategy is right for *that* business. Most organizations that are operating without the support of a data warehouse are compelled to make strategic decisions on the basis of outdated planning processes, consultancy advice, surveys or intuition rather than on facts. The data warehouse reduces the risk of getting corporate strategy wrong because it presents the key decision makers with facts about key indicators such as profitability, risk and customer requirements.

Despite the commonality of purpose that may be observed in the utilization of data warehousing across industry boundaries, some applications are more prevalent in particular vertical industries and these are illustrated in the following table:

Table 2.3 Vertical industry applications

Telecommunications and utilities	• Customer segmentation • Asset management • Resource management
Retail	• Customer loyalty • Supply-chain integration • Market planning
Manufacturing and distribution	• Logistics management • Cost reduction
Financial services	• Risk management • Product design • Customer profitability assessment • Fraud/delinquency detection
Airlines	• Yield management • Route profitability assessment
Government	• Strategic planning • Manpower planning • Cost control

A particular fact that is inescapable in any analysis of the scale of investment in data warehousing is that there is a close correlation between the degree of competition in any given marketplace and the level of investment in data warehousing. Trends in deregulation, liberalization and privatization are all accompanied by intensive investment in data warehousing, which tends to support the thesis that data warehousing is, first and foremost, an investment in gaining competitive advantage. In those countries and markets where there is a high degree of monopoly enterprise, the level of investment in data warehousing is markedly lower than in economies and markets where competition is more intensive. An associated trend that is also observable is the tendency for all those players in a market to invest quickly in data warehousing as soon as one player in the marketplace deploys a data warehouse.

Many companies cite cost justification as an obstacle to making an investment in data warehousing. At an objective level, this is difficult to understand. The applications and benefits of data warehousing that have been outlined in this chapter illustrate, beyond reasonable doubt, that there are tangible measurable benefits and reasonably well-defined applications achieved across a broad spectrum of companies and industries. In the next chapter the process of sponsoring and managing a data warehouse project is outlined, including an exploration of the cost justification process.

3

Managing the Data Warehouse Project

'The means employed determine the nature of the ends produced.'
— *Aldous Huxley*

PREPARING FOR THE DATA WAREHOUSE PROJECT

Successful planning for the data warehouse project requires that a number of issues be addressed at the earliest stage in the project. These issues can be broadly divided into three separate categories — technology issues, organizational issues and skills issues. The technology issues are often addressed via a feasibility study that determines the technological feasibility of the project. And the issue of skills is best addressed by implementing a pilot project or data warehouse prototype that allows both the business and IS staff in the enterprise to grapple with the complexities and possibilities of this type of project. The organizational issues are best addressed by constructing a project charter that addresses the various non-technical aspects of the project that have to do with policies, sponsorship, objectives, expectations and risk. Experience tends to indicate that in the preparatory stage it is the organizational issues which dominate the data warehouse agenda and one of the key issues that needs to be explored is the organizational readiness of

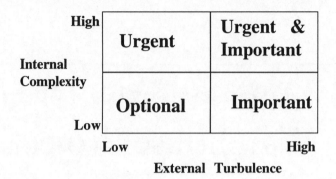

Figure 3.1   Data Warehouse Drivers

the enterprise for a data warehouse. As can be seen from the material in Chapter 2, competition, liberalization and economic turbulence are all key external factors which need to be assessed by the enterprise in seeking to establish the state of organizational readiness for data warehousing. The need for more sophisticated management of large volumes of data can be driven by external turbulence (the market) or by internal complexity (the business) and these factors are plotted in Figure 3.1. The external drivers will tend to force the pace of the data warehouse project while internal drivers will tend to require more architectural rigor. The real problem arises when both internal and external drivers are evident — inevitable tensions arise between the need for infrastructure (which is important) and the need for applications (which is urgent).

In addition to the objective measurable aspects of the enterprise, some account needs to be taken of the enterprise climate and culture. A common error in data warehousing is to see architectural design as essentially a specific business problem-driven activity, not recognizing that an architecture needs to be informed by some knowledge about how the enterprise functions. Successful data warehouse strategies are influenced by a range of non-technical considerations including the sophistication of the organization, the credibility and commitment of the project sponsor and the ability of the organization to embrace change. Some enterprises are

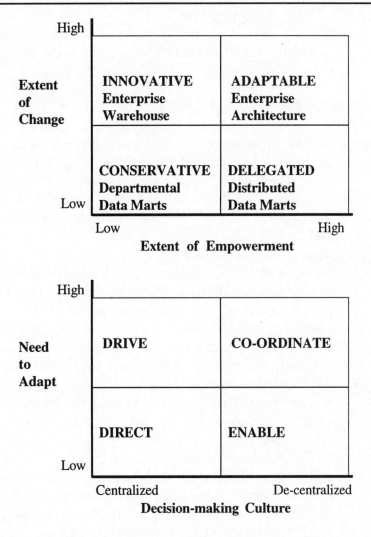

Figures 3.2 and 3.3 Corporate culture

command-led (with implications for highly centralized warehouse management; some are based on the idea of empowerment (with implications for semi-autonomous data marts); some are highly de-centralized (with implications for distributed processing), and some enterprises need to use the data warehouse to advance the process of radically re-engineering the enterprise in the face of significant change and massive external threats to survival. Figures 3.2 and 3.3

offer a high-level mapping tool to use to locate the type of enterprise which is hosting the data warehouse.

DATA WAREHOUSING AND THE IT ORGANIZATION

A number of trends are becoming evident in the scope and organization of corporate IT functions that bear examination in the context of data warehousing. These include apparently diverse tendencies like business modeling, standards and quality metrics, outsourcing, facilities management, consultant-assisted strategy and architecture projects and . . . data warehousing. There is a common thread uniting all of these tendencies into a common theme. That theme is the organizational integration of the business domain and the technology domain. What this means for the traditional corporate IT department is that the scope of their authority is being eroded on the one side by a more confident and computer-literate business community and on the other by the increasing role of external technology specialists and outsourcing contractors. Attempting to stem this tide is futile and the smart IT organization is forging a new role for itself with a focus on more strategic concerns such as architecture, innovation, quality management and risk management.

Those aspects of corporate computing that are being outsourced are usually concerned with facilities management and contract programming — in other words, the production and operations functions. Facilities management (usually) has the benefit of cost reduction. Contract programming and the use of package solutions have the benefit of improving the response time of IT to the needs of the business.

These tendencies reflect a need by corporate IT to respond in a faster and more flexible manner to an increasingly turbulent marketplace characterized by more intense competition and technology-led change. The downside of this approach is that the enterprise is exposed to the risk of a fragmented pattern of application development. Such fragmentation is difficult to avoid in an environment of separate and simultaneous development activities.

Many IT organizations have accepted the need for such a pragmatic approach to the delivery of systems to the business. The data warehouse, which integrates data from diverse sources, helps to ensure that strategic decision making continues to be supported, despite the tactical pattern of application development.

The recognition by corporate IT that data integration is realizable in the short-term while process integration is not, represents a considerably downscaled ambition by the IT organization. In the aftermath of a significant degree of disappointment with the lack of success of repository and CASE initiatives, corporate IT are concentrating at a more strategic level — tying together the complex web of corporate data.

If we turn our attention to the other dominant tendencies in corporate IT, we find that there is a renewed interest in business modeling, inspired in part by the present focus on business process re-engineering. This tendency, as well as the new concern with architecture standards, is also impelled by the need for a more responsive and flexible IT capability. Both of these activities are normally closely associated with the data warehouse and provides a good clue as to where responsibility for the data warehouse project actually rests — with the business users.

The present preoccupation with standards also reflects the need for the enterprise to control the risk represented by a complex web of systems. Increasingly, the end users are becoming more active in corporate computing as sponsors of projects that, like the data warehouse, have more to do with IT strategy than the role traditionally occupied by users.

In fact, much of the application development associated with data warehousing is effectively outsourced to software houses that build end-user applications using SQL or OLAP development environments. The key standards that the data warehouse imposes on the enterprise are architecture standards, corporate data standards and metadata standards.

What all of this means for the data warehouse project is reasonably clear. In the first instance, it is clear that, because the business users own the data, any strategy to integrate, store, or replicate this data is primarily a matter for the business. In the second instance, the technical task of constructing a data warehouse for the business is primarily concerned with creating a set of corporate technology standards for DSS computing. Words like 'framework', 'architecture' and 'infrastructure' are all widely used in the context of the data warehouse project to express (at a conceptual, logical and physical level). the need for a coherent IT strategy. The data warehouse is not widely seen as an application, but as the *means* of delivering applications.

The data warehouse standards are likely to be represented by a corporate IT architecture comprising clear standards for data extraction and transformation, data management and data access. The data warehouse will also create the need for a logical data model of the enterprise and a metadata repository for the enterprise. The data model will enable a common understanding of the key data entities in the enterprise. The metadata repository manager will control the transformation and movement of data in the enterprise. And the architectural standard defines how the data is physically moved around the enterprise.

In the future many of the operational activities will be outsourced to facilities management specialists. Application development will increasingly be dominated by packaged solutions. In the case of DSS applications it is possible that a significant portion may be outsourced by the business organization rather than the IT organization. Apart from expert contractors, on whom IT departments increasingly depend, the traditional IT function is also besieged by a more computer knowledgeable business organization. Undoubtedly, a residual IT organization will stay in place and the size of such a function will largely be determined by the need to protect and maintain mission-critical systems which were developed by the corporate IT function.

The essence of realizing competitive advantage through technology will be retained by the enterprise in a new function which will be concerned with strategy, planning and infrastructure. This strategy and planning function will be concerned with building a model of the business which can be mapped on to a coherent architecture which will also be created by this group. It will be the task of this group to oversee all strategic planning and systems development, as well as addressing deficiencies in the existing infrastructure. Organization ownership for this function is likely to be divided between IT specialists and business specialists and the group is likely to be strongly supported by external consultants.

All data warehouse implementations have exhibited evidence of agonising standards setting, data cleansing, vendor-led systems integration, project structure, consultant-led architecture design, and business-led project sponsorship. Indeed, the new IT job title to have been created through data warehousing — Data Steward — signifies a more strategic than an operational role.

The dilemma for many data warehouse projects is that, while the proper place to start is with IT strategy and planning (in order to create a coherent framework within which applications can be quickly developed), the usual place that the data warehouse project starts is with an urgent requirement for a specific DSS application. Inevitably, this approach leads to a situation where the further development of applications is fragmented, inefficient and dysfunctional. The most common problem experienced in the mature data warehouse is the need to re-engineering the entire strategy because of a failure to take a corporate perspective with the early iterations.

The only meaningful step to take to ensure that a full account is taken of all of the implications of the data warehouse project is to employ a data warehouse-specific methodology which draws on experience of the range of considerations that impact on the success factors of this type of project. While sounding the usual warning about following methodologies slavishly, there is the distinct advantage that roles and responsibilities are clearly defined for the different parts of the organization. Methodological rigor is one of the most pressing requirements of data warehousing at this stage in the maturity of the concept.

CRITICAL SUCCESS FACTORS FOR DATA WAREHOUSING

Project Scope

Deciding on the scope of the data warehouse project is the shared responsibility of the project sponsor, the project manager and the

Table 3.1 List of critical success factors

	Critical Success Factor	Description
1	Information	The data warehouse should have the means of easily converting the mass of data into information and, ideally, as the system matures the ratio of data to information should be reduced considerably.
2	Ease of access	Access to the data warehouse should be enabled in a manner that is appropriate to the skills, preferences and requirements of the user community.
3	Data standards	The data warehouse should impose corporate standards on the enterprise with respect to data definitions, data quality, data access, data exploitation and data presentation.
4	Dedicated resource	The core data warehouse system resource needs to be dedicated exclusively to queries and DSS applications.
5	Adequate performance	The data warehouse technology components, applications and physical data schemas all should be directed at optimizing the performance of the system as a whole.
6	Corporate sponsorship	Because the data warehouse is a pan-corporate project there needs to be corporate approval and understanding of the project at the highest level.
7	Operationally stable	The data warehouse that is deployed needs to be stable and safe from the points of view of performance, availability, security and metadata management of the environment.
8	Agreed infrastructure	The data warehouse should have a distinct and agreed infrastructure to manage decision-support computing that is separate from the operational systems.
9	New user culture	Because the data warehouse tends to precipitate new business processes that could not otherwise exist, users need to change their business culture to be fully aligned with the possibilities of data warehouse technology.
10	Source data	The most obvious factor that is critical to the success of a data warehouse project is that the data needed for the warehouse exists. Care should be taken to ensure that the data required as the raw material for the business information required by users can be sourced inside and outside the enterprise.

project architect. It is undoubtedly the most difficult decision to be made in relation to the overall success of the project. It is critical to the success of the project that the scope is defined correctly. It is instructive, in discussing the question of scope to consider it in terms of both positive and negative outcomes. A scope that exceeds what is achievable will doom the project. Equally a scope that fails to encompass data integration on a wide scale is going to fail to deliver any strategic breakthrough for the enterprise. Therefore, it is instructive to assess the scope initially in terms of a positive and negative scale which illustrates the acceptable range of options. These can be then be narrowed down with reference to a prioritized list of the business goals and objectives.

Key Issues for Users

For most users the data warehouse seems like a good idea in theory but appears to be risky in reality. The key challenge for users, who have grown accustomed to the stove-piped nature of information technology development, is to be able to see the enterprise as a holistic entity rather than the more comfortable perspective of their own individual part of the enterprise. This challenge of being able to envision a pan-corporate system and to be able to exploit the possibilities of integrated data should not be underestimated. Apart from the Chief Executive there is no other single individual in most corporations who have a responsibility to the entire organization. Most managers have developed deeply entrenched and compart-mentalized perspectives of the work that they perform. The first task is to find an appropriate and acceptable sponsor for the project. The next task is for that sponsor to communicate the value of the data warehouse to the many different constituencies in the organization who can benefit from the system. In the early stages of the project most of the time and energy of the sponsor and the project manager should be devoted to communication. This is the only means of assuaging the fears and concerns that present obstacles to the progress of the data warehouse project. It is important to acknowledge that the fears and concerns (and the scepticism) of the user community are legitimate and need to be addressed. The simple message is — communicate, communicate, communicate. The following list of typical user concerns provide guidance to the more common issues that arise in data warehouse projects.

1. Concerns regarding security and confidentiality of the data.
2. Concerns regarding the ownership of the integrated store of data.
3. Concerns regarding legislation protecting data and public concerns over privacy.
4. Concerns regarding the risks associated with large information technology projects.
5. Concerns about the costs and benefits of the project.
6. Concerns about the pan-corporate scope of the project.
7. Concerns regarding the centralized nature of a data warehouse system.
8. Concerns about the definition of applications before the data is available to them to explore.
9. Concerns about the levels of data quality that they require.
10. Concerns about the level of response times for queries that they require.
11. Concerns about the aligning the data warehouse with corporate strategy.
12. Concerns about their lack of knowledge of emerging technologies for data exploitation.

The Project Team Culture

The data warehouse project team needs to adopt a way of thinking and acting that is substantially different from the manner in which traditional information systems development teams function. The need for this shift in attitude derives from the fact that the traditional role of the user — in defining systems requirements in a functional specification — is not appropriate to the data warehouse project. Therefore it will be necessary for the project team to be more aware of the business issues and more pro-active in helping users to arrive at their requirements. They must also realize that the requirements definition process in data warehousing is iterative and that the application designs will never be frozen in the way that operational systems requirements have a definite cut-off point. Therefore the main criteria for membership of a data warehouse project team is the adaptability of the individual.

For many people in the business of developing software this change will be difficult as it requires people to act out of their natural positions. It will also be uncomfortable for information systems personnel who have, traditionally, distanced themselves from the business aspects of systems on the grounds that it was their mission to develop systems that were defined by the business or to align the information systems with the business processes. In the context of data warehousing the real goal is, in many instances, to transform the business processes. This requires people that are part business specialists, part information technology specialists, part management consultants and part business process re-engineers. Many data warehouse projects fail at the point where the information systems personnel realize that the business users do not know what they really want and the business users realize that the information systems people are not equipped to assist them in finding out. The following is a simple checklist of attributes that should be sought in candidates for the data warehouse project.

1. Be strongly customer-oriented and be capable of demonstrating a sense of empathy with the business users at the early inchoate stage of the requirements-gathering process.
2. Be capable of adapting flexibly to changes that occur in the direction of the project.
3. Be capable of demonstrating good political skills, because of the degree of co-operation that is required with the rest of the information systems department (as well as with the business functions) if the project is to be successful.
4. Be capable of demonstrating good communications skills as all members of the team will have a strong role in reinforcing the strategy that underlies a data warehouse architecture as well as

acting in a constant public relations capacity to reinforce the benefits of the project.

5. Be capable of team work and close collaboration within a cross-functional environment where each individual bears a high degree of responsibility for his/her aspect of the project.

6. Be capable of working under pressure in an environment where the project plan contains critical path time dependencies that have the potential to cause considerable delay.

7. Be capable of taking an enterprise-wide perspective and being conscious of the potential of synergies between different applications of the warehouse.

8. Be capable of demonstrating excellent analytical skills and an ability to grasp, at a theoretical as well as a practical level, how the entire architecture interacts.

In short, the data warehouse team members need to be open-minded and creative rather than system-driven in their approach to the project. While the use of a data warehouse-specific methodology will help considerably in managing the risk inherent in the project, there is always in this kind of project a greater need for individual intelligence and initiative than is the case in more conventional projects that are more tightly bounded and specified.

Ensuring the Buy-in of Business Users

It is now accepted wisdom that user commitment to the concept of a data warehouse is critical to the success of the project. User commitment is something that has to be managed by the project team during the course of the project in order to ensure that enthusiasm does not flag, that expectations are managed and that useful applications are developed and deployed quickly in the early stages of the project. In addition, it will be necessary to publicize the data warehouse and its successes in order to maintain the momentum of the project. The following checklist contains a number of actions that should be given active consideration by the project manager and factored into the project plan.

1. The Prototype

An important aspect of the public relations campaign that needs to be managed is to develop and deploy a useable prototype warehouse prior to gaining commitment for a full implementation. This prototype should contain a modest set of integrated data and should offer the use some canned and ad hoc query options. For the purposes of the prototype, an application may be defined as a report, an ad hoc query tool (with a populated repository of metadata), a GUI application developed for a specific purpose and should include an example of data access from a desktop tool (such as a spreadsheet) that is in common use in the user community. The total number of applications that can be demonstrated should include at least five separate screen interfaces.

2. Documentation

Because the user is likely to be overwhelmed by the options available in the data warehouse environment, good documentation is an essential ingredient for success. Where possible, the documentation should be available in electronic form (ideally in a hypertext format) and should be capable of navigating the user around the system and the various query and application options that are available. This aspect will become more and more important as the project expands and the range of data exploitation tools and canned applications become more wide-ranging.

3. Metadata

Providing an information catalog for users is essential if they are to feel confident with the data that is available to them. The catalog should offer an easy-to-use interface and should simplify rather than confuse the definitions (and transformation rules) of the data.

4. Support

Users are going to need a reasonable level of support, especially in the early stages of the project. If the company has an Information Centre, with responsibility for end-user computing, then this is the natural home for the data warehouse support team. Bear in mind that many senior managers in the enterprise are not going to be active users of the warehouse data access tools and are going to require that reports and queries are run for them by the project team. Even the power users are going to require considerable hand-holding if they are to truly exploit the data warehouse environment. In addition to technical services there will be a need to provide consultancy to the business about what queries are likely to be useful and what tools to use to execute the different types of analysis.

5. Publicity

Whatever means is available to the enterprise should be utilized to publicise the data warehouse. Care should be taken at the launch of each new application to publicize what is on offer. Equally, when data is added to the warehouse (or when new aggregate tables are made available) the opportunity should be used to publicize the development. Indeed, a strategy based on successive releases should probably be considered in order to formalize the ongoing expansion and development of the system. But, most of all, publicity should be made to every single success of the warehouse. This is the real guarantee of growing the project and achieving the ongoing funding that will be required.

Summary of Data Warehouse Project Management Principles

Experience has demonstrated that there are a number of factors associated with successful data warehouse projects that are common across industries where data warehousing has been attempted. Table 3.2 lists the key principles that underlie a successful approach to data warehousing.

Because many data warehouse project fail (perhaps as many as half) to meet the expectations of the enterprise, and because a growing number of data warehouse projects have to be abandoned and recommenced, strong project management discipline is especially important. The distinguishing feature of a data warehouse project, compared to most other IT projects, is the architectural complexity of the project. Most other IT projects are clearly defined and the requirements are capable of being clearly specified. Even

Table 3.2   Key Principles

	Principle	Elaboration
1	Strategic focus	The data warehouse should be directed at supporting a known strategic objective of the enterprise.
2	Executive sponsorship	Because of the strategic focus and because the data for the data warehouse will span the corporate organization, sponsorship and support are needed at the most senior levels.
3	Goal and benefits-oriented approach	despite the fact that many of the benefits of data warehousing are unforeseen, the benefits should be expressed in general terms in order to provide clear goals for the project.
4	Communication	A successful data warehouse requires the input and co-operation of many people in the enterprise in many different functions.
5	Enterprise survey	The architecture for the data warehouse should be based on a high-level survey of the entire enterprise.
6	Application delivery	The first, and each successive, iteration of the data warehouse should be based on the deployment of clearly defined application functionality.
7	Iterative deployment	The deployment of each phase of the warehouse should be based on an integrative approach based on an evolutionary model of system development.
8	Opportunistic	The data warehouse project plan should be sufficiently flexible to detour in pursuit of business-oriented opportunities that arise during the course of the project.
9	Rapid deployment of first iteration	The first iteration should be focused on a high-value application of the data and should demonstrate the speed at which applications can be constructed and deployed.
10	Pragmatism	Successful projects rarely fall neatly into a top-down or bottom-up approach and tend to belong to the middle-out school of design that compromises potential with expediency.

where other IT systems are very complex, the complexity resides predominantly in the application functionality. This is not the case with the data warehouse project where the application functionality, while complex, is not always completely apparent at the outset of the project and is delivered in a modular fashion over a long period of time. The risk that is inherent in the data warehouse project is that the infrastructure that must be constructed during the early part of the project must be sufficiently flexible, scalable and extensible to accommodate these multiple applications. The data warehouse itself can be compared to the infrastructure of a large building — it must be capable of accommodating changes in the usage pattern of the building without being radically altered and it must, if it is a truly robust infrastructure, be capable of accommodating new uses for the building that cannot even be envisioned when the infrastructure is being constructed.

One of the most common issues to be encountered in the project is the politically sensitive issue of how to separate the project into discrete phases, each of which delivers sufficient functionality to the business to maintain the credibility of the project, but none of which is so ambitious as to endanger the stability of the project. The 'big-bang' approach is universally condemned as a method of delivering a data warehouse since the scale and scope of such an undertaking would be too complex to attempt in a single pass. When considering how to phase the project there are two alternative and competing approaches to be considered. The first approach may be referred to as *data-driven* and the second as *application-driven*. In the data-driven approach the enterprise makes data available to users in the hope that it will prove beneficial to the business. This approach is based on a belief that the application requirements for a data warehouse cannot be captured and that the structure of the data warehouse will only take shape over time after considerable experimentation by the users. This approach often fails because insufficient attention is paid to the business model and too much to the data model. In the application-driven approach the business model receives all of the attention and the concept of a single enterprise view of the data becomes clouded, as different applications are constructed according to the data requirements of that application only. To be truly successful a data warehouse project needs to incorporate elements of both approaches in a manner that minimizes the risk of failure.

The problem of balancing the long-term scope of the data ware-house (encompassing the entirety of corporate decision-support

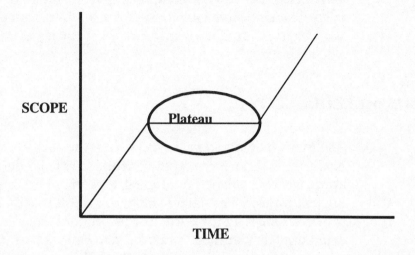

Figure 3.4 Failing to adequately maintain momentum

computing) and a short-term scope (that is sufficiently pragmatic to be delivered quickly and easily) represents a major challenge. The only practical resolution to this problem is to invest some time in an overall high-level model of the enterprise and all of its data and to proceed on the basis of small chunks of iterative development so that, in a piecemeal fashion, the apron of the entire enterprise is covered over time. The failure to adapt such an approach has led many enterprises to falter after commencing the data warehouse project and a surprisingly high number of projects stall after the first iteration is delivered, not because the first iteration was not successful, but because nobody had a real strategy to progress the project *beyond* the first iteration. Because the true value of data integration rises geometrically with the amount of data that is integrated, the value of isolated pockets of data integration is limited. In many instances such stalled projects are re-started from scratch, which is a demoralizing experience for those involved. This experience of stop/start progress is illustrated in Figure 3.4.

What the data warehouse project requires most of all is a new method of software engineering. Many attempts have been made to construct methods and techniques to support data warehouse design and construction. One comprehensive methodology — the Metis methodology (is available from the Data Warehouse Network. (See Web Page at http://www.dwn.com/dwn for more information).

METIS METHODOLOGY

The Metis methodological approach to the data warehouse project is distinct and different in a fundamental way from the methodological approach that might be adopted to a standard application development project. The data warehouse project is actually two separate projects. One is an infrastructure project; the other is concerned with exploiting the business value of the data. Many data warehouse projects that fail because of a lack of clarity about the shape of the project and a failure to distinguish between these different objectives. The data warehouse project does not follow the usual planning, analysis, design and construction phases of information systems development in the same way that a typical stand-alone application would follow, because it is not a stand alone application, it is a complex iterative infrastructure that is being constructed.

Elements and Objectives of the Metis Methodology

There are eight stages defined by the Metis methodology. The methodology framework separates the infrastructure build phase, which is concerned with the overall architectural strategy for the system, with the application development stage which represents the ongoing exploitation of the data. The preliminary stages are concerned with defining the environment and the later stages are concerned with exploiting the data and stabilising the administration environment.

The following stage breakdown of Metis provides a high-level overview of the different elements that need to be addressed in each stage.

1. **Organizational Readiness Assessment**
    This stage is concerned with assessing the key business drivers, the organizational culture, the legacy systems and data quality and the skills required.

2. **Business Strategy Definition**
    This stage is concerned with capturing the business vision for data exploitation and should result in a comprehensive business strategy model for this purpose.

3. **Data Warehouse Architecture Definition**
    This stage defines the logical architecture for the data warehouse i.e. it defines how the business strategy model is to be supported by information technology. And crucially, it defines the scope of the warehouse.

4. **Data Warehouse Infrastructure Design**
    During this stage the physical infrastructure components are assembled and integrated. Issues such as performance, metadata management, copy management, data access and systems integration are addressed.

5. **Design & Build**
    The physical design of the data warehouse database and the data staging strategy are completed during this stage and the first iteration of data is populated on to the target platform.

6. **Data Exploitation**
    By now it is possible to commence the deployment of the applications that are envisioned in the strategy model.

7. **Implementation**
    The implementation stage is concerned with the roll-out of the first applications and is directed at user training, support, publicity and assessing the business value achieved.

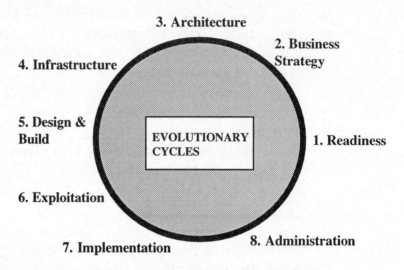

Figure 3.5   An overview of the evolutionary cycle of the Metis methodology

8.   *Administration & Operations*

This stage is concerned with ensuring that the environment is made more robust and rugged with regard to data security, operations and administration procedures (including archiving), system availability and performance tuning.

It is crucially important to understand these stages in the context of evolutionary development, since the data warehouse is a continuous programme of information management and exploitation. As is illustrated in Figure 3.5, the evolutionary cycle is a closed loop of continuous refinement. While all stages should reviewed with each succeeding cycle, the key infrastructure should be relatively stable requiring only slight refinement — with each successive cycle attention and effort should shift progressively from the infrastructure to the applications. In addition, it would be an error to assume that all of the stages are strictly sequential since many activities can occur in parallel. Indeed, as the project matures (i.e. after multiple cycles), it is common for many stages to be worked on simultaneously. A good methodology must also manage to provide routemaps for users, depending on the degree of urgency of the project (or the degree of design rigor required by the project) while managing to control risk.

REASONS FOR PROJECT FAILURE

It is instructive to examine the key reasons for data warehouse system failure that occur in real implementations. These fall broadly into two categories — the technical and the non-technical.

Technical

1. An inability to scale the data warehouse, with reference to the volume of data and/or the number of users.
2. An inability to extend the data warehouse infrastructure to accommodate additional application or technology modules.
3. An inability to effectively manage the exchange of metadata between the different tool components of the data warehouse architecture.
4. An inability to provide real business applications to users as a basis for delivering early 'hits' for the project.
5. An inability to deliver a flexible and robust data warehouse architecture that provides the basis for flexible application deployment.
6. Failure to take advantage of the discoveries made by the data warehouse because of the inflexibility or/and instability of the legacy systems.

Non Technical

1. Failure to engage the business users in a real commitment to the project.
2. Failure to provide a compelling cost/benefit analysis to the board.

3. Failure to specify the application requirements of the data warehouse.
4. Failure to change the organizational culture and make the enterprise information-aware.
5. Failure to take advantage of the discoveries made by the data warehouse because of organizational inertia.

What distinguishes the evolutionary methodologies from other conventional information engineering is that the evolutionary approach manages the interrelationship between the infrastructure project and the applications project while delivering a conctant trickle of benefits.

From a project management perspective, there are five characteristics of a data warehouse project which make it different from other IT investments. These are:

1. The challenge of selecting the appropriate data warehouse strategy and designing the data warehouse architecture that supports that strategy.
2. The challenge of presenting a cost justification for the data warehouse that takes account of the tangible and non-tangible benefits that accrue from this level of decision support processing.
3. The challenge of translating the business vision and the conceptual architecture for data warehouse into a workable technology architecture that delivers the vision expressed in the conceptual architecture.
4. The challenge of combining the infrastructural activities with the application development activities.
5. The challenge of clearly articulating and describing the applications that users require in order to truly exploit the business value of the data.
6. The challenge of managing the multiple iterations of the data warehouse project and supporting the evolutionary and cyclical development cycle that is peculiar to the data warehouse.

As has already been discussed, the traditional "waterfall" method of systems development has no place in the data warehouse project except in the most literal sense that systems analysis, software design and software construction still have to occur. The iterative process of system development is based on the assumption that the requirements for the system are subject to ongoing change and uncertainty, and where rapid functionality is required quickly in respect of a number of nominated priority applications. The iterative approach is based on the principle that there will be a number of successive releases of the data warehouse software and that modules of functionality will be delivered every 90 days. In this way the system can evolve towards a future vision of the enterprise. It is normally a very successful approach to take to the data warehouse project, especially in situations where some clarity exists concerning the immediate functionality that is required and where it is realized that this vision is incomplete and is subject to change. The objective is to deliver that early functionality without compromising the design of an overall enterprise data warehouse infrastructure. Of course, the infrastructure needs to be designed and assembled on the basis of a global architecture for the enterprise and this will take longer than 90 days. It is the deployment of additional applications that roll out in 90-day cycles.

Some approaches to data warehousing regard the infrastructure project and the application development projects as distinct phases with an elaborate modeling of the infrastructure initially. For some enterprises it may be necessary or desirable to take this approach, but it does run the risk of embarking on an intergalactic analysis phase which is unattractive to a project team under pressure to deliver results fast. These two phases are illustrated in Figures 3.6 and 3.7

Figure 3.7 illustrates the sequence of stages followed by the application development team.

PROJECT PRINCIPLES

It is especially useful to enshrine the broad thrust of the strategic framework for the data warehouse project in a set of project principles that are agreed by the enterprise. These principles should

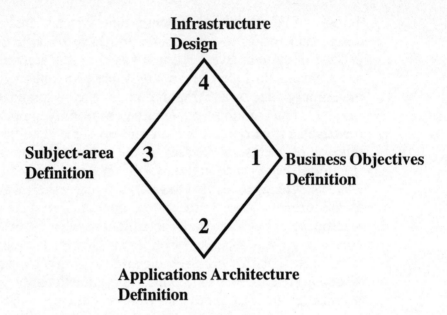

Figure 3.6   The sequence of iterative design

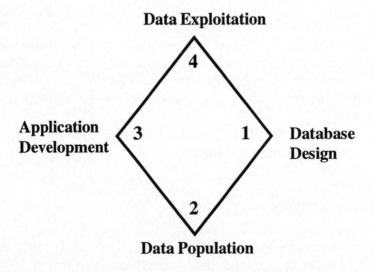

Figure 3.7   The sequence of iterative development

be set out at the very commencement of the project and should capture the underlying strategy for the project. Having principles is helpful in such an ambitious and long-term project as data warehousing. It must be acknowledged at the outset of the project that many elements of the data warehouse infrastructure will change, expand and evolve during the three-year intensive development period common to most projects. But the principles remain an enduring statement of the goals of the data warehouse as well as a high-level description of the architectural and technological solution. The principles should be the foundation stone of the data warehouse from which everything else follows. It is advisable not to record as principles low-level considerations relating to specific technology or specific applications. The principles should be located on a more abstract plane, which ensures that they can remain a reasonably permanent point of reference during the various crises that will inevitably occur during the lifetime of the project.

A typical data warehouse project would have no more than 20 project principles addressing the overall project. The principles should be formulated bearing in mind the full lifetime of the data warehouse system. Principles may relate to budgets, resources, applications, high-level infrastructure standards, project priorities or business goals. Examples of some candidate principles for an enterprise data warehouse system might be:

1. There will be only one gateway from DSS applications to legacy systems data and that gateway will be the enterprise data warehouse.
2. The data warehouse solution will be capable of scaling from 30 to 200 gigabytes of data within two years in respect of the existing enterprise.
3. Substantial new data warehouse functionality (expressed in additional data or/and additional applications) will be released every 90 calendar days.
4. The database implementation must be capable of porting to a different vendor hardware platform.
5. The data warehouse applications will extend the life of the (specified) legacy systems by two years.

6. Priority access to the data warehouse will be afforded to those working on customer relations/sales/marketing/corporate planning, etc.
7. The allocation of resources on the project will be a matter for the project sponsor to decide.
8. The data warehouse architecture needs to include provision for additional data that may arise due to a potential take-over in the next two years.

PROJECT SPONSORSHIP

The manner in which the data warehouse project is sponsored presents both threat and opportunity — done right it can save a considerable amount of difficulty: done wrong it can make the project unmanageable. Why the challenge of sponsoring the data warehouse project is greater than for other IT projects is fairly obvious. The data warehouse is a pan-corporate system that has to be managed outside of the existing organizational boundaries of the enterprise. If the data warehouse sponsor is, for example, the executive with responsibility for marketing, then it is highly unlikely that the pan-corporate creed will be adhered to and, over time, other functional managers will sponsor their own data warehouse systems leading to at least as much confusion about the data as existed before. At the other extreme is the danger of making the project too remote from the real business by sponsoring it only at a corporate level and not having real influence being exerted by those who are facing the day-today business challenges.

What is required for the data warehouse project is a multi-tier model of sponsorship with roles and responsibilities identified at different levels. At the top of this hierarchy is the overall sponsor of the project who should be a senior business manager without a functional role. The ideal candidate is the CEO and the strategic nature of the data warehouse projects does demand some input from the leader of the enterprise. The responsibilities of the corporate sponsor should reflect the position of that person in the enterprise and should normally be confined to the largely political task of agreeing and policing the project principles and authorizing the project budget. The demands on the time of the corporate sponsor are modest and front-loaded to the extend that interpreting the project principles should be a very occasional affair. At this business level of sponsorship the architectural and technological issues are very much in the background.

The next level of sponsorship probably has to reflect the real political and organizational boundaries that make up the enterprise. It would be neater to partition the project along elegant lines of demarcation, like business process, but this is an ambition that is rarely achieved. The more likely division of the project, at least initially, is along the departmental boundaries. As the project progresses and different functional fiefdoms realize that they are all exploiting the same data, then the project tends to become less focused on individual organizational units or individual legacy systems. The functional sponsors will provide the vision to define and prioritise the business prioritize within their own functions so that the resources of the project are best utilized in support of the key goals of the business. This level of sponsorship is really at the level of architecture.

Once the architecture for each module of the data warehouse is designed and deployed, it becomes necessary to define in more detail the actual application requirements of that business area. This is best done by the actual decision-makers and specialized knowledge workers in that business area. For every functional sponsor there are likely to be many application sponsors defining the manner in which they would like to be able to exploit the data.

PROJECT TEAM

The key ingredients in a data warehouse project team are provided in the following list:

1. The team should comprise a mix of business and information systems department personnel. The business users should be selected from the ranks of computer-literate 'power users' who will have a significant role to play in the development and deployment of applications.

2. The team should be independent of existing organizational structures and cultures and should be answerable only to the project sponsor. A clear reporting structure should be contained in the project charter detailing how progress is reported to the sponsor, the project manager, information systems management and the business.

3. The team should be led by a dedicated project leader who has overall responsibility for the management of the project plan, project deliverables and project timetable.

4. The design of the data warehouse architecture should be entrusted to a data warehouse architect who has experience of data warehousing. This person should be recruited externally where such a competency does not exist in the organization or the use of expert consultants should be considered. The remit of the data warehouse architect should extend to all subsidiary data marts that may be defined in the original architecture or which may evolve during the period of the project.

5. The data extraction and transformation should be the responsibility of a dedicated sub-team of people who have a high degree of familiarity with the legacy systems.

6. The development of the data warehouse applications should be assigned to a dedicated sub-team who have a high degree of competency in the area of end-user computing and who are familiar with the tools and platforms that are going to be utilized by the user community.

7. Consideration should be given at the outset of the project to the administrative and operations role to be played when the data warehouse is deployed. A data steward with overall responsibility for the management of the data and the metadata should be appointed for this purpose.

8. The team should be complemented from time to time by end user representatives in order to assess data quality, define the business rules associated with the source data, define the individual application requirements and to inform the data modeling activities. These persons have a very separate role from the 'power users' and are required for their knowledge of the business, not the technology.

9. The team should, where possible, recruit only persons who have a commitment to the data warehouse concept and who are willing to engage wholetime on the project for its full duration.
10. The team size should be kept relatively small to ensure tight integration of the various elements of the project. The maximum team size should not normally exceed ten persons, excluding technical support personnel.

PROJECT TEAM COMPOSITION

The project team composition for a data warehouse project needs to include a wide variety of skills. There are four essential technical competencies required in a data warehouse project team. These four divisions of the project team activities and specialist skills are:

1. *Data acquisition.* The collection of data from the legacy operational systems requires expertise based on a knowledge of the legacy systems and the technical environments in which these legacy systems are located. Data acquisition represents the technological bridge between the source data and the data warehouse and is a key component of the infrastructure.
2. *Data modelling.* This expertise is required to architect the business model and the data model of the enterprise (or that part of the enterprise involved in the project). Skills should include business modeling, entity relationship modelling and multi-dimensional modeling.
3. *Data management.* Data management is concerned with the manner in which the data is structured and the manner in which the data warehouse environment is managed and administered. Important functions such as security, metadata management, performance management and data integrity will normally be performed by this group.
4. *Application development.* Data warehouse applications are directed at exploiting the data in the data warehouse. Most

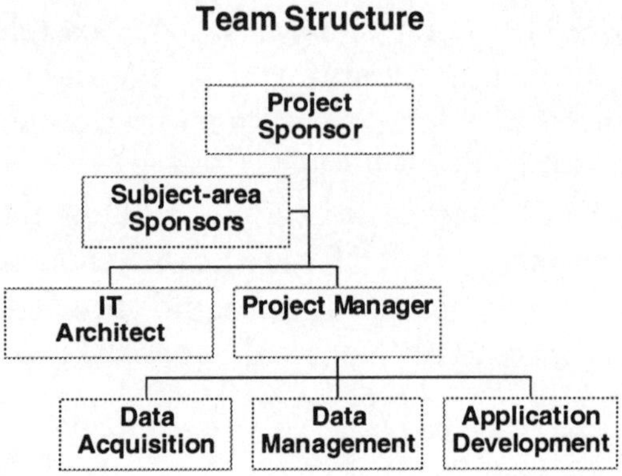

Team Structure

Figure 3.8   The Project Team Structure

data warehouse applications will be based on offering a structured queries or graphical applications that function as query builders. Data exploitation encompasses all those software tools that available for the purpose.

The size of data warehouse project teams vary according to the scale of the project, but in a typical large enterprise data warehouse project there are usually eight to ten persons on the project team. Obviously, not all of the skills are required at the same time and the data modelers will have completed their task long before the application developers are needed.

The project team and sponsorship structure is illustrated in Figure 3.8.

THE PROJECT CHARTER

After the organizational readiness has been assessed and the business drivers identified and agreed, the enterprise should proceed to agree a project charter setting out the objectives of the project, policy issues relating to the project and identifying the scope of the project. The project charter represents an agreement between all those who are party to the project. At the outset of the project the only parties to the project are likely to be some business users and the IS department. As the project progresses other business users, vendors and suppliers, consultancy partners and software contractors may join the project and they will need to have their roles incorporated into the charter. The charter underscores the project plan and is a statement of all of the underlying assumptions of the project. The charter is a written agreement and would normally be supported by a project plan Gannt chart or Pert chart.

Any organizational or technological disputes that may break out during the course of the project will have a reference point in the project charter and should be resolved by adapting or confirming the contents of the charter. The project charter should be reviewed at the commencement of each stage of the project in order to measure progress and identify any changes that occur in the underlying assumptions (and the impact of those changes).

The fundamental purpose of a project charter is to manage the change process. Where objectives, priorities, resources or timescales change, then the process of amending the project charter should illustrate clearly the costs, risks and implications of the change that has occurred.

A typical project charter would include information under the following headings:

- Project roles and responsibilities.
- Budgets.
- Resources.
- High-level timescales.
- Project management methodology.
- Statement of project objectives.
- Statement of project principles.
- Statement of project scope.
- Risk management process.
- Change management process.

PART 2

INTEGRATING THE DATA —
THE DATA WAREHOUSE
INFRASTRUCTURE

4

The Data Warehouse Architecture

'Architecture, of all the arts, is the one that acts the most slowly, but the most surely, on the soul.'
— *Ernest Dimnet*

DATA WAREHOUSING — AN ARCHITECTURAL CHALLENGE

Since the beginning of the data warehousing phenomenon there has been a simmering background debate about the nature of data warehousing that has still to be adequately resolved. This debate centres around the question of whether a data warehouse should be data-centred or application-centred.

The advocates of the data-centred approach have contended, with cogent arguments, that it is impossible to anticipate precisely the benefits that will accrue from a data warehouse and that the data warehouse project is simply a corporate imperative for any enterprise that is serious about decision-support, customer care or strategic planning. The essence of the data-centric thesis is that information is the lifeblood of the modern adaptable enterprise and that the project is justified simply on that precept. According to this view the data warehouse does not need cost justification or application definition.

The advocates of the application-centric approach take the perspective that a tangible measurable business need is a necessary prerequisite for any IT investment and that the first iteration of a data warehouse should be a pre-defined decision-support application. In reality, of course, the actual decisions taken by implementers have not been as clear cut as the stark options presented above, but any cursory analysis of a corporate data warehouse strategy does find that each project has substantially followed one or other of these strategies.

There are now emerging in the data warehouse marketplace two distinct camps around vendors who are, in fact, making quite contradictory assertions about the nature of data warehousing. Because vendors are now offering development frameworks (which are a good deal short of anything that can be honestly be called a methodology) which are based on utterly different premises, there is a real danger that users will embark on a first iteration of the data warehouse project on the basis of a strategy that is inappropriate to their needs and will guide them to a destination that they had not intended. Experience shows that some enterprises that require an enterprise architecture have ended up with disparate decision-support databases and some enterprises that had a pressing business need for a simple application have embarked on a complex enterprise data architecture initiative. The real danger about this situation is that the debate is not out in the open and, as a consequence, users are being confused and misled.

Proponents of both approaches cloak their respective positions with the language of pragmatism. The data-centric camp point to the need to capture large volumes of atomic level data about the entire enterprise and deride the fragmented approach of the application-centred advocates. The application-centred camp point to the enormous cost and risk inherent in investing blindly in a large ill-defined system solution. What both groups fail to comprehend is the real need of the business — to have a fully abstracted enterprise-wide data repository that is based on a data model that is fully application-independent, while at the same time constructing an applications architecture for decision-support computing that meets the needs of the entire enterprise. The absence of such an architecture means that the data-centric solution manages to capture only the data that is available, rather than the data that is required and the application-centric project manages only to solve the most pressing business problem rather than the most important.

Until recently, this debate has simmered quietly among market analysts and consultants, and the consensus view of serious commentators seems to have been that an application-driven enterprise data warehouse infrastructure was the optimum option. In this way many decision-support applications can be delivered over time during the course of an evolutionary deployment strategy. Such advice indicates that the data warehouse project occurs in two distinct phases. The first phase establishes an architectural blueprint. The second phase is concerned with deploying the applications.

The early vendor proponents of data warehousing were the large systems suppliers and, until the early 1990s, a data warehouse was typically an integrated store of corporate data located on an IBM mainframe computer or on a specialised Teradata database machine. Data warehousing was a new philosophy and it usually meant big iron. As the data warehousing concept was emerging from the testbed systems of US Fortune 500 companies, another IT trend — EIS systems — was coming to the end of its era. EIS systems had been a qualified success as a tool for corporate management. What the senior executive saw on the EIS screen was often beguiling and attractive but the manner in which the data was assembled to populate the EIS system was, all too often, inelegant, inefficient, incongruous, incomplete, inflexible and inaccurate.

The complex problems of conflicting data definitions, data synchronization, data pollution, data fragmentation, operational systems resource contention, data transformation and metadata management were being tackled by the data warehouse architects and by a new swathe of software tool vendors. Data warehousing and vendors of data warehouse components were set to completely supersede the EIS experiment. At about this stage (in 1994) four EIS vendors (Arbor, Comshare, IRI and Pilot) formed a defensive strategy that resulted in the formation in January 1995 of the OLAP Council. They were quickly joined by other erstwhile EIS vendors who satisfied the membership criteria — a multidimensional database product. Most OLAP vendors and some RDBMS vendors do not have the capability to construct enterprise-wide solutions for data warehouses in the terabyte range and have a vested interest in selling the application-centric approach or an enterprise approach based on a high level of data summarization. Other vendors who are selling high-end hardware platforms have an equally vested interest in selling the concept of the long-history, enterprise-wide, atomic level data, warehouse solution.

There is no absolute right answer for every situation but there is certainly a right solution for each individual enterprise. It is sobering to note that one in every two data warehouse projects fail and failed data warehouse projects usually have their origin in a failure to select the right approach at the outset. Most often the problem is not that the enterprise selected the wrong strategy from the two competing options available, but that they failed to properly combine the two approaches. Some ended up with databases not optimized for the business applications that became visible after implementation and others ended up with applications that were not supported by an adequate architectural framework. Either way, the end result was an application/architecture dysfunction.

Both the application-centric and enterprise architecture-centric approaches to the data warehouse are directed at constructing a query-intensive decision support system and share certain characteristics such as prototyping, iterative development, some element of data cleansing, and the possible incorporation of external data. However, case studies indicate substantial differences in the two approaches. Table 4.1 contrasts the most common differences that may be witnessed in the characteristics of data warehouses influenced by the competing philosophies.

Different problems require different types of solution and the data warehouse project will mean different things to different organizations. A more real distinction that can be drawn in actuality is between architected and non-architected systems. A data warehouse needs to have an applications architecture, a data architecture and a technology architecture and will suffer from the lack of any one of these.

Table 4.1 Data-centered and application-centered approaches contrasted

	Application-centric	Data-centric
1	Application focused	Data focused
2	Pre-processed data	Transformed data
3	Defined user population	Elastic user population
4	Business problem-driven	Strategic opportunity-driven
5	Easy to cost justify	Difficult to cost justify
6	Low entry level cost	High entry level cost
7	Vendor facilitated	Consultant facilitated

In the final analysis the debate between the application-centric and data-centric camps is actually a cry for more methodological rigor in the initial planning of the data warehouse. Like almost all IT developments that go awry, data warehouse projects that go wrong do so at a very early stage in the project. The most important advice that can be offered to any project sponsor is to try to envisage what is going to exist, not at the end of the first iteration, but at the end of many iterations.

ESSENTIAL COMPONENTS OF A DATA WAREHOUSE ARCHITECTURE

An architecture is best described as a unified way of representing an object. But an architecture also includes all of the policies and standards that underpin that unified representation. An architecture should be complete and distinct. It should provide the developer with a framework within which to work. It should also encapsulate the information technology strategy of the enterprise. And, crucially, it should provide a stable platform to accommodate change, both technological and business, as the enterprise grows. The comprehensive success, or otherwise, of an IT architecture can only be gauged in the years after the initial implementation. Effective architectures will withstand the future demands made upon them.

Ineffective architectures will decay over time and crumble in the face of new business demands and new technologies.

At the core of the data warehouse architecture is the dedicated read-only database which contains the integrated data for decision-support computing. But this represents only part of the architecture. Other crucial activities such as data mapping, extraction, transformation, cleansing, access and exploitation all form part of the jigsaw. But perhaps the most important issue for the data warehouse architect relates to data staging — important because it is difficult to prescribe a standard solution for every enterprise. A strategy for data staging decides where the data and information is located within the overall infrastructure, since it is rare for all of the information to be centrally stored on a single database which is accessed for all queries. Incorporating subsidiary data marts brings benefits in query performance and avoids bottlenecks arising in the network.

It always useful, when creating an architecture, to distinguish what is being built (the conceptual architecture) from how it is to be built (the logical architecture) from the actual technology that will be used to build it (the physical architecture). The data warehouse architecture needs to be completely described at these three separate levels. There is a danger in only having a physical technology architecture when what is really needed at the outset of the project is a clear conceptual and logical architecture which explain what the system is designed to do (the conceptual architecture) and the manner in which this will happen (the logical architecture). It is particularly necessary to express the architecture in abstract terms as well as in concrete technological terms. The following is brief outline of what should appear in a complete three level architecture.

Conceptual Architecture
- The business vision for the system.
- The business objectives of the system.
- The required capabilities of the system.
- The required functions of the system.
- The relationship of the system to other corporate systems.
- The ownership and usage of the system.

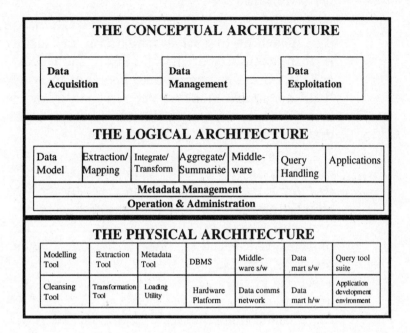

Figure 4.1 The conceptual, logical and physical architecture

Logical architecture
- The scope of the system.
- The applications.
- The data model.
- The infrastructure framework.
- The layers of the framework.

Physical architecture
- The hardware components.
- The software components.
- The data communications components.
- Operational tasks, activities and processes.

Figure 4.1 illustrates these different views of the data warehouse architecture.

Conceptually, the data warehouse is very simple to describe. All that is essentially happening is that data is being acquired from operational systems and from sources external to the enterprise; is then loaded on to a separate platform and, finally, that information is then exploited by the business. In a real world project the conceptual architecture would be likely to be more comprehensive than this simple model since each data warehouse implementation has, for the sponsoring organization, its own particular goal which describes what needs to be achieved.

The logical architecture explains how the goal of data integration and exploitation is to be achieved and is crucially important in describing the scope and boundary of the project. And the physical architecture becomes the working architecture for the implementation and describes the individual software and hardware components that, together, provide the data warehouse infrastructure for the enterprise.

As has already been discussed in Chapter 3, the methodological approach to the data warehouse project should follow a structured route which maps precisely from conceptual to logical to physical in order to ensure that the actual implementation is driven by the requirements of the business which, at the early stages of the project, can only to captured at the conceptual level. One of the commonest project management errors in data warehousing is to allow the project to become embroiled in a technological debate about how best to build the data warehouse before discovering what exactly it is that the enterprise expects to be delivered.

For the sake of simplicity the conceptual architecture should, in essence, contain the vision; the logical architecture should define the mission of the project and the physical architecture should represent the technology infrastructure that will achieve the mission.

Table 4.2 The conceptual, logical and physical views contrasted

Conceptual Architecture	'The Vision Statement'	THE WHAT
Logical Architecture	'The Mission Statement'	THE HOW
Physical Architecture	'The Infrastructure'	THE TECHNOLOGY

The Conceptual Architecture

The conceptual architecture should capture, reasonably precisely, the user expectations of the data warehouse and should communicate how, in general, the data warehouse is going to impact on the business processes of the enterprise and on the existing information technology infrastructure of the enterprise. The conceptual architecture should answer the questions: 'What is a data warehouse' and 'What are the implications of a data warehouse for our company?'.

The conceptual architecture will always contain the three essential ingredients contained in Figure 4.1 but should contain as much additional contextual information as is necessary to communicate the concept to the enterprise and to allow the enterprise to define the boundaries of the system as well as informing the logical design.

The conceptual architecture should also allow for discussion around many of the 'soft' issues that are crucial to the success of data warehouse initiatives, such as overall IT strategy, business strategy, project sponsorship, timescales, costs, priorities and roles and responsibilities.

The Logical Architecture

The logical architecture provides a detailed elaboration of the conceptual architecture. It is here that key questions concerning the frequency of updates, types of updates, volumetrics, application definition, data staging strategy, the query environment, the administration environment and database design are all answered.

The entire data warehouse solution should be expressed in the logical architecture without reference to specific tools or technology products. The logical architecture may have to make some implicit assumptions about technology — for example, a relational platform may be assumed or may even be a prerequisite in the logical architecture. The logical architecture is concerned with the activities, processes, events and overall shape of the data warehouse. The logical architecture describes what needs to happen and not how it is actually going to happen.

The test of a good logical architecture is the degree to which it comprehensively anticipates all of the processes and functions that need to be addressed. These will include:

- Data modelling.
- Data sources.
- Data cleansing.
- Data transformation.
- Data mapping.
- Data extraction.
- Data management.
- Data access.
- Data staging.
- Metadata management.
- Data policy and standards.
- Administration.
- Security.
- Volumetrics.
- Target applications.
- Service level standards.
- Anticipated evolution.

The Physical Architecture

By the time the physical architecture comes to be designed, most of the crucial decisions which will inform the choice of physical tools and platforms to be selected will have been made and can be directly inherited from the logical architecture. One of the many difficulties to be encountered at the physical design stage relates to the degree of overlap of functionality of many of the tools in the marketplace. The real challenge for the warehouse architect at this stage in the project is the challenge of systems integration. In a project where architectural integration is everything, architects cannot fall back on the tried-and-tested mechanism of buying best-of-breed tools. It is not the excellence of the software tools in themselves that should determine the selection, but the degree to which all of the tools that are selected work together to provide the best solution.

Normally the logical architecture will provide the basis for a 'Request for Proposals' to issue to the vendors and the selected vendors are, most likely, to be directly involved in the final design and construction of the physical infrastructure. Once the physical architecture has been defined then, to all intents and purposes, the scope of the base infrastructure is 'frozen'.

The physical architecture needs to define the different components of the data warehouse infrastructure and will normally include the components outlined in the following paragraphs. Many of these aspects (metadata, data quality, data access, data administration) of the physical architecture have been addressed in considerably more detail in dedicated chapters elsewhere in this book. The technical evaluation of the different technologies that comprise the physical architecture are addressed in Chapter 5. All of the key components are included here for the sake of completeness.

Legacy System Impact Analysis

An important aspect of logical and physical design for the data warehouse is the extent to which the architecture impacts on the performance and functionality of the legacy systems. For this reason it is useful to perform an operational systems impact analysis to assess the extent to which the data warehouse will adversely affect performance or resources in the legacy environment. Such an analysis should have regard to the issues described in Table 4.3.

SCOPING THE DATA WAREHOUSE ARCHITECTURE

As has already been discussed in Chapter 3 (Managing the Data Warehouse Project) the issue of scope is a difficult (and often contentious) problem for the data warehouse architect to grapple with. The scope should be defined in the project charter and the architect should be satisfied that the scope is clearly defined and not capable of becoming dangerously elastic during the course of the project.

Table 4.3   The impact on legacy systems

	Impact	Example
1	Performance	The use of propagation tools may adversely impact the performance of operational applications
2	Batch Schedule	The suite of extraction programs may constrict the batch window available in the legacy environment
3	Functionality	The warehouse may substitute many of the reporting requirements of the user population that are served by the legacy systems
4	Standards	Technical or data standards defined for the data warehouse may impact on the future development of operational systems
5	Processes	The data warehouse applications may give rise to changes in business processes in a manner that impacts the operational systems
6	Resources	The effort required to address data pollution on the legacy systems may impact on the available legacy systems maintenance resources

The scope of a data warehouse architecture can be measured by reference to the following elements:

- The number of legacy systems comprehended by the architecture.
- The number of external data sources comprehended by the architecture.
- The extent of data integration and transformation required of the architecture.
- The volume and granularity of the data managed by the architecture.
- The number of users served by the architecture.
- The number of decision-support functions supported by the architecture.
- The range of technologies employed in the architecture.
- The requirements of the administrative and operations environment.

- The extent to which the architecture determines information technology standards and policies for the enterprise as a whole.

ASSESSING ARCHITECTURAL RISK

Risk is always present when architecting an information technology solution and care should be taken to analyse and assess risk during the course of the architecture design. In the data warehouse project the following five areas of risk should be considered:

- *Technological risk.* This occurs where the technological components that are implemented (or that are available) are insufficient to satisfy the conceptual and logical architectures that are defined or where the degree of system complexity is great
- *Business risk.* This occurs where the logical or physical architecture is inappropriate to the needs of the business as defined in the conceptual architecture or where there are changes in the business environment over time.
- *Project management risk.* This occurs where the architectural requirements that are defined at the conceptual and logical levels change, or where the scope or business requirements of the system become elastic.
- *Scalability risk.* This occurs where the proposed architecture is incapable of scaling to meet future needs that can be reasonably be anticipated.
- *Extensibility risk.* This occurs where the architecture is inflexible and is incapable of being extended to accommodate new requirements or new technologies.

TECHNICAL ARCHITECTURE COMPLEXITY

Architectural complexity in the data warehouse project is generally a product of one of three separate factors. These are:

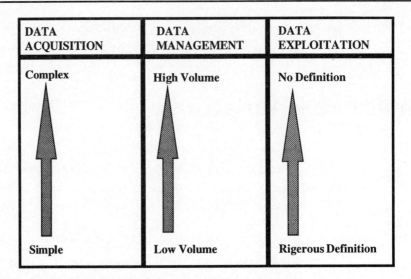

Figure 4.2   Technology architecture complexity factors

- *Transformation complexity*. This reflects the extent to which the data transformations that are required are simple or complex.
- *Data volumes*. This reflects the extent to which the data volumes required are large or small.
- *Application definition*. This reflects the extent to which the applications that are required are rigorously or loosely specified.

Obviously, the degree to which a data warehouse architecture is complex has a direct bearing on the degree of technological risk that is absorbed by the system architect. A data warehouse which has relatively simple transformation rules, modest data volumes and well specified applications has a level of technological risk that is an order of magnitude less than a project which has complex transformation rules, enormous data volumes and loosely defined applications. Figure 4.2 illustrates the data warehouse complexity grid.

TOP-DOWN ARCHITECTURE—STRATEGY-DRIVEN

Some data warehouse projects are driven by the need to make radical changes in the business or follow a methodological course that commences with an analysis of business goals and objectives. Typical examples of strategy-driven data warehouses are to be found in the retailing industry, where the introduction of loyalty cards has transformed the business culture and where there is an urgency to construct systems that exploit the masses of data now being captured about customers at the electronic point-of-sales (EPOS) terminals at retail outlets. Another example is the telecommunications industry which is using data warehouse technology to introduce customized billing for customers. In these cases the enterprise has a clear and visible business strategy and the data warehouse has a clear mission to support that strategy by making available the technological means to realize the business vision.

In the context of architecture the strategy-driven data warehouse has a number of implications. Firstly, it is far more likely to be application-driven rather than data-driven in the sense that the business goal of the data warehouse is clear and well defined. Secondly, the data model for the warehouse is more likely to be constructed on the basis of what data the enterprise needs rather than what data the enterprise actually has — this will, in turn, have implications for the data mapping and transformation layer of the architecture which is likely to be more complex and demanding than taking a bottom-up approach. (Indeed, it is not uncommon in the top-down design activity for the enterprise to discover that the data required to drive the applications that are needed simply do not exist within the enterprise!) And finally, the scope of the strategy-driven warehouse will, almost always, be more clearly defined.

BOTTOM-UP ARCHITECTURE — OPPORTUNITY-DRIVEN

A bottom-up architecture takes, as its starting point, that there is a failure in the current enterprise strategy for decision-support computing. This may manifest itself by a backlog of change requests to legacy systems in order to provide better reports. It may manifest itself by users embracing a diverse (and often incompatible) range of decision-support tools. It may be driven by technology visionaries who are championing the cause of data warehousing. Or it may occur in circumstances where a clear business vision does exist, and where outlines of business applications have been defined, but where the enterprise is unwilling to undertake any extensive enterprise modeling.

The bottom-up approach takes as its starting point the fact that certain data exists in the operational systems of the enterprise; that this data has some value to the enterprise, and that it should be released into the hands of users as a matter of urgency. The bottom-up approach is far more likely to be data-driven than application-driven and is likely to take the existing data (along with existing data models, data definitions and data policies) and massage them into a unified whole. The data transformations that arise in this scenario are likely to be less daunting than in the top-down approach and the overall design stage of the project is completed much faster. However, since no attempt is made to model the business strategy and to map the data and applications back to business goals and objectives, the risk of delivering a data warehouse that is inappropriate to the real needs of the business is magnified considerably.

When reviewing data warehouse implementations, it is always abundantly clear which architectural route has been followed. The top-down approach tends to be more effective but takes a long time. The bottom-up approach is less effective and often requires re-engineering but can be delivered quickly. Some implementations attempt to make a compromise between the two with an approach that may be described as 'middle-out' and it should be observed that, since it is not possible for any enterprise to take an absolutely 'pure' top-down approach to designing information systems, there will always be some level of compromise. It should also be noted that some enterprises follow a non-architected approach to decision-support computing and deliver multiple, isolated mini warehouses. This phenomenon is discussed in more detail later in this chapter under the heading 'point-solution data marts'.

Figure 4.3 offers a concise picture of the choices that are open to the data warehouse architect. The title of this illustration reads: 'Pick any two'. You can have goodness and cheapness if you

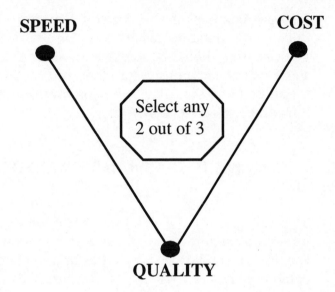

Figure 4.3 The menu of options

sacrifice speed. You can have speed and goodness if money is no object. You can have a quick cheap solution if the quality of the solution is not critical. In short, there never is a free lunch.

THE BURDEN OF INFRASTRUCTURE

At the heart of the data warehouse project there is a tension between the need for rapid deployment of functionality on the one hand, and the need for a comprehensive and robust infrastructure on the other. The burden of infrastructure is generally borne by the first data warehouse iteration. The first application that is deployed requires that the pipeline to the operational systems be constructed, and this pipeline can then be used for subsequent applications which build into a full data warehouse architecture. Except in the case of multiple point solutions, each of which has a separate pipeline (a non-architected approach which inevitably becomes dysfunctional), the architecture needed to deliver a full-enterprise solution requires more or less the same design effort for one application as it does for multiple data exploitation projects. Therefore, the strategy adopted initially for data modeling, mapping, extraction, transformation, and cleansing should be reusable for all applications. This implies a single logical architecture for all decision-support systems as well as a standard and scaleable technology architecture to provide a base infrastructure for such systems.

CRITICAL SUCCESS FACTORS FOR DATA WAREHOUSE ARCHITECTURE

The key goal of the data warehouse architect is to develop an infrastructure for query-intensive information processing which is capable of supporting all of the decision-support systems in the enterprise that rely on data as an input. The success of an architecture can be measured with reference to its capacity to absorb change and uncertainty in the environment. The sign of a failed architecture is the inability of the infrastructure to support a new application or a new technology without significant and costly alterations to the existing infrastructure. An information technology infrastructure is no different to the infrastructure of a building — if a change in the use of a building occurs, most of the existing infrastructure should be capable of being adapted without having to rip out the all of the existing infrastructure. Because the data warehouse concept is constantly maturing and evolving and because the technological components of the data warehouse are also changing, managing future change is the overriding critical success factor. Table 4.4 contains the eight key critical success factors that apply to the data warehouse architecture and can be regarded as eight essential 'rules' of data warehouse architecture.

STRATIFICATION OF DATA

Data, like geological formations, exists at different levels of stratification ranging from the detailed atomic level data to aggregate data with a high information content. This stratification needs to be

Table 4.4 Critical Success Factors for data warehouse architecture

	Critical Success Factor	Elaboration
1	Logically layered	The architecture should not be rooted in an exclusively physical framework.
2	Robust	The architecture should be capable of supporting current (and anticipated) performance-related service level agreements with users.
3	Holistic	The data warehouse architecture should be located within the overall IT architecture of the enterprise and should be not be separate or isolated.
4	Scalable	The architecture should accommodate growth in the volume of data being stored and processed.
5	Extensible	The architecture should be capable of accommodating new applications and new technologies.
6	Safe	The architecture should address the issue of security and confidentiality of data.
7	Administrable	The architecture should be capable of being easily administered without undue risk, complexity or prohibitive cost-of-ownership.
8	Appropriate	The architecture should be appropriate to the needs of the business and the culture of the enterprise.

reflected in the architecture that is implemented to exploit the data, since each layer is refined directly from the layer underneath. The dilemma presented to the data warehouse architect relates to critical decisions which have to be made about the related topics of granularity of the data and the flexibility of the data warehouse. Granularity refers to the level of detail reflected in the data — low levels of granularity are displayed in summary tables and high levels of granularity are displayed in detailed transaction data.

The critical issue is whether there is a need for detailed transaction level data in the data warehouse. Two questions need to be posed to answer this question.

The first question is straightforward: 'Will the data warehouse applications need detailed data in order to satisfy the needs of the application?' For many retailing and utility companies which relate promotions and pricing to individual customers, and where a clear link exists between the analysis on the data warehouse and the operational systems that serve the customer, the requirement for point-of-sales transaction level data is obvious. For other data warehouse projects, in the financial services industry for example, the primary goal of the business may be to extract trending information from the data and the need for transaction level data may not be as pressing.

The second question is less easy to answer: 'Will changes to the business over time require that the refined information be reconstituted in order to reflect changes in the actual data, the data definitions or the business rules that underpin the data?'. Take for example a company that implements a data warehouse that contains only summary and aggregate data concerning product sales in ten categories of product. Let us postulate, for the purposes of this example, that the company then undergoes a radical re-organization which eliminates some of the categories; bundles other categories and assigns some products to entirely new categories. Naturally the data warehouse structure will have to be altered to reflect these new categories and possibly also to reflect organizational changes that have wrought on the company. But the manner in which the summary data is then captured and presented in the data warehouse is completely different from the historical data. Because the historical data is held only at summary level it cannot be reconstituted to reflect the new arrangement of product categories. Thus no time series analysis is now possible between the data that was populated prior to the re-organization and the data that was populated after the re-organization. In effect, the data in the data warehouse prior to the re-organization is rendered null and void for the purposes of supporting the re-organized business units. Of course, it may be possible to recover the original detailed transaction data that would be archived from the operational systems that generated the detailed data in the first place, but this is a laborious and high-risk option that would be difficult to execute or to justify.

The most apt metaphor that this author has come across to communicate the risks associated with summary data in data

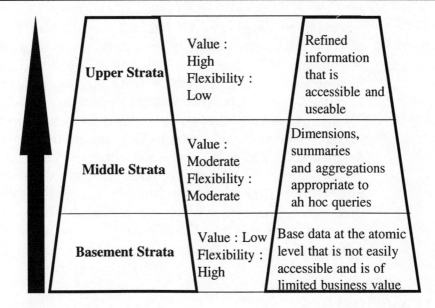

Upper Strata	Value : High Flexibility : Low	Refined information that is accessible and useable
Middle Strata	Value : Moderate Flexibility : Moderate	Dimensions, summaries and aggregations appropriate to ah hoc queries
Basement Strata	Value : Low Flexibility : High	Base data at the atomic level that is not easily accessible and is of limited business value

Figure 4.4 Data stratification

warehouses is the simple cup of coffee. A cup of coffee contains many components — coffee beans, water, sugar and milk. Once these ingredients have been transformed into a cup of coffee it is no longer possible to reduce the cup of coffee to its constituent components. Equally, it is not possible to significantly alter the flavour of the cup of coffee. A person confronted with a cup of coffee that is unsatisfactory generally throws it away and brews fresh coffee. The same is substantially true of summary data sets that prove unsuitable for the users for whom they were intended.

Figure 4.4 illustrates the stratification of data in a data warehouse. The key aspect of this illustration is to recognize that each layer is a product of the strata beneath. Highly summarized data that is not connected to the layer from which it was refined is less likely to be adaptable to changes that occur in the manner in which it should be refined. Equally, if there are gaps in the boundaries between the strata (due to inadequate metadata to describe the manner in which the data was refined from one stratum to another or where the transformation process is poorly documented or is performed in an ad hoc fashion), then the ability to drill-down from summary to detail will be lost. In cases where the logical and physical data stratification is not comprehensively architected, then disharmony will occur in the strata which will make it difficult or impossible to navigate lucidly from the upper layer of refined information to the basement strata of detailed data.

One change that is occurring in the data value proposition relates to the value of detailed data. The traditional wisdom held that detailed data was too dense to be of high value to the business except in so far as it provided the raw material to refine information. This assumption is now being challenged by the use of data mining techniques which can scan and analyse atomic data in a manner that was not feasible with traditional query tools. The subject of data mining is explored in more detail in Chapter 10.

DATABASE DESIGN

When the enterprise has completed the architectural design for the data warehouse, the design focus quickly moves to the database. Database design is a three-stage process which begins with a business model of the enterprise which identifies the key goals, objectives and criticall success factors for the enterprise. This is then translated into a logical model for the data. The logical model is then translated into a physical schema which optimises the performance of queries and applications. This overall process is illustrated in Figure 4.5.

The Logical Model

This element of the project is critical from a technical perspective, since the logical design of the database fixes the scope of the system. The logical database design for the data warehouse must be sufficiently broad and generic to accomadate change and must also be sufficiently precise to be interpreted for the purposes of designing the physical schema for the system. If a design error is going to occur in the data warehouse project, the likelihood is that it is

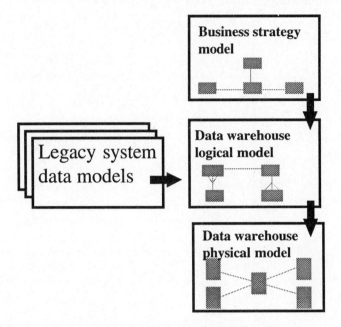

Figure 4.5   The data warehouse database design process

going to occur during the logical database design phase. It is not uncommon for data warehouses to be constructed solely on the basis of a physical design, but it is also not uncommon for such systems to fail to meet the changing demands of the business users in the enterprise.

The key issues that need to be addressed during the logical design activity are as follows:

1. Achieving adequate *performance* for query intensive processing, bearing in mind the query environment that is anticipated (see section on query domain analysis in Chapter 8).
2. Achieving adequate *flexibility* to support future unknown requirements.
3. Defining the *scope* of the data warehouse with reference to the subjects that are included.
4. Defining the level of data *granularity* (how detailed the data in the data warehouse will be) and how multiple applications will be supported by the data structures.

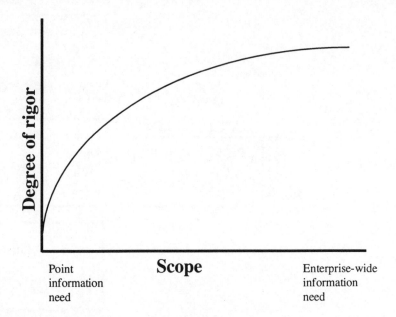

Figure 4.6 The relationship between scope and rigor

Ideally the data warehouse logical database design should start from the position of what the enterprise needs rather than what data actually exists. The modeling process should not be concerned with the data that exists in the legact systems; it should be concerned with what data is needed to run the business. The fundamental goal of good logical modeling is to model an abstraction of the enterprise independently of how the model may be used. The purpose of such abstraction is to yield benefits through future flexibility and reusability. The degree of abstraction and the overall degree of rigor that needs to be applied to the logical model will vary with the scope of the project as illustrated in Figure 4.6.

Sometimes it is useful to use generic data models as a means of kickstarting the modeling process. Vertical industry generic data models (e.g. for airlines, retailers, utilities etc.) are available from vendor and consultancy organisations. These are useful in forming the modeling process but rarely constitute a solution in themselves. Becasue every enterprise has its own particular requirements and because the business benefits of data warehousing come from innovation rather than standardisation, the advantages of generic models is limited.

The Physical Model

Query-intesive database design is fundamentally different from transaction-intensive database design. Getting data out of a database fast requires a completely different approach to achieving subsecond response times when getting data into a database. The main goal in a query-intensive system is to minimise the number of table joins by minimising the number of tables and by optimising the level of indexation of the tables without hampering the load processing performance.

A number of different bottlenecks can arise in the data warehouse. Because of the large amounts of data being accessed, a bottleneck can occur in the transfer of the data from the disk drives to the processor. A second, equally dangerous, bottleneck can occur in the network because of the volume of data that is moving from the server tothe client. Various options have been developed, from both a hardware and software perspective, to tackle the issue of performance of the physical database and these are outlined in Table 4.5. (One of the most popular means of managing query performance is the Star Schema and this is discussed at greater length later in this chapter).

Timestamping Data

Representing time in the data model presents a particular challenge to the designer since conventional modelling assumes a static view of the data. Relationships that are represented in the data model may be true at the time of modelling, but may not have been true in the past (i.e. in respect of historical data) and may not be true in the future. Because the time dimension is a common component (perhaps the most common component) of a business query, all data must be timestamped. Timestamping is also important for database

Table 4.5 Approaches to optimising data warehouse performance

Solution	Hardware impact	Software impact
Parallel processing	•	
Subsidiary data marts	•	
Distributed data warehouse	•	
Relational OLAP tools		•
Subject partitioning		•
Query regulation		•
Advanced indexing		•
Data aggregation/pre-processing		•
Star Schema		•

administration. Because the design may incorporate time cycles for data coverage, (for example, a utility may maintain 52 weeks of detailed transaction data where the oldest week of data is removed each time a weekly update occurs), effective administration of the data warehouse requires reliable timestamping of the data.

Timestamping the data warehouse data normally occurs during the extraction process and data can be timestamped at field level, record level or file level. Field level timestamping is an enormous overhead and is not generally recommended unless extremely detailed pattern analysis is required. Record level timestamps will suffice for most decision-support applications since data analysis normally is applied at row level in the warehouse. Where data is refreshed (i.e. where point-in-time data is updated and replaces the previous data) the data is generally timestamped at file level where time granularity is not critical to the decision support application. For example, the address field might be refreshed periodically where the business value is achieved by maintaining the current address in the data warehouse (i.e. there is no business value in storing the previous addresses). Transaction data, on the other hand, needs to be captured and maintained in timestamped increments since there is a business value in observing changing patterns of transaction behaviour.

In many instances the transaction logging on operational systems will not provide adequate timestamping of data and the data warehouse designer may have to have recourse to identifying those records on the production system that have changed. This may involve a comparison of the production data being extracted against the previous extract in order to identify changes. Opinions differ about where this task should be located but, where practicable, the match and compare process should reside in the legacy production environment.

THE STAR SCHEMA

Most data warehouse developers, for reasons of security, standards, openness and scalability will wish to deploy the data warehouse on a relational database engine. Yet, one of the lessons of data exploitation that has been learned is that very many queries are multi-dimensional in nature and structure. Whenever one hears the '*by*' word, one knows that the query has multiple dimensions. For example, the query 'I want to know the breakdown of customers *by* region, *by* demographics, *by* value and *by* segment' is a classic multi-dimensional query. The critical issue for the database designer relates to the data partitioning strategy that is pursued. Getting the partitions wrong can be an expensive mistake and predicting all of the possible queries that will be requested by users an impossible task. Therefore, many database designers base the partitioning strategy on the star schema approach pioneered by Ralph Kimball. The star schema is a mechanism by which the relational database can be configured to optimize queries that are naturally dimensional.

The star schema (Figure 4.7) takes its name from the star configuration that is represented by this approach. A (very large) fact table containing the detailed transaction data forms the axis of the star with (much smaller) satellite tables containing the dimensional data. The fact table normally contains the performance data relating to the business, i.e. data that can be expressed in units. The dimensional tables normally contain textual values which equate to constraints. For example, in the query 'select all of the purple-coloured motor vehicles' the colour 'purple' is a constraint. A full

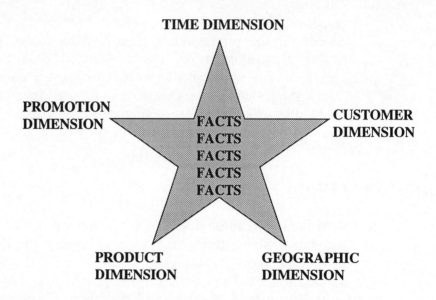

TIME DIMENSION

PROMOTION
DIMENSION

FACTS
FACTS
FACTS
FACTS
FACTS

CUSTOMER
DIMENSION

PRODUCT
DIMENSION

GEOGRAPHIC
DIMENSION

Figure 4.7   A representation of the star schema

table scan of a fact table would only occur when the business
needed to look at all of the records in the database without having
any constraints identified. Fact tables are fully normalized while
dimensional tables tend to be deliberately denormalized into a flat
structure.

The obvious benefit of this approach is to minimize the number
of table joins that need to occur to satisfy a dimensional query. It
should be noted that some relational database products have limits
on the number of rows in a table and therefore it may not be
possible to actually have a single 'fact' table containing all of the
transactional data.

The benefits of the star schema are many and perhaps the most
important is that it is an approach that is readily understood by
business users. Presented with a dimensional model of the data and
an entity-relationship model of the data, it is clearly no contest in
terms of comprehension. In addition, the star schema has the
advantage of being easy to develop and deploy quickly. But perhaps
the most beguiling attraction of the star schema is that, since it
assumes that all queries can be satisfied by combining dimensions,

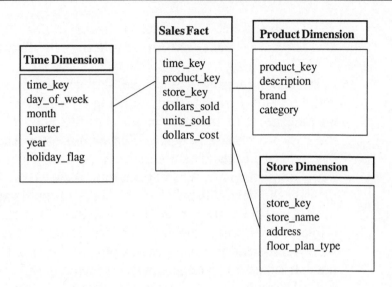

Figure 4.8 Typical data dimensions[3]

it neatly avoids the nasty business of having to define the precise requirements of the data warehouse from the perspective of the business. However beguiling this may be, it is a highly dangerous trap for many developers. Not all queries are naturally dimensional. For many industries the data warehouse query environment will require complex computational logic and for many others the real promise of the data warehouse will only be realized when they can deploy now types of operational applications having refined and integrated detailed data. Therefore, the star schema, while highly attractive and representing an important innovation, should not be the only option considered in the approach to database design. An example of a typical dimensional model is provided in Figure 4.8.

In arriving at a star schema for a data warehouse the critical things that need to be established by the architect are:

1. The grain of the fact table that is required.
2. The dimensions that are required.

---

[3] From *The Data Warehouse Toolkit*, by Ralph Kimball, John Wiley & Sons 1996.

3. The hierarchy of members (of each dimension).
4. The actual facts that are required in the fact table.

To a considerable extent the star schema is a reaction to the standard entity-relationship modeling approach which tends towards normalization of the data in the data warehouse. Whether data in the data warehouse is normalized or not often excites considerable debate, but in this author's opinion, is not a point of principle. For many implementers where transaction-level data is being used to provide the flexibility to alter the types of aggregation that may be needed in the future, then normalization is attractive. For other implementers, where the data is refreshed rather than being updated, then normalization is simply not possible. It should be obvious that the star schema is a denormalized schema with limited potential for radical change once it is deployed. This becomes the critical issue for anyone considering a star schema approach. It should also be noted that a variation on the star schema which involves an additional ring of satellite tables — the so called snowflake schema — is, in fact, an attempt at a normalization of sorts. But extreme caution should be exercised in migrating from the standard star schema to a snowflake schema since the main advantage of the star schema — that of performance — is, to a considerable extent, sacrificed in the process.

There is clearly a need to keep large quantities, terabytes, of very detailed transaction history for decision analysis. The primary reason for this is that because the world changes and consumers change their buying habits, it is not possible to predict in advance the single correct way to analyze, summarize and aggregate this data.

Figure 4.9 contrasts data entities and elements with data dimensions.

Star schemas are highly effective in some types of industries, such as retailing (for basket analysis or customer profiling), but less so in others such as airlines or where individual customer detail history comes into play. New, complex algorithms, such as customer segmentation and clustering analysis, also point to the fact there is no single 'right' schema for all types of data store. What is likely to happen in many instances is that cleansed detailed historical

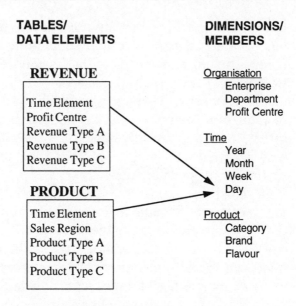

TABLES/
DATA ELEMENTS

DIMENSIONS/
MEMBERS

REVENUE

Time Element
Profit Centre
Revenue Type A
Revenue Type B
Revenue Type C

PRODUCT

Time Element
Sales Region
Product Type A
Product Type B
Product Type C

Organisation
  Enterprise
  Department
  Profit Centre

Time
  Year
  Month
  Week
  Day

Product
  Category
  Brand
  Flavour

Figure 4.9   Entities and elements mapped on to dimensions

transaction data will be kept in one enterprise data warehouse and that relational technology will evolve to include new ways of processing different types of data. In this way subsets, summaries, aggregates and derived data will be extracted from the enterprise data warehouse and processed by more specialized software engines at the level of the subsidiary data mart.

POINT-SOLUTION DATA MARTS

The concept of the data mart has excited a lot of attention in the trade press and many commentators are incorrectly positioning the data mart as an alternative to the data warehouse. Like most concepts in IT the term 'data mart' means different things to different people. A rigorous definition of a data mart locates it as a data store that is subsidiary to a data warehouse of integrated data and which is directed at a partition of data that is created for the use of a dedicated group of users. It is in this specific sense that the term 'data mart' is generally used in this book. However, the term has come to be associated with an entirely different concept — that of an isolated store of data that is used for query processing but which is not necessarily connected with other similar isolated marts in the enterprise. Therefore a subsidiary data mart might, in fact, be a table of summarized or aggregated data on the data warehouse rather than a physically separate store of data. A point-solution data mart has no ambition other than to satisfy the needs of a single business requirement.

In most instances, the subsidiary data mart is a physically separate store of data and it is normally resident on a separate database server, often on the local area network serving the dedicated user group. Sometimes the data mart simply comprises relational OLAP technology which creates hypercubes of data for analysis by groups of users with a common interest in a limited portion of the database. On other occasions the data warehouse architect may incorporate data mining tools that extract sets of data for a particular type of analysis. All of these types of data mart have a high value because, no matter how many are deployed and no matter now many different enabling technologies are used, the different users are all accessing the same single integrated version of the truth.

Of course, it has to be borne in mind that every data warehouse project — even enterprise data warehouse projects — commence with a single iteration. Therefore a point-solution data mart might be the genesis of a full data warehouse strategy. Whether the decision-support strategy of the enterprise is architected or non-architected only becomes apparent when the second business requirement is voiced. If the response of the information system department is to build on the first system (i.e. by extending the logical data model and scaling the logical and technological architecture of the first system), then the enterprise is following an architected strategy which will, presumably, blossom into a full enterprise warehouse architecture. If the response is to deliver another isolated solution, then it can be assumed that the enterprise is engaged in the construction of a new generation of legacy systems, since each isolated data mart will contain the fragmentation of the original legacy systems and will replicate all of the weaknesses associated with fragmenting the corporate data.

Confusion about data marts arises because the term has been applied by many commentators and vendors to describe small subject-area data warehouses which are in fact fragmented point solutions to a range of business problems in the enterprises. This type of implementation is rarely deployed in the context of an overall technology or applications architecture and is missing the ingredient that is at the heart of the data warehousing concept — that of data integration. In fact, this type of implementation would be better described as a standard business intelligence system which does not purport to offer the benefits that data warehousing achieves. Simply off-loading operational data onto a separate server where more attractive end-user tools can be employed to analyze the data may well be necessary for urgent business requirements but there is nothing new about the concept. Information systems departments have been delivering fragmented point solutions for decades — it is simply more of the same.

In an effort to avoid the onerous tasks of data modeling, data integration, data transformation and an architected response to the needs of decision-support users, these stand-alone business intelligence systems achieve the goal of rapid delivery of enhanced decision-support functionality to end-users. The business drivers of these developments include the fact that some requirements are extremely urgent, the absence of a budget for a full data warehouse strategy, the absence of a sponsor for a pan-corporate decision-support strategy, the decentralization of business units and the attraction of ease-of-use tools and a mind-sized project. In short, the point-solution data mart is an effort to avoid the burden of infrastructure.

Ever ready to offer a silver bullet, many of the vendors have rushed to endorse the concept of the point solution data mart. Many vendors of database products with limited scalability have a vested interest in touting the point-solution data mart since the technological capacity of their products prevents them from offering a complete data warehouse strategy. This is short-sighted, since there is more to be gained from exploiting the opportunities presented by data warehouse implementations which require increasingly sophisticated and diverse data exploitation solutions in subsidiary data mart implementations. In any event, playing in both the data warehouse space and the point-solution data mart space will, for these vendors, become untenable in the long term. One does not complement the other but, in fact, contradicts the other.

The point-solution data mart is not always a bad thing: it is often a necessary and valid IT solution to a pressing business problem. The chief difficulty with the point-solution data mart is that it is a term that was coined by the data warehouse community and which is marketed either explicitly, or by inference, as having the same benefits as a scaled-down data warehouse. This is palpably untrue.

The dishonesty of the marketing hype about data marts has to do with vendor reassurance that these data marts are scalable and can evolve into an enterprise solution. There is no example that this author has been able to source anywhere where multiple independent data marts have evolved seamlessly into a coherent integrated data architecture for the enterprise. The chances of multiple data marts being successfully integrated are negligible. It is not, of course, an impossible feat but it requires that the enterprise first commission a comprehensive model of the corporate data and then enforce compliance by the different data marts. The reason why such a scenario is unlikely is that it contradicts the main marketing message of the data mart adherents — that it is quicker, cheaper and easier.

The real cost of the kind of data mart that avoids the detail-oriented central repository can only be gauged in the longer term. Readers should brace themselves for a barrage of cynicism in the trade press in a few years time when the full implications of a disjointed strategy for decision-support computing becomes visible in enterprises which have adopted the data mart strategy.

Data marts are essentially a marketing concept designed to sell the idea of a simpler, quicker, cheaper data warehouse. Data marts are simply smaller data warehouses and, generally, are used to support the decision-making of an organizational unit of the enterprise. This considerably diminishes the political and financial obstacles that are inherent in the data warehouse project. Architecturally it is difficult to distinguish the data mart from the data warehouse. In both cases there is probably data being extracted from a number of sources; there is probably some element of data integration; there has to be, in both cases, some kind of database design that reflects the need for query-intensive processing and finally there has to be an application layer to exploit the data. The thing that is singularly different is that the data mart is an isolated development, while the data warehouse is a pan-corporate project. Even this distinction is inadequate since there are, in the world, very few genuine enterprise data warehouses in production. Perhaps there never will be, as some data in the enterprise is not of interest to the core business. Therefore all enterprise data warehouses are incomplete to some extent.

The only key difference in the two concepts relates to the scope of the project. The data warehouse is perceived to be doomed to cultural resistance from the organization while the data mart finds willing sponsors within existing business units. The data mart is a more natural fit with the enterprise cultures which obtain in many organizations. These cultures are characterized by the following factors:

1. They are normally highly sensitive and resistance to change of any sort.
2. They are normally deeply antagonistic to large-scale technology projects.
3. They are normally hidebound by the political dynamics imposed by existing organizational boundaries.
4. They are normally driven by short-term considerations and are unwilling to consider the merits of any initiative that takes longer than six months.
5. They are normally unaware of the potential of new technologies until the benefits can be demonstrated by a competitor at which point they panic.

In short, the problem has to do with an appreciation of the benefits of infrastructure. People understand applications because they can clearly see the benefits that can accrue from an application. People can also easily assimilate the benefits of enhancing a business process because this clearly impacts on the real world of the business. Investing in infrastructure that can bring about more sophisticated applications and can support more complex business processes is more difficult to sell. This is a central challenge in the data warehouse project that does not really arise with a data mart because a data mart is, essentially, an application for a dedicated group of users. The data warehouse is the enabling platform to support multiple integrated applications that can be resident on multiple different subsidiary data marts. But it is the applications that sell the concept, not the concept itself. Therefore, care should be taken to focus on applications when selling the data warehouse and hope that the benefits of having multiple synchronized and consistent applications will become evident to the business rather than having multiple different isolated applications. This is the stark choice. The information systems department has a clear responsibility to counsel the business about the likely outcome of a corporate strategy based on isolated point-solution marts.

CONCLUSIONS

Successful data warehouse architectures are achieved by striking the right balance between competing demands. A correct balance must be struck between the need for infrastructure and the speed of development; between the temptation to select best-of-breed tools and the need for systems integration of all of the tool components; between the need for detailed data and summary data; between the flexibility offered by normalised schemas and the immediate business benefits of denormalised data; between the needs of application users and ad hoc query users; between the requirements for query performance and load performance, and between enterprise data warehouses and autonomous marts. Achieving this balance is the mission of the data warehouse architect and it is a skill that remains, for the moment, more an art than a science.

5

Data Warehouse Technology

'Take care of the means, and the end will take care of itself.'
— *Gandhi*

Parallel Processing

Parallel processing has become the favored means of ensuring scalable performance for data warehouse implementations. The reason for this choice is twofold. Users want to ensure that, as they add more and more data, the data warehouse will be capable of expanding without necessarily sacrificing performance. Secondly, users want to ensure that complex SQL queries, that would take days to execute on a conventional platform, can be broken down into smaller components and worked on in parallel, thus ensuring reasonable response times.

But what exactly does parallel processing mean? Almost every different vendor of parallel processing hardware technology employs different hardware architectures to achieve parallelism. In the area of database parallelism the variations are just as evident. And when the user comes to evaluate the combination of parallel hardware and parallel database engines the scope for confusion is immense. The hardware platforms range from symmetric multi-processing (SMP) machines to massively parallel processors (MPP) and now includes the parallel mainframe S/390 from IBM. Within the SMP camps and MPP camps there are considerable differences in architecture, processor technology, operating systems and component technologies. In the market for parallel database engines the range of options spans databases which were specifically engineered for parallel computing to traditional databases which were extensively re-engineered for parallel processing.

Differences between massively parallel computers, symmetric multi-processing computers and the CMOS mainframe from IBM are debated endlessly within the industry. At any one point in time the relative advantage of one over the other changes. For example, in the early days of data warehousing, those who were deploying very large databases tended to opt for the MPP solution. More recently, with the ability of SMP vendors to cluster SMP platforms, users have tended to opt for this route to scale their data warehouses.

Because of advances in the design for interconnects between CPU's in MPP machines, the performance of MPP machines significantly exceeds the performance of networked servers. With speeds of 1GB per second now available, this compares to ATM bandwidth forecasts of half that in the next few years. In addition, interconnect technology now enables memory to be shared across multiple processors and this development is having the effect of blurring the distinction between MPP and SMP platforms. This new generation of platforms are commonly referred to as NUMA (Non-Uniform Memory Access) machines and allow for greater flexibility in managing the processing load.

And now that IBM have arrived on the scene with what is effectively a parallel mainframe computer, with impressive performance benchmarks, the situation is even more confusing for the prospective data warehouse purchaser. To make matters even more confusing some vendors, notably NCR with their Worldmark 5100, can configure the system as an MPP or SMP. With advances in fully paralleled databases the transition from SMP to MPP is not as daunting as it was a few short years ago. For example, any application written for the IBM RS/6000 can be ported to the IBM massively parallel SP.

Because of the increasing difficulty in locating the precise boundary between SMP and MPP systems many commentators have ceased to make clear-cut distinctions between the world of SMP computing and the world of MPP computing. And because many vendors offer both types of platform in the marketplace, they too tend to avoid positioning SMP and MPP as irreconcilable options. But there are real differences and these are explored in the following section.

Massively Parallel Processing (MPP) and Symmetric Parallel Processing (SMP) contrasted

As a general rule of thumb, any data warehouse that is expected to exceed 400–500 GB in size properly belongs to the world of MPP. Warehouses that are not expected to exceed the 200GB threshold can scale comfortably within the SMP world. Where the expected data volume is the grey area between 200 and 400 GB, considerable care needs to be taken in arriving at the best decision. In weighing up the MPP/SMP option, the following separate factors need to be considered:

Advantages of SMP
- More affordable technology.
- Requires less specialized knowledge for application programmers.
- Requires less specialized knowledge for systems management.
- More mature technology.
- Greater availability of software products.
- Has the advantage of shared memory.
- Continuing advances in data capacity.

Advantages of MPP
- Higher threshold for data volumes.
- Linear scalability.
- Improved query performance (especially for complex queries).
- Faulty tolerance.

Future trends in MPP/SMP

- Progressive blurring of SMP/MPP boundaries.
- Hybrid processing comprising dual architecture for transaction-intensive (SMP) and query-intensive (MPP) processing.
- More emphasis on high availability and contingency tending, in the short term, to favor MPP.
- SMP supporting rising data volumes.

MPP Platforms

Different vendors of massively parallel hardware have found different solutions to the problem of designing interconnect mechanisms. The earliest was Teradata's (now NCR's) Y-net. IBM uses the Vulcan switch. Pyramid uses the mesh interconnect. Tandem have developed an innovation on the interconnect called the Servernet architecture, whereby the data can be passed through the system without having to go through the processors. All vendors of MPP platforms have developed their own mechanism for tackling the problem of I/O-intensive activities, such as queries, that lead to memory bus bottlenecks.

Table 5.1 includes the more common massively parallel platforms employed in data warehouse solutions:

Table 5.1   Vendors of enterprise parallel servers

Hewlett Packard	Enterprise Parallel Server
IBM	PowerParallel SP2
NCR	Worldmark 5100M & 3600
Pyramid	Reliant RM1000
Tandem	Himalaya K20000

Parallel Database Products

The database engines listed in the following table are available for parallel hardware platforms. The number of reference sites for some products are still relatively few and are confined to large enterprises.

Table 5.2 Vendors of parallel database engines

IBM	DB2 MVS
IBM	DB2 PE (Unix MPP)
Informix	Online Dynamic Server (SMP)
	XPS (MPP & Cluster)
NCR	Teradata
Oracle	Oracle Parallel Query (SMP)
	Oracle Parallel Server (MPP)
Redbrick	Redbrick Data Warehouse XPP
Sybase	Sybase 11 (SMP)
	Sybase MPP
Tandem	Nonstop SQL MP

EXPLORING DATABASE PARALLELISM FOR MPP — THE TERADATA DATABASE[4]

Parallel databases are designed to handle the complexity of distributed memory in the multi-node shared nothing architecture of MPP systems. Because distributed memory systems are extremely difficult to program, most data warehouses rely on using paralleled databases and query tool products which are engineered for the parallel environment. Paralleled databases allow the enterprise to run applications that are not paralleled and standard SQL can be submitted with the database handling the complex parallelization. What this means, in many cases, is running the queries across multi-node instances of the database. However, understanding how the database manages the parallelization is still important for the system designer since decisions on data partitioning strategy can function to support or inhibit the optimization of the query performance. Because different parallel DBMS products manage parallelism differently, a knowledge of how to optimize the design of the database can only be achieved through knowledge of the DBMS product being used.

The Teradata database was the first and most successful parallel database to be engineered specifically for a massively parallel

---

[4] This source material for this evaluation is provided in the NCR White Paper 'Born To Be Parallel' (August 1996) authored by Carrie Ballinger and Ron Fryer.

environment (originally called a database machine). The Teradata database avoids all single-threaded operations. All tasks are parallelized from the entry of SQL statements to the smallest detail of their execution. Teradata developers, not knowing where the future bottlenecks might spring up attempted to weed out all single points of control in order to eliminate the conditions that breed gridlock in a system. Interconnect pathways, optimizers, host channel connections, gateways and units of parallelism can be defined which increase flexibility and control over the performance of query-intensive systems. The Teradata database still remains a benchmark for other parallel database vendors because it operates as a single, integrated parallel unit with all units intrinsically aware of the entire system. Many other parallel databases operate as discrete copies of the database resident on each processor in the system — so called 'instances' of the database with software co-ordinating the flow of data between the instances.

The original Teradata unit of parallelism was the AMP which was a physical processor — a standard Intel processor which provided a physical connection between the system and the data. This method has come to be known as 'closely-coupled' architecture. Because the data is closely coupled with each unit of parallelism in the system, it becomes crucially important for the data warehouse data to be evenly distributed across the entire system. An obvious bottleneck would occur if all customer profile data in a customer data warehouse was allocated to one disk unit since every query would need to access that data, thereby obviating the benefits of parallelism. This is managed in the Teradata database by a data loading utility that attempts to evenly balance distribute the data across all available units of parallelism. This is an important consideration since traditional data placement schemes are designed to balance data across disks or nodes, but this does not necessarily guarantee that the queries will be equally balanced. What is needed is a scheme that enforces an even distribution of data regardless of changes in the pattern of growth or access.

With Teradata version 2, the AMPs became virtual processors (VPROCs) with many co-existing on a single node as a collection of UNIX processes. With the virtual processor as the fundamental unit of apportionment, it can deliver basic query parallelism to all work in the system.

The following list highlights aspects of database parallelism that need to be probed by any prospective parallel DBMS purchaser:

1. Query parallelism
Query parallelism is enabled in the Teradata database by hash-partitioning the data across all of the virtual processors (VPROCs) defined in the system. A VPROC provides all of the database services on a pre-defined allocation of data blocks. All relational operations, such as table scans, index scans, projections, selections, joins, aggregations and sorts execute in parallel across all of the VPROCs. Each operation is performed on a VPROCs data independently of the data associated with the other VPROCs.

2. Within-a-step parallelism
A second dimension of parallelism that naturally occurs during query execution is an overlapping of selected database operations which are referred to as within-a-step parallelism. The system optimizer splits an SQL query into a small number of high-level database operations called 'steps' and dispatches these distinct steps for execution to the processors in the system. A step can be simple, such as 'scan a table and return the result', or complex, such as 'scan two tables with row qualifications, join the tables, redistribute the join result on specified columns, sum the redistributed rows and return the result'. The complex step specifies multiple relational operations which are processed in parallel by pipelining. Pipelining is the ability to begin one task before its predecessor task has completed. This dynamic execution technique, in which a second operation jumps off of a first one to perform portions of the step in parallel, contributes hugely to increasing the capability of the system to execute a complex query in parallel.

3. Multi-step parallelism
Multi-step parallelism is enabled by executing multiple steps of a query simultaneously, across all units of parallelism in the system.

One or more processes are invoked for each step on each processor to perform the actual database operation. Multiple steps for the same query can be executed at the same time to the extent that they are not dependent on results of previous steps.

4. Multi-statement parallelism

Multi-statement parallelism allows several distinct SQL statements to be sent to the database optimizer as if it was one single statement. These SQL statements can then be executed in parallel. Any sub-expressions that the different SQL statements have in common can be executed once and the results shared among the different SQL statements. Sometimes called 'common sub-expression elimination', multi-statement parallelism means that if six SQL select statements were bundled together, and if all contained the same sub-query, that sub-query would be executed only once.

5. Multi-load parallelism

Multi-load parallelism is the ability of the DBMS to support insert parallelism. Many data warehouses suffer from severe problems with loading the data during limited windows for updating/refreshing the data and most data warehouses suffer from difficulties during the initial load of data (which may represent tens or hundreds of gigabytes of historical data) when the data warehouse is first commissioned. In addition, DBMSs which do not support insert parallelism will need to create all intermediate answer sets serially, which may become a serious bottleneck. This bottleneck arises when the insert part of the insert/select statement is not paralleled, and occurs where complex queries require temporary tables between SQL statements.

6. Workflow management

An ever-present danger in any query-intensive system is the danger of 'thrashing'. Thrashing (sometimes called 'churning') occurs when, in a virtual memory system, the memory swapping becomes unstable. In practice, thrashing can occur when too many queries of a particular type are concurrently introduced. The physical memory is filled with pages of active processes, and where there are too many active processes needing access to too many pages, it results in paging between physical memory and the disks. In order to operate near the resource limits of the system, without causing the system to thrash, the system software needs to include effective workflow management. This is a crucially important issue for any data warehouse architect since the absence of sound workflow management software will require instead a considerable number of database administrators to manage the workflow which is a high cost of ownership in the long-term. The Teradata database, for example, monitors the utilization of critical resources (such as CPU, memory and interconnect). Where any of these reach a threshold value it triggers the throttling of message delivery, thereby allowing work already underway to complete.

Data Partitioning in a Massively Parallel Environment

Traditional data placement schemes may be used to partition data in a data warehouse environment. However, many of these techniques are inappropriate to a data warehouse environment and, in addition, can be inconsistent with a parallel computing environment. The following four data placement techniques comprise the range of schemes that are generally employed by database designers and the weaknesses of each are considered in the context of deploying data warehouse data in a massively parallel computer.

1. Data set partitioning
Data set partitioning occurs when incoming data is batched into data sets when it arrives into the system. Each segment of the data that is received is assigned one load file at a time. The problem with this method is that a small sub-set of the files will contain the most recent data and a high proportion of queries consist of operations that compare recent data to historical data. In MPP or clustered environments the DBMS has no way of telling if rows from two tables which are to be joined are located on the same processing

node. Any join activity using this approach is likely to pass enormous amounts of data across the interconnect, reducing overall system throughput.

2. Range partitioning

Range partitioning can work well if there is regular repetitive access based on the same constraint, because the DBA can partition the table into multiple collections of rows based on those particular values. But range partitioning presents a considerable ongoing challenge to the DBA. Firstly, a thorough analysis of the data distribution must be undertaken to start setting up the partition across nodes. Second, a method to locate commonly joined rows from different tables onto the same nodes to reduce interconnect traffic needs to be considered. Third, a method of balancing the data for each table across multiple nodes must be achieved. Fourth, since data demographics change over time, the partitioning scheme must be revisited regularly and recalculated and reorganised.

Even this effort may not achieve success since most range partitioning strategies are, at least to some extent, a function of time. Query behavior, on the part of users, changes over time and certain queries can be seasonal or cyclical. And, because some of the processing nodes will always contain significantly more current data than others, this will tend towards unbalanced processing.

3. Random partitioning

Random partitioning is the assignment of data to data sets based on a random number calculation. Unlike the hash partition, the random partition is non-repeatable, meaning that the DBMS never understands where a particular row for a table resides and so has no direct hook into a specific data row. While this technique will evenly spread data across nodes, it also means that rows will always require redistribution for a join or an aggregation, or even for the final sort of a result set.

4. Schema partitioning

Schema partitioning is the assignment of data to specific physical processors or nodes and has proven useful when there is a need to restrict portions of the hardware to handling certain groups of tables, or schemas. While this is generally viewed as a means of increasing performance for specific tables, and can be applied in a useful way in an SMP environment, it has not proven hugely successful in the MPP environment. In most cases to join data from two schema partitioned tables all rows have to be redistributed across the interconnect for each query. This data movement may significantly impact performance for the affected queries and the increased interconnect traffic may also impact overall system throughput.

Lock Management in the Parallel Environment

Care must be taken to ensure that locking does not consume large amounts of CPU resource and create a bottleneck. In the Tetadata database, for example, each row is owned by a particular VPROC, and only that VPROC can create, read, update or lock that data. Therefore all transaction logging is under local control. Because of this both locking and logging are parellelized, control of data is consistent and interconnect traffic can be reduced. Some systems attempt to deal with the locking problem by suspending locking. In such a system, any number of database processes could be attempting to update, insert, read or delete one row simultaneously. While not ideal, this may not be a critical problem since only the DBA will have the authority to update, insert or delete and users in a data warehouse environment are normally confined to read-only operations. However, in cases where the locking mechanism cannot be switched off, the task which wishes to use a row must retrieve a lock and then pass control to the next process wishing access. While this is quite feasible in an SMP environment where shared memory pointers are available, it would quickly saturate any MPP interconnect.

SELECTING A RELATIONAL DATABASE ENGINE

Selecting the appropriate database engine for the data warehouse is, arguably, more important than the hardware platform. While the problems associated with inappropriate hardware platforms become evident over time the deployment of an inappropriate database engine will be evident at the very outset of the development phase of the project.

For many enterprises the nature and scale of the data warehouse can be accommodated by a multi-dimensional database and these are discussed in more detail in Chapter 9. For most data warehouse implementations a relational (or quasi-relational) database will be mandatory for the enterprise.

It is self-evident that databases that perform to a high level of satisfaction in a transaction-processing environment are not necessarily appropriate to a query-intensive environment. Putting data into a database quickly and getting data out of a database quickly are distinctly different challenges and many of the traditional database vendors have struggled with the challenge of offering a product that satisfies both requirements. For example, a key challenge in data warehousing is preseted by the need to update large volumes of data (hundreds of millions of rows) on a daily basis. Achieving this update within the narrow batch window available requires a database utility capable of loading the data while at the same time achieving format conversions, integrity checking and indexing. Where an update fails, for whatever reason, the system should be capable of recovering and restarting while maintaining the integrity of the update process. In terms of performance, the database must support a query intensive environment where there will be a mixture of complex and simple queries, different types of analysis (ROLAP, SQL, data mining), and different patterns of usage. The database should be capable of managing online data (on magnetic disk) as well as offline data which is less frequently accessed (on optical disk or or other media). It is crucially important for the database administrator to be capable of managing the impact of complex computationally intensive queries and have the ability to anticipate potentially 'runaway' queries. Because the pattern of usage of a data warehouse changes over time it is useful to have query behavior tracked in order to evaluate what changes need to be made to physical schemas, access paths and disk layouts. The scale of the data warehouse database also presents new challenges since tasks such as database reorganization, unload, backup and restore need to be achieved within reasonable time-scales on databases with massive volumes of data. All of these requirements combine to create an environment which is distinctly different to the OLTP database administration environment.

Table 5.3 outlines the most important aspects, (in addition to the obvious considerations of basic performance and price), that need to be explored in any evaluation process for a database engine for a data warehouse implementation.

The TPC-D Benchmark Test

The Transaction Processing Council have defined a benchmark test for query-intensive processing (TPC-D) which is measured on the basis of a five year cost-of-ownership of the server processor, disk storage and software. The results are expressed in terms of cost per query (K$/Q) and the query environment represents a defined set of 17 SQL queries and a defined database schema. Different tets are performed at 1, 30, 100, 300 and 1000GB of data[5]

There is widespread agreement that the TPC-D benchmark test are still immature as a basis for real comparison. The main difficulty arises because of the problem of replicating a real-world query environment. Almost all production data warehouses will vary considerably in terms of the type and complexity of queries, the mix of concurrent and serial usage, the database schemas, the hardware/ DBMS combinations and configurations and the types of query tools used to analyse the data. In addition to these difficulties, many aspects of data warehouse performance are not addressed such as load performance (including indexing, format conversion, integrity checking), the building of aggregate and summary tables and the performance of multi-dimensional analysis. TPC-D should be regarded as a useful stress test for the database engines being tested rather than an authoritive statement of comparitive

---

[5] The full TCP-D specification is available at http://www.tpc.com

Table 5.3　key issues in the selction of a DBMS

	Issue	Elaboration
1	Query governor	All runaway queries should be anticipated and aborted before substantial systems resources are consumed.
2	Query optimizer	The query optimizer should enable the database to optimize the parsing of SQL syntax that is expressed inefficiently by the user.
3	Query management	The system resouces should be capable of being monitored and balanced between queries of different type and complexity.
4	Load utility	The performance of the data loading utility should be measured in gigabytes per hour and the DBMS should support recovery and restart in the event of load processing failure.
5	Metadata management	The database should support an active catalog that contains both internal and external metadata (see Chapter 6).
6	Administration and operations	The database needs to support the activities of the Database Administrator and Data Steward with regard to data movement, data updates, query prioritization, resource limitation, unload, backup, restore, archiving and security.
7	Scalability	The database should be capable of scaling with regard to both users and data volumes.
8	Query tool APIs	The database should support the use of all query tools selected by the enterprise.
9	Copy management tool APIs	The database should support the copy management tools selected by the enterprise.
10	Extensibility	The database should support hybrid extensions to the data warehouse architecture, including OLAP databases, data mining, groupware environments, the Internet and specialized applications.
11	Portability	The database should be capable of being easily ported across hardware platforms.

performance.One of the more interesting aspects of the benchmark test results is the ratio of raw data to disk storage for the different database engines. In the case of the 100GB benchmark test published in 1996, the disk storage requirements of different vendors ranged from 350GB to almost 900 GB.

Assessing the Relevance of Database Reference Sites

The issue of scalability is of considerable concern in selecting a database engine. Many vendors will quote reference sites with enormous volumes of data being accessed by knowledge workers, thereby creating an impression of safe scalability. In many of these instances the volume of raw data is actually a fraction of the data volumes being quoted. Users should be aware that the difference between the disk storage capacity of a data warehouse and the actual volumes of data is considerable — in some cases this ratio can be as high as 10:1 and is, in most instances, at least 3:1. The questions that needs to be posed to vendors by the prospective purchaser at a reference site should include a breakdown of the following statistics:

(a) The volume of spinning disk,
(b) The volume of allocated disk space,
(c) The level of indexation and the space consumed by the indices,
(d) The volume of raw data,
(e) The proportion of raw data that comprise summary and aggregate tables of the base data.

In addition to the above questions the evaluator should establish if the star schema design approach is applied to the table schemas in the reference site since use of the star schema (explored in more detail in Chapter 4) can consume a larger amount of disk storage.

With regard to building and maintaining the data warehouse database two important considerations need to be assessed. The first relates to the number of separate physical tables that are needed to implement the logical design. A telling question here is to enquire how many DDL statements are needed to construct the database at the reference site in question. From an operational perspective it is important to establish how many DBAs are needed to support the operation and administration of the database. Some merchant databases require a considerable amount of support from database administrators while others (such as the Teradata database) require very little management. Data stewardship considerations (explored in more detail in Chapter 7) should also be included in the evaluation from the perspective of administration tools for the Steward.

But the single most common omission made in the selection process for data warehouse database engines relates to the issue of data loading. For most enterprises the time it takes to load the data into the database is a critical success factor and, all too often, it is an aspect that is overlooked in the evaluation and selection process. Users need to bear in mind that significant data volumes need to be refreshed and updated on the data warehouse within a limited batch window. A common ploy of vendors is to optimize the performance of SQL queries on the database through blanket indexation of the tables without pointing out to the user that, as a result, it is unlikely that the weekly update/inserts can be loading within their lifetime! A separate problem often arises in respect of the initial loading of the legacy data. It may be that of gigabytes of historical data need to be loading initially and this may stretch the capability of some database engines.

MASSIVELY PARALLEL PROCESSING AND MAINFRAME S/390 COMPARED[6]

IBM announced, in late 1996, the results of their data warehouse benchmark test for the System/390, thereby allowing a direct comparison to be made with the same test that had previously been used to benchmark test the RS/6000 SP massively parallel platform.

---

[6] The source material for this evaluation is provided in the IBM White Paper 'Sizzling S/390 Query Performance' (1996) authored by David Heap.

The result, according to IBM, 'explodes the myth that S/390 mainframes cannot handle decision-support queries'. And, while the evidence available from these new tests supports this view, the old perception of the mainframe probably had more to do with the performance of older versions of DB2 than any mistaken impression created by analysts, users or commentators in the past.

The Atomic Performance Benchmarks were developed by IBM to provide customers with factual information on the performance of large-scale IBM systems and were specifically directed at measuring query-intensive (as opposed to transaction-intensive) computing environments. The 13 atomic tests provide repeatable results that represent the basic 'atomic' building blocks necessary to estimate the performance of large-scale data warehouse systems. Each of the 13 tests focuses on a different aspect of decision-support systems performance. The benchmark database is similar to the specification for TPC/D 1.0 (the Transaction Processing Council Decision-support benchmark test) and was constructed from 60GB of raw data distributed across six major tables. The largest table is the 51.4GB LINEITEM table.

What is really valuable about these benchmarks is that they offer an opportunity, for the first time, to directly compare the performance of machines of a different architecture — the RS6000 SP and the S/390 mainframe. Of course, one can argue (and IBM does) that the CMOS mainframe is effectively a massively parallel computer and that the technological chasm that traditionally separated the mainframe from the new generation of MPP platform is synthetic and no longer relevant. However, the technical architectures of the RS/6000 SP and the S/390 are distinctly different and the DB2 database engine used on each platform is distinctly different in terms of its architecture, functionality, performance and behavior. S/390 has always had powerful SMP capabilities and since shipping S/390 sysplex and MVS v4 in 1994, S/390 has had the hardware and operating system capability to manage up to 320 engines in parallel. This is, in effect, S/390 MPP.

The S/390 tests were run on a 9672-R42, an SMP system comprising four 'concerto' CMOS engines, 2 gigabytes of memory, and a single copy of MVS 5.2 and DB2 4.1. A total of 60 3390 disk devices were attached to the 9672 ESCON channels via four 3990-6 cached storage controllers.

The RS/6000 SP tests were run on a 14 node SP system with 12 thin nodes and two wide nodes. Each node was a 66mhz POWER2 processor with 256MB memory running AIX 4.1.3 and DB2/PE 1.0. 180 2.2 gigabyte disks were attached to SCSI channels of the 12 thin nodes via 7135-210 storage controllers.

The following four queries are selected from the benchmark results as they represent a range of classic tests of a data warehouse query-intensive environment.

Query 1 — Full table scan
This query is a full scan of all 360 million rows in the largest table (51.4 LINEITEM table). With no index field for this query, every row is read and processed.

Results:
S/390 : 16.1 minutes.
RS/6000 SP : 25.1 minutes.

Comment: The traditional perception of the System 390 was that performance on I/O intensive tasks was poor. An interesting comparative analysis demonstrates that a full scan of 180 millions rows (23GB table) with 1991 DB2 ran in 172 minutes, while the same query running on DB2 (version 4) ran in 4.6 minutes.

Query 2 — Select, aggregate and sort
This test simulates a user application requesting summary data created by selecting 9 million rows from the 360 million row LINEITEM table.

Results:
S/390: 3.8 minutes.
RS/6000 SP: 2.6 minutes.

Comment: The 9 million rows selected for this query were all located on 2 disks which illustrates the real world problem that arises when the data paths between these two disks and the processors become bottlenecked. In the actual test the S/390 processor utilization was only 48%. It should be noted that a similar query that scanned 36 million rows spread across 6 disks took only 7.8 minutes to complete and ran the processor at 93% busy.

Query 3 — Co-located joins

This test illustrates the joining of one very large 'fact' table (the 360 million row LINEITEM table) with the 9 million row ORDER table. It returns 1 million unsorted rows to the requesting application.

Results:
S/390: 5.1 minutes.
RS/6000 SP: 38.2 minutes.

Comment: The processing power and I/O bandwidth of the S/390 is clearly superior to the SP in this type of query. The bottleneck in both the S/390 and the SP turns out to be the serial processing of the 1 million rows by the receiving application.

Query 4 — Ad-hoc joins

This test requests two large tables to be joined by a common field that is not an index.

Results:
S/390: 6 minutes.
RS/6000 SP: 26.9 minutes.

Comment: The differences in architecture are at their most stark in this query because of the different behavior of the two platforms in executing an ad hoc join. DB2 for MVS selects 9 million rows from the 360 million row LINEITEM table and sorts them in about 4 minutes. It then selects 9 million rows from the PARTSUPP table and sorts them. Finally it merge-joins the two result tables to complete the whole query in 6 minutes. DB2/PE selected 9 million rows from the PARTSUPP table and broadcasts them to all other nodes. Each node then matches these rows with the LINEITEM rows on its disk using a merge-join technique, completing the query in just under 30 minutes.

Clearly the results are exceptionally good news for S/390 advocates. For the first time we have a reasonably good basis for comparitive analysis between a massively parallel architecture and a mainframe architecture. But the differences in operating system (MVS and Unix) and database software also contribute to the results that are achieved.

However, price performance is the real test for most users, not absolute performance. In addition, the report of the benchmarks acknowledges that each result depends not only on the differences in the underlying architecture but on data placement, partitioning, indexing and query optimization. However, these factors which bedevil the analysis of most benchmark test results are less pressing in this case since it is not a benchmark test of one vendor product against another. Clearly, IBM themselves were interested to know what the results would be in a fair contest between their own massively parallel Unix platform and their mainframe product. One must assume that the S/390 and the SP/2 groups within IBM were equally happy with the nature of the test and that both groups optimized the features of both products to achieve the very best result possible.

IBM has had, and continues to have, a twin track product strategy for large-scale decision support servers. The RS/6000 SP is a high performance Unix MPP solution, for those customers who want a 'mix and match' Unix solution, and a S/390 MPP solution, with S/390 and DB2 v4, for those customers who prefer to build on their existing MVS applications, DB2 data resources and people skills.

An estimate of S/390 linear scaling in the terabyte range is more difficult to predict, but an indication of the linear capability of the new IBM 10 engined 9672-RX4 at the DB2 technical conference in Miami in October 1996 offers some insight. Two coupled RX4s were unleashed at a monster 6 billion row 750 gigabyte table of the same rowsize as the 23 gigabyte table used in the atomic benchmark tests.

These 20 engines scanned and read all the rows and completed the task in 50 minutes. So the data table was about 33 times bigger than the table used in the benchmark test, about four times the processor resource was applied and the scan took about nine times longer.

COPY MANAGEMENT

The first problems encountered in the task of building a data warehouse are the data migration and data conversion aspects of the project. Capturing and moving legacy data from source systems to the target database is, for many organizations, an extremely complex task. Problems arise because of the need not to impact adversely on the performance of the legacy systems. Problems arise because of the complex transformations that need to occur in the data, if it is to be truly useful. Problems arise because of the need to manage the metadata. Problems even arise because there is no clear semantic definitions for some of the legacy data. For the purposes of this section all of these issues will collectively be labeled as copy-management.

One observation that needs to be made about copy-management tools generally is that the use of such tools is not pervasive and a majority of data warehouse sites, at the time of writing, use custom-developed extraction and transformation programs rather than the copy-management tools that have been designed for this function. The reason for this is twofold. Some enterprises with relatively simple requirements consider these tools to be overspecified and too expensive to cost-justify. Other enterprises, with extremely complex transformation requirements from a hetrogeneous database environments (especially those including older versions of hierarchial databases) find these tools not to be sufficiently rich in functionality to meet their requirements. The relatively low level of adoption of these tools is a factor of the immaturity of this segment of the market, and the development of more modular tools that are more functionally rich can be expected.

Change Data Capture Critical Success Factors

The following list of CSFs summarize the issues which need to be managed to ensure the success of the data capture process and tool evaluations should be guided by reference to these CFSs:

- Minimize operational systems impact.
- Allow data snapshots to be refreshed.
- Allow delta changes to be transferred.
- Allow trickle feed of data.
- Allow real-time transfer of data.
- Allow undo of warehouse updates.
- Exploit target database features/utilities.
- Read data from different platforms.
- Meet specific service levels.
- Support operational management of warehouse environment.
- Schedule extractions and related dependencies.
- Detect and highlight source system changes.
- Ability to hold data mappings between layers, including logical and physical.
- Ability to import LDMs and PDMs.
- Ability to reverse engineer schemas.
- Ability to support configuration management, including version control.
- Ability to support security administration.

Constructing a Copy Management Tool Specification

The key concerns when selecting the hardware platform and database engine are performance and scalability. Assembling the right suite of software tools for the data warehouse architecture provides the key to an elegant and manageable environment. There are a number of different tools which may be required, but the essential tools are going to be the data extraction tool (to capture the data), the repository tool (to manage the metadata), the and the information catalogue tool (to support end-user access and downstream data marts). In addition to these tools there will also be CASE tools and data cleansing tools and project management tools that are desirable and may be needed. The key concern when selecting the tools for staging the data is the issue of integration. Put another way, the key question that the project manager must pose when considering the suitability of software tools is, will they exchange metadata? Bearing this over-riding consideration in mind, the following sets of questions in respect of the main tool categories should provide the reader with a guide to the issues that need to be addressed. Because of the fast-moving nature of this marketplace any structured evaluation of tools using the criteria here, or other criteria devised by the user organization, should be assisted by competent external consultants.

Key Questions when Evaluating Repository/Metadata Management Tools

- Does the tool have a metadata catalog where the data can be described?
- Does the catalog support administration functions, including security?
- Does the catalog support end-user access for browsing?
- Is the catalogue active or passive (e.g. does it respond to events such as updates)?
- Does the product have a graphical interface environment?
- Is the metamodel extensible by the user? If yes, do subsequent releases preserve these extensions?
- From what data environments can the tools automatically import/export schema definitions?
- What type of user interface does the tool provide for browsing and querying the metadata?
- Can the tool flexibly exchange metadata with other tools?
- Is the vendor organization a member of the Metadata Interchange Initiative?

Key Questions when Evaluating Extraction/Transformation Tools

- What operating system/desktop platforms does the tool reside on?
- Can the tool import business metadata from CASE tools? What CASE tools can the tool access in read mode? In write mode?
- Does the tool support the emerging CDIF (CASE Data Interchange Format) standard?
- Can the tool dictionary automatically import metadata from repository products?
- What repository products can the tool access in read mode? In write mode?
- Can the tool dictionary export data, table and attribute definitions to database catalogues? If yes, which database products are supported?
- Can the tool dictionary export data, table, and attribute definitions to data access tools? If yes, what data access tools are supported?
- How does the tool import/export schema information?
- What other metadata does the tool maintain and can this be exported?
- What program language does the tool generate?
- Is the code readable and/or customizable?
- Can the program include user exit routines?
- Does the tool support calls to proprietary routines?
- Does the tool create the control language (DCL, JCL, TACL, Unix scripts) for compiling the Cobol source statements, running the Cobol programs and loading the SQL databases?
- Does the tool support user functions?
- Does the tool support conditional logic?
- Does the tool support look-up tables?
- Does the tool support generating programs that perform selective retrieve and changed data capture?
- Can data be merged from multiple sources during the retrieval process?
- Is the vendor organization a member of the Metadata Interchange Initiative?

Key Questions when Evaluating Replication/Propagation Tools

- What source data environments are supported by the tool (specify database product versions)?
- What target data environments are supported by the tool (specify database product versions)?
- Is there any mechanism for supporting the transformation of data values in the replication process?
- Can the tool operate in synchronous and asynchronous mode?
- Does the tool support scheduled transmissions in asynchronous mode?
- Does the tool support complex broadcast requirements such as store and forward for moving subsets of data to successive levels?
- Does the tool support both refresh and update copying?
- Does the tool capture changes by reading the database log or by another method (e.g. triggers)?
- Do applications require to be altered for replication — do they require re-compilation, re-bind or re-link?
- Is the tool fault tolerant — i.e. does it require that a network be continuously available?
- Does the tool support bi-directional replication?
- Is the vendor organization a member of the Metadata Interchange Initiative?

CONCLUSIONS

It should be noted that the data warehouse project is a systems integration project and requires specialist systems integration expertise. One thing that should not be done in the data warehouse project is to purchase separately the different technology components of the warehouse on the basis of separate criteria. The objective is not to buy the best-of-breed in each separate category. The objective is to buy a suite of products that work together. Ideally, a conscious decision should be taken to only accept proposals from consortiums of vendors who undertake to ensure the interoperability of the different vendor components that are proposed. This measure will help to manage the risk that is inherent in the project.

User organizations faced by the prospect of a data warehouse solution that combines products from a number of different suppliers should enquire:

- What testing there has been of this particular combination of products working together, the results of those tests?
- What is the extent of live implementations based on the combination of product components?
- What detailed performance reports are available?
- What reference sites exist for the component combination under consideration and an assessment by the system architect at that site of the strengths and weaknesses of the combination?

6

Metadata Management

'There is a great difference between knowing and understanding: you can know a lot about something and not really understand it.'
— *Charles F. Kettering*

Metadata is a term that is applied to the data that describes data. A thorough understanding of the role of metadata is essential in any understanding of data warehousing. Metadata indicates the source, value, use and function of the data in the data warehouse and describes how data is changed or altered as it passes through the various layers of the data warehouse architecture.

The concept of metadata should have, in the context of data warehousing, the broadest possible connotations and should not simply refer to the semantics and syntax of the data. In order to understand what the data in a data warehouse represents (from a user's perspective), and in order to manage and administer the data in a data warehouse (from a system administrator's perspective), the management of metadata is indistinguishable from the management of the data warehouse itself.

Metadata management is, for most data warehouse projects, the single greatest technical challenge. The copy management environment, the database environment, the applications development environment, the data access environment and the data administration environment all need to know about metadata and, crucially, at all times have the same metadata.

INTERNAL AND EXTERNAL METADATA

Because metadata is used to support both the activities of the data administrator and the enduser, it is useful to draw a distinction between these two uses of metadata. For the purposes of distinguishing these two perspectives of metadata, the administrator's view of metadata may be referred to as "internal metadata" and the enduser's view may be referred to as "external metadata". Obviously, the external and internal views overlap and must be consistent, one with the other. These separate views are defined in Table 6.1:

Table 6.1   Internal and external metadata

Internal metadata	Internal metadata is primarily concerned with describing the sources, transformations, business rules, update and refresh schedules, staging, physical locations, logical to physical mappings, aging, purging, archiving, synchronization, database representations, table names, access patterns, movements and security constraints that pertain to the data.
External metadata	External metadata is primarily concerned with describing the definitions, aliases, ownership, quality, units of measure, summarizations, aggregations, access criteria, currency, coverage, volumes, conversions and relationships that pertain to the data.

Traditionally, database administrators used dictionary products to help to manage the database environment. Endusers rarely had any user-friendly mechanism to help them to understand the data, but some tools had information catalogs to assist in this task. The data warehouse user needs to have more sophisticated support in order to fully optimize the value of the warehouse and to prevent users from drawing incorrect conclusions from the analysis that they are conducting. Users need to know more than just the meaning of the data: they need to know when the data was last re-refreshed, what the pedigree of the data is (i.e. what is the quality, accuracy and source of the data), the business terms that describe the data, as well as a knowledge of pre-defined reports that are available to them.

The data warehouse environment requires a metadata management and presentation environment which contains the complete metastore of data that satisfies both the constituency of business users and that also satisfies the needs of those information technology personnel who are tasked with developing applications, administering the database, extending the architecture and ensuring that adequate controls exist to guarantee that the data is valid for the purposes for which it is being used.

THE CHALLENGE OF METADATA MANAGEMENT

Because each separate software tool has its own proprietary metadata, the main challenge facing data warehouse developers relates to achieving a common metadata standard which ensures that all of the different tool components of the data warehouse architecture contain a common subset of metadata that is sufficiently complete to enable the effective management of the data warehouse environment. Then the metadata must be synchronized as data ripples across the different parts of the physical data warehouse infrastructure. In order to do this correctly the system architect has to ensure that the correct item of metadata at the correct level of detail is copied from one software tool to another tool where it has to be mapped on to the correct metadata there. In the course of this transfer a number of semantic, syntactic and algorithmic differentials need to be incorporated into the conversion.

The challenge is further complicated by the fact that data may change in the source systems or changes may take place in the data transformation rules or even to the underlying physical schema. Up until recently developers were severely constrained from automating the exchange of metadata from one tool to another. This challenge is now being addressed by the Metadata Coalition, an industry body which is described later in this chapter.

Table 6.2 identified the different elements that need to be addressed in constructing a comprehensive metadata strategy for the data warehouse:

Table 6.2   Elements of metadata strategy

Metadata exchange	Metadata needs to be exchanged between different software tools that comprise the data warehouse physical infrastructure.
Metadata standardization	The representation of metadata needs to be standardized so that different metadata repositories represent the same metadata in the same way.
Metadata replication	As changes occur in metadata within the physical infrastructure of the data warehouse, these changes need to be rippled throughout the rest of the infrastructure.
Metadata synchronization	At all times the metadata that is available at different locations within the physical data warehouse infrastructure should present the same metadata concerning events, updates, archiving, purging, etc.
Metadata versioning	Legacy operational systems are only concerned with the current definition of data, but the data warehouse which contains historical as well as current data needs to be concerned with historical metadata that may have changed over time.

A wide variety of problems exist in trying to create a common, accurate metastore and many of these problems have their roots in the historically inadequate (or non-existent) corporate information technology planning process. In the same way that data is fragmented across the enterprise, so too is the metadata. The following list indicates some of the more common problems encountered in the quest for a unified metadata standard:

- Conflicting data naming conventions.
- Conflicting data definitions.
- Conflicting data attributes.
- Conflicting values.
- Conflicting sources.
- Conflicting business rules.
- Different time periods.

- Different units of measure.
- Different means of measure.
- Missing data.
- Lack of, or poor quality, documentation.
- Different data structures.
- Inadequate data validation.
- Indiscriminate use of aliases.
- Conflicting syntax.
- Conflicting standards and formats.

In the long term the solution to the problem of metadata management lies in the adoption of a metadata standard by the software industry. Because of the wide variety of proprietary metadata that occurs at present, it must be anticipated that the vendor community will resist any standard metamodel because it would force them to radically re-engineer and retrofit their products. The best that can hoped for in the short to medium term is that some degree of agreement will be reached on a metametadata standard which would allow for user-defined metadata structures and which would facilitate greater degree of tool interoperability.

The real cost of managing metadata relates to the cost of maintaining the data warehouse infrastructure. Many enterprises are finding that the data warehouse maintenance challenge is becoming increasingly complex, prone to error and prohibitively expensive in terms of the cost of human resources.

Locating Metadata within the Physical Data Warehouse Infrastructure

Metadata is trapped and used throughout the data warehouse infrastructure. Source data dictionaries contain metadata but are unlikely to be sufficiently complete to satisfy the needs of the data warehouse. The source systems are likely to have multiple dictionaries which contain metadata, and changes in the application systems as well as database re-organizations will complicate the task of discovering what metadata is relevant to what data. Different legacy systems will have been implemented over a long period when different data standards existed and will be resident on different technologies. Data will be transformed during the extraction process and data relating to a specific subject (e.g. customer data) will need to be consolidated and reformated. The description of these transformation rules will be resident on separate dictionaries that reside in the copy management tool environment. In addition, data cleansing will apply changes to the source data which also need to be trapped and consolidated with the other transformations. The data warehouse database will be based on a design that is, most probably, contained in a modeling tool that identifies the logical model for the data and the data warehouse database catalogue will contain information about the physical schema of the data warehouse database implementation. Also the mappings from the source systems to the target database also need to be captured. Most data warehouse infrastructures will comprise multiple front-end data access tools and applications development environments and each of these software tools will have their own metadata environments. The complexity of this entire data warehouse physical infrastructure is illustrated in Figure 6.1:

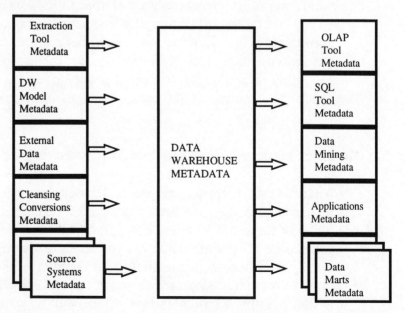

Figure 6.1 The location of metadata within the data warehouse infrastructure

This illustration of metadata duplication through the entire architecture of the data warehouse appears complex but is, in fact, over-simplified. In many data warehouse implementations, data is being updated in data marts with a requirement for bi-directional data replication from the central enterprise warehouse to and from the marts. In addition, the central warehouse physical structures are subject to continuous change, as summary and aggregate tables are constructed to satisfy performance considerations and new derived data is resulting from queries and calculations. The data warehouse environment is dynamic and constantly changing and the metadata needs to keep abreast of all these changes.

SOURCES OF METADATA

It is unusual to find metadata already defined and captured in an enterprise. Therefore, the task facing the data warehouse project team during the initial modeling phase of the project includes discovering what is known about the existing data and defining what changes are going to take place to that data within the data warehouse environment. The search for metadata is often onerous and difficult because of the poor level of documentation that exists to inform the analysts about legacy applications. And where documentation does exist it is unlikely to have been adequately updated as changes occurred as the original application was altered and as the original database design was changed. The following list includes some common sources of metadata:

- Operational data dictionaries and catalogs.
- Corporate data repositories.
- 4GL repositories.
- COBOL copybooks and file structures.
- Business models.
- CASE tool repositories/encyclopedias.
- Word-processed documents.
- Paper documents.
- Data models.

- Job streams.
- Comments embedded in application programmes.
- Inside the heads of users and systems developers.

DATA STEWARDSHIP

The concept of the Data Steward, with responsibility for managing the entire metadata environment, has been introduced by the phenomenon of data warehousing. The mission of the Data Steward extends beyond the traditional remit of the database administrator and is a new job role that is now regarded as an essential feature of the data warehouse environment.

Once the data warehouse construction staff deliver a new chunk of functionality responsibility for managing the additional data and or the new application environment normally passes to the Data Steward. All responsibility relating to data quality, data availability, system performance, system security and metadata management are vested in the Data Steward.

The list of responsibilities that are normally included in the job specification of a Data Steward is contained in the following list:

- To manage metadata capture, maintenance, synchronization and replication throughout the data warehouse architecture.
- To accumulate and compile knowledge concerning the available data.
- To unify data definitions, naming conventions, business rules and data quality indicators.
- To identify sources of corporate and syndicated data.
- To decide on the archiving strategy for the data warehouse.
- To administer the security rules that apply to data warehouse access.
- To assess the accuracy of data elements.
- To assess the overall quality of available data.
- To ensure the consistency of data definitions and ensuring compliance with data models.

- To capture and analyze access patterns and to construct summary and aggregate tables as necessary to relieve congestion and avoid performance problems.

As the data warehouse matures the role of the Data Steward becomes more central and the views of the data Steward should be canvassed by the warehouse Architect and by application developers. Inevitably, since the Data Steward occupies a control role, he or she may eventually become to be regarded as an obstacle in the ongoing evolution of the warehouse. This is a necessary role to play since the potential for the data warehouse to evolve in an ad hoc manner and degenerate into chaotic dysfunction is quite real. The Data Steward is a role that bridges the many gaps that exist in the pre-warehouse information processing environment. For example, the marketing department may understand how to use the data, but not how to manage it. Individual developers may understand the requirements for their own application, but not that of other developers. The information systems department may understand the underlying processes that create the data, but have no authority to make business decisions which are needed to improve the quality or accuracy of the data. Endusers who wish to implement downstream data marts will have a clear vision of the data that they require to populate the mart, but will have little understanding of the performance impacts that replicating the data from the warehouse will have on other applications. So the Data Steward must stand at the various intersections and manage the traffic in data that will become increasingly complex as the data warehouse expands. It is a role that requires both business and technical skills and the creation of a fully empowered Data Steward is the single most important decision that will be made by the enterprise to contain the risk of system degeneration that is inherent in every major data warehouse project.

DATA WAREHOUSE ADMINISTRATION AND MAINTENANCE

The universal problem that is experienced in mature data warehouse sites is managing the data warehouse environment. Because the data warehouse architecture comprises many different tools doing different tasks (modeling data, extracting data, transforming data, loading data, managing data, building views of data) the challenge has always been to manage the complexity of integrating the entire framework. The solution lies in implementing a layer of metadata management software that spans the entire architecture from data acquisition to data management to data access. It is increasingly critical to the enterprise to find a way of effectively managing this environment as the potential for chaos in the movement of data around the enterprise is considerable.

Operations and Administration

This aspect of data warehousing is, at present, poorly supported by tools in the marketplace and the current state of data warehouse operations support is extremely primitive. Because the data warehouse architecture has evolved in an ad hoc manner, taking advantage of various technology innovations as they occur, most real world data warehouse logical and technology architectures consist of complex data staging strategies that are considerably less elegant than the conceptual architecture that is defined. Most data warehouse implementations are based on multi-tier approach to delivering the data to endusers whereby the central warehouse distributes data to subsidiary data marts. These data marts tend to employ a wide range of technologies ranging from relational database servers, OLAP servers, data mining servers and application environments. The use of data marts serves to:

- Relieve the processing load on the central server by using cheaper server technologies.
- Reduce the design challenge of the central data warehouse database by allowing highly specialized aggregations to be made available to users and by maintaining a sense of application independence of the enterprise data on the central server, which guarantees more flexibility in the architecture as the requirements of the system change over time.

- Reduce the complexity of navigating the central server, which will contain a lot of data that is not of interest to large groups of users.

- Reduce the monolithic nature of the data warehouse which is often a barrier to effective use of the data warehouse, and foster a sense of ownership by groups of users who have a sense of control and ownership over these local servers.

- Allow users to employ a wider range of data exploitation techniques and allow users a location to store result tables (from SQL queries) and hypercubes (from relational OLAP operations).

- Insulate the user from downtime on the central server and data communications failures.

The challenge of managing a complex data architecture where data is physically located at a number of points in the architecture is considerable. The end user should perceive the data warehouse as a seamless system and should not be required to have any knowledge of the physical location of the data or the physical structure of that data. The challenge of managing the environment can be divided into two separate aspects. First there is the problem of presenting the user with a fully abstracted level of access. Secondly, there is the challenge of facilitating the system administrator in the task of knowing what the precise status of data in this fluid system at any one time and all of the time.

TYPES OF END USER

There is no such thing as a typical end user of a data warehouse but there is compelling evidence to suggest that there are distinct user types:

1. *Operations.* One type of user is the routine user who has a repetitive pattern of usage and whose decision-making is highly programmed in nature but where the level of detail required is often highly granular. This type of user usually has a

requirement for a limited amount of data, but very often requires detailed data that is near real-time in terms of currency. Typically this user is seeking data to support an operational process such as financial management, logistical supply analysis, account management, etc.

2. *Planning.* The planner has a requirement for highly predetermined data but it is generally of a summary or aggregate nature. Very often this type of user will have a requirement to maintain result tables for modeling purposes and for iterative analysis.

3. *Strategy.* Another type of user has a requirement to access data in a manner that is generally ad hoc and not amenable to being predetermined. This user may require access to all or some of the data and to detailed and summary data.

4. *Executive. T*he Executive user is concerned with monitoring the key performance indicators of the enterprise and is therefore concerned with having access to pre-defined reports and to calculated fields.

Table 6.3   Different categories of user

User	Detailed data	Summary data	Pre-determined	Calculated
Operations	●	●	●	
Planning		●		●
Strategy	●	●		
Executive			●	●

The demands of the user community for a more comprehensive data warehouse administration and maintenance software environment has been steadily building for a number of years. The early data warehouse developers focused most of their attention on the challenge of building a data warehouse. The equally demanding challenge of maintaining the entire data warehouse architecture only became evident when the complexities of managing these early implementations became clear. It is precisely because the data warehouse is an architecture (and not an application) that it becomes essential to have administration tools to ensure that the different components of the architecture can interact in a standardized, synchronized and dynamic fashion.

The list of questions in Table 6.4 represents a cross-section of concerns that are being voiced by data warehouse managers and which illustrate the need for enhanced data warehouse administration tools

The demand for metadata management tool is finding a response from many different vendors. One of the most innovative tools to be developed for the purpose of data warehouse administration came from an unusual source. Bank of Boston constructed a data warehouse in 1992 and in the course of implementing the solution they found a gap in their architecture. Nobody had a tool to support the activities of the database administrator who was responsible for the administrative and operational aspects of the system. Bank of Boston quickly discovered that this situation was potentially disastrous. What would happen if a table name was changed or a new table was added? What would happen if there were orphan data elements? How would they manage to ensure synchronization and replication of metadata from the copy management tools to the database catalog to the data access tool catalogs? How would they manage the delivery of data to the many data marts and DSS applications that were spawned by the enterprise warehouse? As happens in an mature data warehouse site the problem of managing the environment was immense. But Bank of Boston's Jack Sweeney decided to do something about it. He and his team developed their own software tool to manage metadata and it was such an outstanding success that it is now marketing by a separate company — Intellidex Systems.

Established data warehouse vendors have also seen the need to develop data warehouse administration tools. SAS Institute has developed the *SAS Administrator* (launched in the first quarter of 1997) to provide complete control over the end-to-end data warehouse solution.

What is needed for effective data warehouse administration is an intelligent metadata catalog that can be accessed and used at one level by the data warehouse administrator and at another level by the enduser. Within the tool environment the metadata should be

Table 6.4   The key issues for data warehouse administration

Location	Issue
External data	• What happens when users want to incorporate external (syndicated) data into the data warehouse? • What happens when the corporation merges with another corporation which has different data types, definitions etc? • What happens when we want to share data with another corporation for a joint promotion?
Data warehouse	• What happens when we need to mask data on the data warehouse for reasons of confidentiality? • How do we control the runaway query? • What happens when we need to restrict access to users on the grounds of security? • What happens when we need to restrict access to users on the grounds of balancing performance and workload? • What happens to the transparency layer that was constructed to hide the data structure complexity from the users when we find that we have to change or alter the physical schemas? • How do we analyze the ad hoc queries that are being generated by users to see if there are any patterns that would be useful in defining summary tables?
Data marts	• How do we manage metadata replication from the data warehouse to the many subsidiary data marts? • What happens if the data on the data marts and data on the data warehouse are not synchronized? • What happens when users change the data definitions on the data marts? • Who controls the data definitions and table names of derived data that is produced by the data marts?
Source data	• What happens when data changes on the source systems? • What happens when business rules or application logic changes on the source systems? • What happens when new data is introduced into the source systems? • What happens when we discover that data needs to be cleansed on the source systems after we have populated the polluted data on to the data warehouse? • How do we audit the logical and physical mappings from the source to target system on an ongoing basis?

presented in terms of the physical description, the logical description and a description of the transformations. What the *Intellidex* tool seeks to do, in the words of company President, Jack Sweeney is "to overlay a semantic business context layer on top of the enterprise data".

Any data warehouse administration tool should incorporate the ability to manage the movement of data around the full warehouse architecture i.e. data coming in from flat files or copy management tools and data being delivered to downstream data marts. Once metadata is integrated into the metadata repository, users should be able to navigate, browse and search for whatever data is contained in the warehouse. They could request on-line extracts to be built for their query, analysis and reporting tools. They could request subscriptions of sub-sets of the warehouse data to be sent to local database servers/data marts. Therefore, the ripple effect of changes and data transfers is managed within a single control centre.

Having one central metastore has many advantages. It allows for the import of the target DBMS catalog metadata into the metastore. An editing facility can provide the capability to synchronize the logical and physical metadata contained in the warehouse system. Analysis and reporting functions include referential integrity checking (matching the metadata model to the real data warehouse), orphan object analysis and consistency checking.

There are also significant advantages for the end-user in having one central metastore. It should empower the user to discover what data is in the data warehouse and present him/her with the facility to browse the metadata rather than experimenting with the live database. The end user could navigate through the metadata discovering what data exists, what the status of the data is, what the definitions of the data are, etc. He/She could then build extracts for the query tool of choice and the information catalog of that query or reporting tool will be populated with the metadata selections of the end user. The end-user catalogue view could also includes an administrator function that assigns and enforced individual and group security, as well as individual database/table/column authorization.

The central metadata repository should also provide the basis for automating the interrelationships of events within the overall data warehouse architecture. Data movement events, such as data requests and recurring tasks can be scheduled, monitored and executed. This effectively automates the complex operational aspects of data warehouse administration. This capability is reasonably rich in terms of functionality and incorporates a filter capability to refine the data being moved as well as an integrity checking capability that ensures that the entire event of moving data is monitored and validated.

The ability to use a central metastore to refresh local servers and business intelligence applications is a powerful advance on the current situation. This increased resilience in the data warehouse environment is all the more necessary as the tendency in data warehousing heads in the direction of having data marts doing not only DSS processing but also including hybrid data marts which incorporate elements of operational processing.

THE METADATA INTERCHANGE SPECIFICATION

The metadata interchange specification is an initiative of the Metadata Coalition which comprises virtually every vendor organization that stores or uses metadata. Coalition membership is open to all vendors whose products create, access or are dependent on metadata as well as end users who have an interest in influencing the direction of the initiative. The purpose of the initiative is to enable full-scale enterprise data management. In order to so this different tools must be able to freely and easily access, and in some cases manipulate and update, the metadata created by other tools and stored in a variety of different locations. The process of evolving the standard is vested in the Metadata Council, which initially comprises the founding members but will be elected by coalition members after an initial period.

The only viable mechanism to enable disparate tools from different independent vendors to exchange metadata is to establish at least a minimum common denominator of interchange specifications and guidelines to which the different vendors' tools can comply. It should be noted that the Metadata Coalition is not a standards body and does not intend to create or impose a standard definition of all of the possible information contained in metadata or of a standard format for representing it. Therefore, all software tools that capture, store or use metadata will continue to have proprietary metadata — but that a common subset of metadata will be identified and applications programming interfaces (APIs) will be defined for exchanging this common metadata.

The short-term goals that were agreed by the founding members of the Metadata Coalition are listed in Table 6.5:

Table 6.5   Goals of the Metadata Coalition

Goals of Metadata Coalition

1   Creating a vendor-independent, industry-defined and maintained standard access mechanism and standard application programming interface for metadata.

2   Enabling users to control and manage the access and manipulation of metadata in their unique environments through the use of interchange specifications-compliant tools.

3   Allowing users to build tool configurations that meet their needs and to incrementally adjust those configurations as necessary to add or subtract tools without impact on the interchange specifications environment.

4   Enabling individual tools to satisfy their specific metadata access requirements freely and easily within the context of an interchange model.

5   Defining a clean, simple interchange implementation infrastructure that will facilitate compliance and speedy adoption by minimising the amount of modification required to existing tools to achieve and maintain metadata interface standard (MDIS) compliance.

6   Defining a clean, simple interchange implementation infrastructure that will facilitate compliance and speedy adoption by minimising the amount of modification required to existing tools to achieve and maintain metadata interface standard (MDIS) compliance.

Source : Version 1.0 Metadata Interchange Specification.

The implementation of the MDIS metadata model must assume that the metadata itself may be stored in any type of storage facility or format — relational tables, ASCII files, fixed format or customized format repositories etc. Therefore, the MDIS metadata access methodology must include a framework that will translate an access request into MDIS syntax and format for the metamodel of choice. Four different approaches were considered by the Metadata Coalition to achieve this. These alternative options are outlined in the Table 6.6:

Table 6.6   Alternative options considered by the Metadata Council

Overview of Potential Approaches

Approach	Description	Strength	Weakness
Procedural	A procedural approach requires that the intelligence to communicate with the standard API be built into the tools.	Maximum flexibility to accommodate changes in the standard.	Significant re-engineering of tools is required.
CDIF	The CASE Data Interchange Format is an existing standard for transferring information between CASE tools.	It is an existing standard that is already defined and is likely to be adopted as an ANSI standard.	Control would shift to a different standards body which is driven by a different mission.
Hybrid	A hybrid approach could be based on using a table-driven API.	Changes to the tools would be minimized.	Changes to the standard would be more difficult.
ASCII Batch	In this approach the entire ASCII file containing the MDIS schema and access parameters is reloaded whenever a tool accesses the metadata through the API.	Minimizes the need to retrofit tools without impacting on the evolution of the standard.	Is resource and process cycle intensive.

Source: Version 1.0 Metadata Interchange Initiative.

Having considered these competing options the Metadata Council decided, in the interests of brining a standard to the market as quickly as possible, to adopt the ASCII-batch approach for version 1.0.

The original metadata interchange specification was defined with four layers:

1. Interchange standard metamodel, which consists of the ASCII file format used to represent the metadata being exchanged.
2. Interchange standard access framework, which describes the minimum number of API functions a vendor must support.
3. Tool profile, which is a file (supplied by the tool vendor) describing what aspects of the standard metadata model the tool supports.
4. User configuration, which is a file describing legal interchange paths for metadata in the user's environment.

In the Metadata Council document that was agreed in July 1996 the semantics and syntax of the specification were set out. This included agreement on the metamodel which describes the entities and relationships used to represent the metadata as well as a mechanism for extending the metamodel. In addition, agreement was reached on the interchange specification access framework, which includes versioning information, a tool profile and a con-figuration profile. This framework enables the bi-directional flow of metadata while maintaining its consistency.

Ultimately the success of the Metadata Coalition will determine the extent to which the ongoing success of data warehousing maintains its momentum. If the initiative fails to evolve a standard that enjoys widespread compliance, this failure will dampen enthusiasm for data warehousing since it places a threshold on the scope of data warehouse systems beyond which it is not possible to venture without descending into chaos. Two aspects of the Metadata Coalition initiative are encouraging — the pragmatic manner in which speedy and simple implementation is being pursued and the active involvement of the user community. Success in the achievement of a metadata standard will have implications for information technology that far exceed the domain of data warehousing and decision-support systems, and will become a prime driver in the reintegration of operational and decision-support computing.

7

Data Quality

'*Poetry does not belong to those who create it, but to those who need it.*'
— *Old Chinese saying*

THE CONCEPT OF DATA QUALITY

One of the most underestimated aspects of the data warehouse project relates to the challenge of addressing data pollution. It is the experience of all seasoned data warehouse practitioners that organizations uncover significant levels of data pollution as a result of embarking on data warehousing and that most enterprises are astounded at the scale of the problem. The main reason why data pollution comes as such a shock to the organization has to do with the concept of aging. Data, like matter, decays. This is not a critical issue for the source system where the data has aged because the data was probably current when the transaction that placed that data there took place. The problem is that the data warehouse is concerned with both historic data and current data, while transaction systems are only concerned with data quality at the point in time of the transaction.

The reason why the issue of data quality is consistently underestimated is that organizations tend to have only narrow measures of data integrity and where audits have been performed they have tended to focus on measuring physical data integrity, data security and access controls, and identifying data corruption has occurred as a result of faulty application software. It has not, generally, been the practice to measure the completeness of data, the consistency of data in different systems, the consistency of data entry, the accuracy of data, the uniqueness of account numbers or the durability of the business rules that underpin the data. All of these issues are critical for decision-support computing and many organizations only begin to address this agenda when they commence the data warehouse project.

In the 1996 Data Warehouse Network DRUID survey of data warehouse practice in Europe, data pollution featured as the second most common (after technology-led project sponsorship) cause of failure in data warehouse initiatives. This situation is mirrored in the USA, where Datamation observed in October 1995: 'The data warehouse effort . . . may be wasted if you don't clean up your data first'.

One of the difficulties that obstruct progress in tackling polluted data is the narrow definitions that are applied to the concept of data quality. Most attention has been paid, by database administrators, to data integrity, which has a narrower scope than data quality. Consider the following two definitions:

Definition of Data Integrity:
- Data integrity reflects the degree to which the attributes of data associated with a specific occurrence of a given entity accurately describe that occurrence of the entity.

Definition of Data Quality:
- Data quality is measured with reference to fitness for purpose as defined by the business users of the data and conformance to enterprise data quality standards as defined by systems architects and administrators.

Clearly the concept of data integrity is located in the domain of database technology. The wider concept of data quality is rooted in the business. It is this latter definition that should inform our efforts in the context of data warehousing. Traditionally data quality was measured in terms of a transaction processing environment where, if the business process was adequately supported and if the record level data conformed to the field validation constraints, then the system was considered to have good data quality.

Within the data warehouse environment the idea of data quality is different. It is not only the quality of individual isolated items of data that is of concern, but the quality of the total integrated system. Transaction systems are concerned only with the transaction and the data that is required to complete the transaction. Quite a lot of data that is captured on transaction systems does not serve any specific purpose in completing the transaction and much of this data is of poor quality. Take, for example, customer service order transaction systems where the primary purpose is to provide service to the customer. Some data that is required for a service order to be processed is obligatory — name, address, payment details, contract conditions and a precise description of the service that is required. These are all necessary in order to close the transaction. Other items of data such as demographic data — age, sex, industry sector, customer profile — are not necessary to close the transaction and may not receive the same level of attention from the sales clerk.

This author encountered a utility company where 90% of their commercial customers belonged, according to the service order system, to the non-ferrous metal industry. The code for the non-ferrous metal industry was 9999. It was simply the most convenient code for the key-punch operator to enter to get by the field. Attention was never drawn to this practice because the management, who were responsible for the service order system, were concerned only with the operational aspects of the business, and the marketing department, who did have an interest in the data, were never allowed access to the system because of resource constraints. When the marketing department finally sponsored a data warehouse to gain access to this coveted data they found, to their dismay, that much of the data was useless. Unfortunately, anecdotes such as this are not uncommon and reinforce the need to perform data quality audits in advance of making the data warehouse investment.

There will always be a temptation to fastpath the data warehouse project by populating the data warehouse with data of an unknown or indifferent quality, in the hope that the data quality issue can be re-visited at a later stage. There may be rare circumstances where this is an appropriate strategy, but extreme care must be exercised when using data of unknown quality, because of the dangers of being misled by the discovery of an interesting pattern that may appear to have business significance, but which is fact no more than a pocket of data pollution.

When discussing the required quality of data warehouse data it is important to consider the fitness-for-purpose principle carefully since not all data in a data warehouse needs to be of premium quality and not all data warehouses will have the same data quality requirements. Thus, the concept of absolute data quality is an abstraction that is rarely achieved (or needed) in real world implementations. Consider the difference between the requirements of a marketing manager to use a data warehouse to identify lists of prospects with the requirements of a financial manager to use the warehouse to determine customer credit ratings. In the former case the desired data quality is achieved if the result tables are reasonably accurate. In the latter case there is probably a need for more stringent data quality standards.

At all times the project sponsor and project manager must balance the effort that is required to cleanse the data with the benefits that will accrue to the business. As a general rule the sales and marketing oriented data warehouses have a lower quality threshold and can be designed, constructed and deployed quickly to support promotions, advertising, market planning and segmentation analysis. On the other hand, data warehouses aimed at detecting fraud and delinquency, supporting supply-chain integration, reporting on expenditure and calculating discounts require more rigorous data quality assurance.

It should be noted that the issue of data quality is likely to become more urgent and important as the data warehouse concept evolves. In the final chapter in this book, which addresses the next generation of data warehouses, the evidence clearly points towards an accelerating tendency for the data warehouse to become 'operationalized'. This marks a critical transition in the use of integrated data by enterprises, since the data warehouse then becomes a mission-critical system which is directly supporting operational processes. When this transition occurs it is likely to precipitate a complete review of the data quality standards that are required in this new situation. Organizations that have failed to address the issue of data pollution adequately will find it impossible to make the transition from a 'pure' decision-support role for the data warehouse to an operational role.

Tales from the Trenches

Anecdotes abound concerning data warehouse projects that have encountered bizarre instances of data pollution. This author's favourite story relates to a utility company that constructed a marketing-oriented data warehouse and discovered, to their dismay, that queries that attempted to discover the value of their major customers were only returning a small fraction of the accounts of those customers. The origin of the problem did not lie in either the marketing department or the information systems department, but in the personnel department. The personnel department of the utility company had initiated an incentive bonus scheme for salespersons that paid a bonus every time a new account was opened. Therefore, every time a major customer opened a new premises the salesperson opened a new account with a new account number and entered a unique account name for each individual premises. After many months of unsuccessfully attempting to integrate the accounts the utility company had to endure the embarrassment of approaching each major customer and acquiring a full listing of account numbers and names. It was an inauspicious beginning to the data warehouse project.

The real insight provided by this example is that the operational billing system that provided the source data for the data warehouse functioned perfectly. The right bills for the correct amounts were issued to accurate addresses every month. Nobody was aware of any problem with data quality. It is only in the context of the data warehouse that the problem was uncovered. This anecdote is more typical of many data warehouse projects and explains why, very often, not sufficient time is allocated on the project plan to addressing the problems of data pollution because organizations are blissfully unaware that any problem exists.

Another anecdote relates to an insurance company that offered both comprehensive motor insurance and third-party motor insurance. The same operational processing application system was used to process both categories of claim. However, data was presented in the claims documentation concerning the circumstances of comprehensive claims and there was no computer field to store this data. At some point in time a decision was taken by a supervisor to use the Third party field (which was unused in a comprehensive claim) to identify the object struck by the motorist. Only when the data warehouse was implemented did the insurance company discover that thousands of third party motorists had improbable names like 'wall', 'ditch' and 'tree'!

In the UK it has been reported that there are 50% more national insurance numbers in circulation than there are persons eligible for insurance purposes. In virtually every developed country the total number of banks accounts that are recorded on computer implies that each citizen has multiple bank accounts ranging from 5 to 15 in different countries — this is patently not true and simply reflects that proper aging, purging and validation of accounts simply does not occur.

There are well publicized studies which have drawn attention to the problems of data consistency like that reported in *DBMS Magazine* in December 1994. In an article on a 20TB database of meteorological data maintained by the European Centre for Medium Range Weather Forecasting, concern was expressed that the rules that were in force at the initial implementation of the system differed from those that were in force later. Obviously this creates a severe problem with any trend analysis as the historical data is not consistent with the current data. One could go on ad nauseum citing examples of data pollution. What an enterprise embarking on a data warehouse needs to be conscious of is that the scale of pollution they are going to encounter is likely to be far greater than anticipated.

BUSINESS RULES

Business rules are defined by the business and reflect what constraints are placed on data by the business. The definition of the data and the business rules associated with the data provide the basis for the *semantics* of the data — what the data actually means. Very often, changes that occur in business rules provide the basis for data contamination and deserve the same level of analysis as the base data. Business rules may be implicit, explicit or institutional as illustrated, (for a banking enterprise), in Table 7.1:

Table 7.1 Explict, implicit and institutional business rules

Explicit	When a customer balance exceeds £300,000 for a period of 6 consecutive months in any one year, the name of an account manager should be entered on the account manager field.
Implicit	Consecutive months are measured with reference to the calendar year.
Institutional	When a customer balance exceeds £700,000 the name of the retail bank manager where the customer has his/her account is normally entered in the account manager field.

The problem with business rules is that explicit rules are often poorly documented, change over time and are interpreted differently by different personnel at different locations. The problem with implicit business rules is that they are documented nowhere and are prone to even greater change over time than explicit rules. Institutional business rules are often a throwback to procedures that existed prior to the computerisation of the current operational system and rely heavily on the experience of staff members and are particularly vulnerable to new staff members simply not being aware of the institutional knowledge.

CUSTOMER INTEGRATION

One of the commonest problems that exists for data warehouse designers is the difficulty of the large customer who has multiple accounts. This happens over time as the customer becomes a consumer from different parts of the supplier organization for different products and services in different regions. Take a customer of a telephone company which has many different physical locations in a country and which consumes different services at these different locations. Table 7.2 illustrates the type of problem encountered:

Table 7.2   The problem of customer fragmentation

COMPANY	REFERENCE NUMBER	PRODUCT
Acme Limited	12345-888	Telephone service
Richard Green M.D.	**********	Consultancy
Acme Corp.	45765876	Leased line
Acme Limited	67546-777	Telephone service
Acme	BLU-8657654	Freephone service
Acme Equipment	76586-555	Telephone service
Acem (sic)	56921-222	Telephone service
Acme Services	8765487GT	Telex service
Acme Corp.	00-987657846	Mobile service
Acme	678907-99G	PABX equipment
AEL	87650-001	Telephone service
Acme Equipment Ltd	VX-Bl4563	Premium response

Bearing in mind that a telephone company (or any large utility) could have thousands, or tens of thousands, of accounts that are all related to the same customer, then the scale of the problem becomes obvious. Where no standard representation exists for customers and other entities, then the first step is to identify what possible range of products, reference numbers and customer names might exist for that same customer. Few enterprises will have implemented keys to join the data and even fewer will have implemented data models which allow for a super account number or single reference.

INVESTIGATING THE DATA — PATTERN PROCESSING

Pattern processing is used extensively to scrub data that is inconsistently represented in fields. Investigating the patterns in data is useful since it simplifies the conversion process by identifying every pattern that the data exhibits. It also provides a bottom-up validation of any top-down design that may be considered. But, perhaps the greatest value of all is to be gained by providing an insight into the degree of pollution that exists in the legacy data. Pattern processing is also a good preliminary measure when considering any new instructions on data entry or new field validations because it identifies what the most common non-standard structures are, and where they are occurring. The following example is taken from a presentation by Vality Technology Inc., a Boston-based vendor of data cleansing tools.

Table 7.3 Vality pattern analysis

Pattern Code	Frequency	Representative data sample
AIA	428,700	EILEEN M. RUTHERFORD
AA	278,900	ROBERT JOHNSON
AIAS	103,700	CHARLES S. HORTON JR
AAS	60,200	RALPH GABRIK II
AACAA	36,000	MARYL DANTA AND KAY LONGO
ACAA	29,000	NICOLAS & CLAIRE MOORE
PAIA	1,000	REV. PASCAL L. ACQUAVIA
AIABBB	570	RICHARD H CARR ET AL TRUST
%BB	1	ATTN:ACCOUNTS PAYABLE

Source : Vality Technology Inc.

DISCOVERING THE EXTENT OF DATA POLLUTION

The first task facing the data warehouse project manager is to determine the nature and extent of data pollution that exists on the legacy systems. Because data pollution can arise for a number of separate reasons, the first task is to isolate the different potential causes of pollution. Table 7.4 illustrates when, where and why data

Table 7.4   When, where and why data pollution occurs

When/Where	Why
System conversions, migrations or re-engineering	• Inadequate data quality testing on conversion process. • Conversion programs introduce new errors. Re-engineering does not consider data context, usage or definitions.
Heterogeneous system integration	• Data is inconsistent or contradictory across systems. • Inadequate data quality testing on integration.
Database design	• Record and field definitions are too loose, unstructured or are not normalized. Schema lacks sufficient validation and integrity rules.
Production software	• Software requirements were incomplete or errors were introduced in the development process. Lack of applied software engineering or production controls.
Data ageing	• The company cannot track the age of data, or has no programme to update or enrich data.
Customer (un-)response	• Data never fully captured. Customer form is badly designed or no incentive is given to the customer to ensure a complete and accurate response.
Fraud	• Physical and logical system security is lax or compensating controls are absent.
Systems internationalisation/ localisation	• Overlapping or inconsistent interpretation or usage of codes, symbols and formats due to national differences.
Input error	• The system input method is badly designed, or lacks automatic validation. Human errors easily introduced.
Business rules	• System requirements lack adequate or current reference to business rules for data.
Policy and planning	• Lack of management attention, policy or audit of data quality management.

Source : Data Quality Systems, Cambridge Market Intelligence, 1996.

quality problems arise and offers a guide as to where to start looking for data pollution.

There is a close relationship between metadata management and data quality management since many of the problems that arise in the quality of the data are caused by the absence of a pan-corporate strategy for managing data. Many organizations use legacy systems (that were originally developed decades ago) to support critical business processes without having adequate knowledge about the data definitions or business rules associated with these systems.

In particular, the importance of a metadata catalog is important since the problems of data quality may be compounded by user ignorance concerning the meaning of the data that is available on the data warehouse.

When attempting to measure the scale of the problem a framework is required to support the analysis. The essence of any examination of data quality relates to the extent to which the data conforms to the business rules of the enterprise and the expectations of the users. Conformance is what should be measured and is normally expressed as a percentage with 100% representing absolute conformance.

The following approach, set out in Table 7.5, to examining data quality is based on data quality dimensions which provides a framework against which the extent of conformance can be measured:

DATA QUALITY — ROLES AND RESPONSIBILITIES

One of the main obstacles to cleansing data is that there are rarely clear roles and responsibilities defined by the enterprise for this key activity and accountability for data quality is diffuse and unclear. This is accentuated in the data warehouse project where the business owners of the legacy data are, typically, the production managers, billing managers and accountants and are not always actively involved in the data warehouse project. The users of decision-support systems are, typically, the sales managers,

Table 7.5 Data quality dimensions

Data quality dimension	Conformance example	Non-conformance example
Accuracy	A credit score of C1 is stored as C1.	A credit score of C1 is stored as B1.
Consistency	A customer demographic profile of C1 is stored as C1 on system A.	A customer demographic profile code of C1 is stored as C1 on system A and as B1 on system B.
Business rules	A sale is defined in the same way on all systems.	Sales are defined as incoming orders on sales systems and paid invoices on financial systems.
Accessibility	Data containing customer contact details are stored in a structured field designated for this purpose.	Data containing customer contact details are stored in a free-form remarks field.
Clarity	A date is stored as 11 June 1996.	A data is stored and displayed as 11061996 (could be read in some countries as 6 November 1996).
Completeness	Name, age and occupation is known for all customers.	Age and occupation is missing for some customers.
Temporal integrity	All customer addresses represent the place of dwelling.	Many customers have changed their address without informing the company.
Structural integrity	All customer names are entered as First Name, Surname (e.g. Sean Kelly).	Customer names are entered with and without titles, prefixes, suffixes, initials and abbreviations (e.g. Mr. Sean Kelly, Sean Kelly, Sean Kelly Esq., Sean Kelly Jnr., Sean G. Kelly, S. Kelly).
Referential integrity	All customers must have an account number.	Some customers have no account number or multiple account numbers.
Customer integrity	Customer information is stored once for each customer and all customers have a single unique reference number.	All customers have different reference numbers on different systems for different products and in different regions.

marketing managers, corporate planners and financial planners and they do not tend to have operational control or influence over the running of the operational systems which gather the corporate data.

Likewise, the information systems team who are designing and constructing the data warehouse are often in a separate organizational unit to the information systems personnel who are responsible for maintaining the legacy systems. One of the many causes of political friction that can occurs in data warehousing arises when the data warehouse team present a list of legacy system data quality deficiencies at the door of the hard-pressed operational management who, very often, regard the data warehouse as a system that is remote from the day-to-day activities of the business. Most legacy applications will, in any event, have a backlog of change requests, enhancements and fixes to contend with, and the data pollution concerns of the data warehouse team simply gets added to the end of the list.

As is illustrated by some of the anecdotal evidence offered earlier in this chapter the problem of data quality is often not visible to those who operate the legacy systems because the data pollution that exists often does not impact on the efficiency or effectiveness of their systems. Therefore, it has a very low priority on their agenda and the data warehouse project may be held hostage to people and events over whom the project manager has no direct control. For many legacy system administrators the boundaries of data quality do not extend beyond ensuring data integrity, access controls and the prevention of fraudulent or inadvertent data corruption.

The key to resolving the data pollution issues in a timely manner that does not impact adversely on the timetable for the rollout of the data warehouse lies in involving the business owners and application maintenance personnel at the very early stages of the projects. Encountering a dysfunctional level of data pollution after the data warehouse project is underway and commitments have been made to users is disastrous. Therefore achieving an acceptable level of data quality to support the applications architecture that is defined by the business users of the data warehouse should be regarded as a prerequisite for data warehousing and should be addressed in at least a preliminary manner prior to making any investment. It should also be an inclusive process and should involve the key personnel who have control over the legacy systems. In addition it should be tacked in a methodical manner (using, for example, the framework that is suggested later in this chapter).

Different participants in the data warehouse project have different roles and responsibilities for ensuring that data pollution is held in check. These roles are set out in Table 7.6:

Table 7.6 Data quality roles and responsibilities

Participant	Role	Description	Organization
Data warehouse user/business analyst	Data consumer	Requires or uses data to perform their job	Business
Legacy system data owner	Data producer	Is responsible for the quality of data that is input to the legacy applications	Business
Legacy system applications users	Data expert	Is the data and subject-matter expert for the data that is produced	Business
Data warehouse data owner	Data policy	Is ultimately responsible for resolving data pollution issues as well as ensuring the quality of transformed, aggregated and derived data	Business
Legacy systems database administrator	Data integrity	Is responsible for ensuring that the legacy data conforms to the data policies and standards that apply to the legacy systems	Information systems department
Legacy systems maintenance	Data correction	Is responsible for the amendments and enhancements required to address the data pollution that is identified	Information systems department
Data warehouse data steward	Data consistency	Is responsible for ensuring that the data within the data warehouse architecture (data warehouse and data marts) are consistent and synchronised	Information systems department

Source: Data Warehouse Network.

The most sensible way to proceed to tackle data pollution is to form a steering committee which represents all of the key players and which has joint responsibility for tackling the problem. This requires the involvement of legacy systems data owners and information systems personnel as well as the key players on the data warehouse project. This steering committee should commission the data quality audit at the earliest possible stage in the project and have responsibility for resourcing the effort that is required to correct the problem.

An important issue that arises from a discussion on roles and responsibilities is the issue of data warehouse data ownership. While the legislation regarding data ownership and registration of systems differs from one country to another, there is a reasonably consistent application of the principle of customer data ownership and restrictions on the use of customer data. This principle has been undermined somewhat by the data warehousing phenomenon whereby data about customers is integrated from a number of different sources in the enterprise so that the customer data that is resident on the data warehouse can have multiple legal owners. This matter becomes further complicated by the introduction of external data and by new data that is derived on the warehouse. The most pragmatic action to take to address these complexities is to regard the data on the data warehouse as sufficiently transformed and integrated as to represent a separate data store that has a separate data owner. This is valuable for a number of reasons, not least because it finally creates a role for a single corporate executive with pan-corporate responsibility for data.

THE DATA QUALITY PROJECT

Having agreed a framework for tackling data quality and having assigned agreed roles and responsibilities, the data quality project should proceed in tandem with other concurrent activities of the data warehouse project. It is essentially a sub-project of the data warehouse project, albeit an important and politically sensitive one.

The ten-point plan that is recommended for the management of a data quality project are set out in Table 7.7:

Table 7.7

1. Establish data quality steering committee
2. Agree data quality framework
3. Define fitness-for-purpose benchmarks
4. Agree data quality policy and standards
5. Determine priorities
6. Develop implementation plan
7. Perform audit (using data quality dimensions)
8. Identify highest impact pollution
9. Evaluate and select tools
10. Perform conversions and test results

It may be useful when performing the quality audit to use Pareto charts to identify where the highest volume of errors are occurring since experience shows that the 80/20 rules generally applies to the incidence of errors in data. In addition it may be useful to use cause-and-effect diagrams when analyzing how the errors are happening. It should be noted that while software tools do exist for the purpose of cleansing data, many difficulties that may be encountered may have to addressed using manual effort. It is essential to address only those data quality problems that need to be addressed for the purposes of the data warehouse project using the fitness-for-purpose principle. Bear in mind that the fitness-for-purpose principle can only be used where the data warehouse applications have been defined and where the knowledge workers who are going to use the data warehouse have had the opportunity to define the boundaries of acceptability for the data that is going to be provided to them.

It is natural that those members of the steering committee who have responsibility for the management of the legacy operational systems will also want to address problems that are identified that have no impact on the data warehouse project but which may represent a threat to the integrity of the business processes. This is a key component in selling the idea of a data quality steering committee to these participants and should be fully accommodated by the data quality management process. However, those data pollution discoveries that impact on the legacy systems (but not on the data warehouse) should, where possible, be addressed by the legacy systems administrators and maintenance personnel and should not consume the resources of the data warehouse project team.

Cost justifying Data Quality

For very many organizations the cost of cleansing data represents a large proportion of the initial cost of the data warehouse. In some cases the cost is easily justified where the extent of data pollution that is discovered is potentially disastrous for the enterprise or where the operational systems are discovered to be severely dysfunctional. It is more difficult to justify where the data pollution is confined to data that is only of interest to the data warehouse users and where changes need to be made on the operational systems. The task is made more difficult by internal debates within the enterprise on what constitutes fitness-for-purpose as well as a general vagueness that often permeates the data warehouse project in the early stages on the precise objectives of the data warehouse applications.

In order provide some focus on the cost of quality, close attention should be paid to the most common use of the data in the typical marketing/sales data warehouse environment. The key items of data that are used for sales prospecting are name, address, and demographic data. The primary concern with name and address data is that it is structured in a consistent manner and that it is up-to-date and accurate. The primary concern with demographic and behavioral data is that it is of sufficient quality to be used as a basis for customer segmentation.

Table 7.8 illustrates the various costs that may be associated with a direct mail campaign for a customer base of 1 million customers.

Table 7.8   The cost of quality — a direct mail example

Customers	Fine Segment (10,000 customers)	Coarse Segment (100,000 customers)	No Segmentation (All customers)
99% accuracy	9,900	99,000	990,000
90% accuracy	9,000	90,000	900,000
80% accuracy	8,000	80,000	800,000
70% accuracy	7,000	70,000	700,000

The vertical axis identifies the different levels of accuracy that may exist in respect of name, address and post code. It should be noted that, for many direct mail campaigns, up to 30% of the mail is not deliverable usually because of inaccurate postal codes. The horizontal axis provides a measure of the quality of the customer attribute data that would be used a basis for effective segmentation.

The optimum solution to the mailing would be to direct the mailing only to those customers with a high propensity to respond positively to the promotion and to ensure that every customer in this segment receives the promotional material. The cost to the enterprise is minimized and the opportunity is maximized. In addition, the enterprise has avoided the negative impact of issuing vast quantities of junk mail. The worst possible scenario for the enterprise is to have no reliable customer attribute data which would enable it to identify those prospects with a high propensity to be interested in the promotion and have to resort to a mass mailing with its attendant costs. If data accuracy is also an issue, it is possible that only 70% of the mailings will be delivered and the likelihood is that many of those in the high-propensity segment will be among the lost mail. This is a clear illustration of the costs of bad data quality which, if repeated by the enterprise on a few occasions, would easily cost justify (on the basis of cost savings alone) the effort required to clean the data.

When considering the business benefits of having good quality corporate data, it may be useful to consider the benefits under a number of separate headings. The cost of the data cleansing effort can be assessed in the context of benefits as expressed in Table 7.9:

Table 7.9 The benefits of high quality data

1	Customer service	The most obvious benefits relate to the level of customer service that is being provided. Poor data quality may lead to mistakes, errors, misdirected communications, misunderstood communications, duplication of effort.
2	Increased opportunity	An inability to identify a measure of the value exchange that exists between the enterprise and the customer or to offer the customer a customised level of service based on that value.
3	Reduced risk	Poor quality data can lead to disastrous decisions, system breakdown, process dysfunction, wasted time and the possibility of legal action.
4	Reduced costs	Poor quality data can lead to increased costs due to the randomness of promotion and advertising campaigns, the cost of mass mailings and the loss of time that is consumed by manual data reconciliation.
5	Improved Strategic Decision making	No true decision-support systems are going to add value to the business until the data that fuels those applications is adequate.
6	Improved IT system maturity	In an age where a stable information technology infrastructure is the means by which large corporations demonstrate their adaptability, optimizing the quality of the data moves the information systems through the maturity curve and allows for future systems to be constructed more quickly and with greater confidence.

Quality and Credibility

Data pollution on a large scale can destroy the credibility of a data warehouse. It has even caused projects to be abandoned or radically scaled down. One of the 'laws' of data warehousing is that users will want most frequent access to larger customers who are most likely to have complex fragmented accounts, rather than Mrs Smith who has a simple account. It is probably axiomatic that, the more valuable the subject of the data, the more polluted will be the data.

A lot of the blame for this situation lies with vendors and industry commentators that portray the data warehouse as rapid relief — a quick fix that releases the data that has been confined in data jailhouses. This is misleading and dishonest. In most instances the data warehouse is being introduced in an environment where there are no real data standards, no rigorously specified data models that enjoy enterprise-wide compliance and no metadata catalogs. With a very few exceptions, that describes the data environment of most large corporations.

The data warehouse is not the end of the journey to the land of information — it is the first step in discovering the scale of the problem and painstakingly addressing it. No data warehouse project should be embarked upon by an enterprise until they know: (a) what is it is they want and (b) what it is that they have got. This is a simple message that is often ignored.

PART 3

EXPLOITING THE DATA — THE DATA WAREHOUSE APPLICATIONS

8

Data Access and Exploitation

'A great part of the information I have was acquired by looking up something, and finding something else on the way.'
— Franklin P. Adams

Once the data warehouse data has been cleansed, transformed and integrated the challenge now shifts to exploiting the data. There are, in broad terms, three separate data exploitation environments that can be utilized for data exploitation.

Managed Reporting Environment (MRE) refers to software tools that have been developed with an emphasis on generating and distributing reports to those users in the enterprise who require prescribed information at pre-defined intervals. The key determinants of a good MRE relate to the distribution capabilities and presentation richness of the tool. Because MRE tools are deployed and closely controlled by the information systems department the users need not have any special knowledge of the data and the quality of the data can easily be checked and assured prior to deployment.

Managed Query Environment (MQE) refers to software tools that have been developed with an emphasis on providing flexible ad hoc query capabilities to end users whose reporting needs cannot be identified easily in advance. Using MQE tools requires considerably more training and familiarization than the MRE environment which is passive. Providing database abstraction through an effective information catalog (containing external metadata) is the key determinant of a good MQE tool. Despite significant advances in database transparency with MQE tools, there always exits the danger that the user will misinterpret the data or will be ignorant of the quality of the data. Considerable care must be taken with MQE tools to ensure that users are fully familiar with these risks. The MQE category includes OLAP as well as SQL tools.

Knowledge Discovery in Data (KDD) is a term that is commonly applied to the range of data mining tools and techniques including statistics, machine learning, artificial intelligence, data visualization and a range of specialized algorithms. KDD as a field of research has its roots in previous research on the subject of expert systems and artificial intelligence. This technology is now being revived and enhanced to deliver decision-support solutions within the data warehouse environment.

It would be wrong to present these different environments as separate alternatives since what they are intended to do is, in each case, different. Some users will be awed by the power of MQE tools and their needs are better satisfied by an MRE. Other users will be frustrated by the constraints imposed by MRE tools and will thrive on the flexibility offered by MQE tools. Users with a sophisticated understanding of statistical analysis will gravitate naturally to data mining. Many data warehouses employ more than one category of data exploitation technology and most mature data warehouses employ a wide variety of data access tools.

The differences between the three separate technologies that are used to exploit data are presented in Figure 8.1. The critical issue, which is represented on the horizontal axis, relates to the amount that is known about the information required by the business. MREs assume that there is a rigorous definition of the users requirements. The MQE environment is intended for business user's whose requirements are known only at a high level and/or where there is a high degree of change in the user requirement. Data mining represents a category of techniques that are used to discover hitherto unknown patterns in data. Therefore the critical issue is the

MRE	MQE	KDD
MANAGED REPORTING ENVIRONMENTS	MANAGED QUERY ENVIRONMENTS	KNOWLEDGE DISCOVERY IN DATA
- Information Push - Inflexible - Control-oriented - Pre-formatted - Distribution enabled - Server-based	- Information Pull - Flexible - Navigation-oriented - Ad hoc - Metadata enabled - Client-based	- Information Discovery - Immature - Model-oriented - Unknown - Algorithm enabled - Server-based

Known   REQUIREMENTS   Unknown

Figure 8.1 The range of data exploitation technologies

degree to which the requirements are known or the extent to which they can be adequately expressed.

Data mining is, at present, an emerging and highly specialized data exploitation environment and is explored in detail in Chapter 9. This chapter is devoted to the more traditional means of accessing and exploiting data — MRE and MQE tools.

At present, the data warehouse represents a store of integrated corporate data that may be accessed by end-users without having to endure the constraints imposed on them by the operational demands of transaction-oriented systems. The data warehouse contains raw data which is not necessarily useful, but it can be converted into information by consolidating it and integrating it with other data and by applying business rules to the data which provide it with the context that is essential in the conversion of data into information. In future data warehouses this reliance on the fallible human component will be considerably diminished through the use of data mining algorithms, software agents and knowledge-aware applications. For the moment though, the nuggets of information are usually to be discovered by human intelligence equipped with the necessary data access and data discovery tools. For the most part, the ad hoc query offers the best chance of discovering previously unknown and significant things about the business. As ad hoc queries are developed and run at frequent intervals it becomes possible to begin developing decision-support applications that users with a minimum of knowledge of the data or its structure within the data warehouse can effectively utilize.

MODELING THE QUERY DOMAIN

The activity of modeling the query domain is an important aspect of the logically modeling activity that has been discussed in Chapter 4 and is informed by the Business Strategy model that identifies the key information needs of the business. It is necessary to create a model of the query environment because of the number of variables that arise in real-world data access behaviour. These variables are illustrated in Figure 8.2.

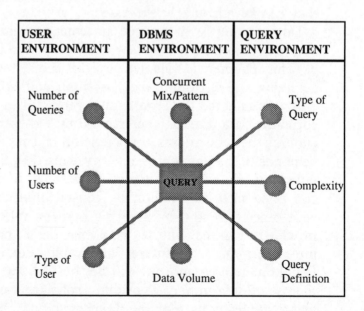

Figure 8.2 The Query Domain Model

In order to fully optimize the database design and the data staging strategy and in order to select the appropriate data access tools, a comprehensive model of the query environment needs to exist. For example, the total number of queries executed, the number of end-users and the type of end user (executive, operational, analyst) will influence the warehouse data management and data access layer of the architecture. In addition, the volume of data being accessed (atomic or summary) and the mix of serial and concurrent queries represents an important influence. But the most important influence on the data access layer of the architecture is represented by the type of query (table scans, multiple join, pre-processed aggregates and reports); the complexity of the queries (ranging from simple multi-dimensional to complex computational) and the degree to which the query is defined (i.e. the extent to which the requirements are known).

ADDING VALUE TO DATA

Data in its rawest form is not genuinely useful because it lacks any kind of context. For example, the fact that 1,000 copies of this book are sold represents a piece of data. But it is not actionable data. It becomes actionable if we know what is the context of that item of data. Therefore, if we know that the target sales for the book is 500, then the actual sales figure becomes meaningful. Or if we know that the cost of producing the book requires that 300 be sold to recover these costs, then the figure of 1,000 sales becomes interesting and amenable to further analysis. Or, alternatively, if we know that, on average, books on data warehousing sell 1 million copies, then the actual sales figure has a context that provides a basis for action. It is in this sense that the revelation provides a basis for action by the decision maker that differentiates data from information. Of course, information is itself not the final product. In the advanced data warehouse the application layer will contain a complex web of business rules and pattern recognition tools that have embedded in them information about the business and which are capable of alerting the decision-maker to circumstances and events that are of interest. This represents a transition from a model of the data warehouse that is passive (and therefore requires interrogation before information can be uncloaked from the data) and a data warehouse that is active and has the capability to alert the enterprise without being explicitly interrogated by a user. A definition of these three tiers of value is set out as follows:

Data — Raw facts that are not necessarily relevant to any business problem but which have the potential to be converted into meaningful information. Data may be of interest to the decision maker but are rarely actionable for any specific business problem.
Information — That which is derived from raw data in the data warehouse by combing data into patterns that have meaning to the business. Information is uncovered by the decision maker and is actionable by the decision maker.
Knowledge — That which is embedded in the data warehouse system and which is capable of triggering reports, conditions, events and alerts without the active interrogation of the system by the decision maker.

It is the task of the data warehouse architect to provide the data to end-users in a manner that it can be easily converted into meaningful information. Ideally, the data warehouse should contain some pre-processed data which offers the user tables containing summarized data, aggregated data, consolidated data and derived data. This pre-processed data is, in fact, raw information which can be more easily recognized and utilized by the end-user. The danger that exists is that a lot of complex processing of the data on the data warehouse unsupported by adequate metadata, makes for complex navigation by the end-user and presents considerable opportunity for error. Therefore, for data to be converted into information and knowledge there needs to be good cataloging of the data in order to display the metadata to the users as well as good database transparency so that the complexities of the physical schema are hidden from the user.

ACCESSING OPERATIONAL DATA

Not every single query is going to be appropriate to the data warehouse and some routine queries that are application-specific (for example, a query relating to the current stock levels of a given stores item, or the account balance of a customer) are better served by the operational systems where the data is completely up-to-date. The type of query that is proper to the data warehouse belongs to the strategic and tactical domains of decision-support rather than the operational environment. In circumstances where sub-second response times are required for predictable queries on up-to-the-minute data, then this functionality properly belongs to the operational system supporting the specific operational process. In most cases the operational query is part of the business process or service and is not likely to be generated by a manager concerning with policy or planning. However, every data warehouse strategy must define the extent to which the operational systems are going to provide reports and a clear division must be defined between the functionality offered by the legacy environment and by the new data warehouse environment. In some circumstances it must be necessary for the data warehouse user to have the facility to reach through to the operational system containing the detailed source data, in circumstances where the data warehouse contains only aggregated data or where updates are not sufficiently frequent to meet the needs of some queries.

THE SUCCESSFUL QUERY — AN EIGHT STAGE PROCESS

There are a number of discrete steps involved in defining a query. These may be separated into the following eight stages:

Stage 1 — Defining the business issue
The business issue that is the subject of the query may be a business problem expressed as a question or series of questions, a simple enquiry or an exploration of a hypothesis by a business user who is

seeking to confirm that a threat condition, opportunity condition or action needs to be responded to by the business.

Stage 2 — Data discovery

Once a business question has been formulated it will be necessary to establish whether the raw data required to respond to the question is available in the data warehouse, and some information will be needed by the business user about the definition of the data that is available, the recency of the data, the source of the data and any security constraints that have been applied to the data.

Stage 3 — Define the query

The business question needs to be translated into a structured query that represents the various elements that need to be included in the query statement. Obviously, the query needs to be expressed in a manner that is consistent with the query statement and must be capable of being expressed in the syntax of the query tool being used. The key issue to be considered in this stage is the effectiveness of the query (i.e. is the query statement syntactically consistent with the data structures and is it semantically consistent with the business question).

Stage 4 — Executing the query

The key issue to be considered in this stage relates to the efficiency of the query (i.e. is the query statement constructed in a manner that is going to consume the minimum system machine resource to return the result). Here consideration must be given to optimizing the query using whatever utilities are available in the query tool and the database product.

Stage 5 — Manipulating the data

For most useful queries there will be some element of calculation or manipulation of the result table to consolidate the data, to rank the data, or to present the data as percentage variations, standard deviations or other statistical manipulations. Most of the this functionality should be resident in the query tool.

Stage 6 — Information presentation
Most users will want to be able to present the data visually using charting techniques such as standard bar charts, pie charts, or trend lines on x/y axes or, in the case of presenting multiple results in a scatter-graph or distribution curve. Depending on the nature of the information the user should be able to present the data in different formats for different audiences or, in the case of lists, should be able to present the data in a report format with customized headings.

Stage 7 — Analysing the information
Because the answers to so many business questions beg even more questions, the user should be able to analyze the resulting set of data and store that set of data in other packages such as spreadsheets, local databases, statistical packages or in custom-made applications.

Stage 8 — Distributing the information
Once the user has reached some conclusions about the business implications of the information that has been discovered, he/she will wish to disseminate the information to other users or to present the data in written reports or visual displays. Therefore, the information and associated graphs and charts should be capable of being loaded into word-processing packages or visual display packages, groupware packages, or distributed via internal e-mail or on the Internet.

Categories of User

It is a reality of data warehousing that there are different kinds of business user and that these have different requirements that will not easily be satisfied by a single data access tool. Business users range in sophistication from novice to experienced in their ability to use the technology. A separate, and equally importantly, distinction needs to be made between users who have an essentially operational role in the business and those who have a strategic role. One of the dilemmas for many enterprises is that those who have the more strategic role at senior management level, and therefore should have a requirement for more complex and resource-intensive query processing, have poorer IT skills than more junior managers. It would be a failure of the data warehouse project if the integrated corporate data was used purely for tactical and operational purposes, when the greatest potential of the data warehouse is to impact on the core strategy of the enterprise.

In the domain of the organization some account must be taken of the nature of corporate decision making as well as the individual organizational culture that pervades the enterprise that is implementing the data warehouse. In a previous commentary (*Data Warehousing, the Route to Mass Customization*, Wiley 1994) on the relationship between the process of making decisions and the data warehouse environment, I observed the following:

> 'In what is possibly the seminal work on the subject of the relationship between decision making and organizational design, H. A. Simon divides the decision making process into three phases. The first phase, which Simon called the intelligence activity, is concerned with gathering data. The second phase, which is called the design activity, is concerned with modeling and analyzing the different courses of action that are possible in the circumstances. And the third phase is called the choice activity and is simply concerned with selecting a solution. Simon correctly identified a common misconception with decision making which focuses almost entirely on the final phase — the moment of decision – while ignoring 'the whole lengthy, complex process of alerting, exploring and analysing that precedes that final moment.'

It is from Simon's distinction between programmed and non-programmed decisions that the distinction between ad hoc queries and decision-support applications, can be made. Simon associated programmed decision making with the middle layer of management. His definition of programmed decisions as 'repetitive' is an accurate reflection of those decisions which are amenable to being supported by decision support applications which may be built for a defined set of users and which allows them to navigate through the data within a reasonably structured environment. 'Decisions are non-programmed', according to Simon, 'to the extent that they are novel, unstructured and consequential'. This category of decision making is associated by Simon with senior management in organizations where their requirement for data would encompass the external environment as well as the internal corporate sources of data. Therefore unstructured decision making can only be supported by ad hoc queries of a wide range of data. From a decisional point of view and from a software point of view it is essential to comprehend and acknowledge that these two kinds of decision making each require a different approach from the system designer.'

This distinction between programmed decisions and non-programmed decisions is central to an understanding of the decision-making dynamic in the enterprise. The data warehouse can perform effectively as an engine for the vast quantity of programmed and semi-programmable decisions but it is in the area of nonprogrammed decisions that the data warehouse reigns supreme.

Over time many decisions that are perceived to be non-programmable will, in fact, become amenable to being captured in applications, and various rules may be embedded in the application layer of the data warehouse architecture that will function as a knowledge base that alerts the enterprise to internal and external events. But in the early stages of data warehouse implementations the ad hoc query will be a more common form of data exploitation.

Consideration must also be given, when considering what query tools to deploy, to the organizational culture of the enterprise. While bearing in mind that the data warehouse will itself be an agent of organizational change, some account needs to be taken of the culture of decision making. Some organizations with strong command-and-control characteristics will wish to enforce strict rules concerning access to data by various users and access to data and various classes of data may be severely restricted. Other types of organizational culture will require complex matrix reporting structures to be supported. Whatever the culture of the organization, the data access strategy and query tool selection will have to attempt to accommodate these requirements.

It should also be noted that different types of enterprise will have a requirement, not only for different types of interface to the data, but for fundamentally different types of data warehouse architecture. For example, enterprises that are under pressure to deploy an application-centred warehouse quickly are likely to select query tools that are closely coupled to the application environment. In other circumstances an enterprise may have to deploy a data warehouse at short notice because of the urgency of meeting a competitive threat, and there may be little time available for the system architect to construct the metadata layers and layer of database abstraction that would normally be required. And there will be inherent differences in data warehouse implementations that have large volumes of atomic level data from those that contain only pre-processed summary and consolidated data. All of these organizational and architectural factors will influence the design of the data access layer.

Query Tools

For the end user to fully exploit the software tools on offer for ad hoc analysis of the data, he or she must begin with some idea of what they wish to know. This initial idea may represent an intuitive feeling about some business condition or, alternatively, may be arrived at following an event in the business. This initial idea may be called 'the hypothesis', a hypothesis being a proposition that is assumed for the sake of proving or disproving it by reference to the facts. If sufficient number of the facts (i.e. data) are available, then the hypothesis can be tested. In the pre-data warehouse enterprise there may any number of hypotheses held by different decision makers but they have not the means of testing their ideas because the data required to prove or disprove the hypothesis are incomplete or unavailable. What it means for an enterprise that can quickly test various hypotheses about the market, customers, suppliers and other real world business objects is that their ability to anticipate changes and respond quickly to threats and opportunities is hugely enhanced. Therefore, having the data is never enough — the data warehouse architecture must have the means of exploiting the data. The most common tools used to exploit the data will be SQL-based tools, although OLAP tools are becoming more common and data mining is emerging as a key technology in the field of data exploitation.

A key critical success factor for the data warehouse is that the access layer of the architecture is constructed with the end user firmly in mind. If the data warehouse is to fulfill its promise of unfettered access to the enterprise data, then the access must be delivered using query and reporting tools that hide from the user the complexity of the underlying data structures and which empower the user by making the data easy to comprehend. What is required for the business user is a tool that provides a layer of database abstraction, so that the user can query familiar business objects rather than having to know the names of tables and columns in a relational database. In addition, it will be necessary to consider having more than a single query tool to satisfy the requirements of the user population because there are three distinct query operations that may be required and each of these categories of query is best served by a query tool dedicated to that specific type of enquiry.

Most query tools are dedicated to giving users the ability to select, browse, analyze, consolidate and present data in a useful manner.

The three categories of query are queries which have natural dimensions (such as time, geography, product, etc.) and which are best dealt with using OLAP tools. There are complex queries which do not have natural dimensions and these are best executed using SQL tools. And then there are routine reports that users will define and which are run at pre-defined intervals and these are, very often, best generated using reporting tools.

It used to be the case that were two types of data access tool — those that were easy to use but were not very powerful and those that were very powerful but which required experienced and skilled users. This distinction is still, to some extent, true but the gap between ease-of-use and functional richness is being narrowed rapidly. It is still the case that the relational model presents serious challenges to business users who are ignorant of the niceties of relational theory. The danger of SQL novices generating result tables that are incomplete or misleading is diminishing, but is still a very real threat. For example, one misplaced 'Where' clause can produce results that are wildly inaccurate and runaway queries that run the risk of crashing the system are more often the result of faulty SQL syntax than of over-ambitious users.

STRUCTURED QUERY LANGUAGE (SQL)

SQL continues to have the advantage of being the open standard query language for the past decade and SQL syntax is clear, concise and reasonably easy to comprehend for users with some technical grounding. However, there are many simple operations that SQL cannot perform (such as elementary statistical analysis or ranking). Unfortunately, SQL is beginning to look its age and even the next ANSI release of SQL is not expected to be able to handle the multimedia objects which will, increasingly, be a feature of the data warehouse.

While SQL can easily tackle the straightforward query it often struggles with the more complex requirements of decision-support computing and the complexities of many-to-many entity relations. For example, some tools will handle computation logic reasonably elegantly; some will have to resort to a long series of SQL statements to construct the query, and some, it has to be said, will not handle them at all. The following types of queries are relatively simple but should be demonstrated by any tool vendor selling their wares to establish how the tool handles the rough as well as the smooth:

- *Ranking* — e.g., for each product show the top 100 customers in the first quarter of the fiscal/calendar year.
- *Variations* — e.g., show the variation in sales of product X by reference to target sales in each year for the past three years.
- *Percentages* — e.g., show the current years sales of product X as a percentage of product Y.
- *Calculations* — e.g., list all those customers which have generated more than 1000 sales of product X in month Y where the customers' annual purchases exceed 5000 units of product.

- *Comparisons* — e.g., show the mean average number of sales of product X in each region compared to product Y.
- *Correlations* — e.g., show all those customers who purchased product X within three months of purchasing product Y.
- *Statistics* — e.g., calculate the standard deviation in the sales of product X over a two-year period.

In a, by now, famous declaration by Ted Codd in 1994 to the effect that SQL was never intended for data analysis, a considerable amount has been written about the efficacy of SQL as an ad hoc query tool and the usefulness of the relational model in decision support computing. Leaving aside the argument about whether it is the relational model or SQL that is at fault, the following list of strengths and weaknesses are submitted to guide the reader in any assessment of the appropriateness of SQL as a query tool.

Strengths
- SQL is a mature standard.
- Most software applications can generate SQL.
- SQL is independent of physical storage.
- SQL is cheaper than other options.
- SQL can provide database transparency.

Weaknesses
- SQL is difficult for end-users to master.
- Many SQL functions can only be exploited using proprietary extensions.
- SQL performance is difficulty to predict.
- SQL is not inherently multi-dimensional, cannot easily rank data and is therefore not intuitive.
- SQL will become more limited as multimedia objects become more common in data warehouses.

ONLINE ANALYTICAL PROCESSING (OLAP)

OLAP databases are databases that are architected to provide a multi-dimensional view of data. These are specialized databases. As has already been discussed in Chapter 4 the relational database can be used to implement a multi-dimensional (Star) schema to aid multi-dimensionality. In addition, there are relational OLAP tools (ROLAP) which create dynamic hypercubes of multi-dimensional data from two dimensional relational tables.

Many, in some cases most, queries that are required in a decision-support environment have natural dimensions. For example, a query that asks how many products were sold in sales region X during September is a natural multi-dimensional query. It has three dimensions — product, time and geography. OLAP tools excel at this type of operation but that does not necessarily mean that the data warehouse must be implemented on a multi-dimensional database. R-OLAP tools are available to create hypercubes of multi-dimensional data out of the two-dimensional relational tables in a standard relational database. There is, of course, a systems overhead required to create the hypercube but the subsequent performance advantage to be gained from more efficient queries may make the investment worthwhile.

Figure 8.3 demonstrates how a number of different dimensions, with members identified in respect of each dimension, would be modeled for the purposes of an OLAP cube.

The following twelve 'rules' of OLAP were defined in 1993 by E.F. Codd, S.B. Codd and C.T. Salley in a White Paper commissioned by Comshare. These rules were intended to identify the fundamental components and criteria that defined OLAP.

1. Multi-dimensional conceptual view
Because most business users view of the data is multi-dimensional, the OLAP tool should provide a multi-dimensional conceptual schema to facilitate model design and analysis as well as inter- and intra-dimensional calculations.

2. Transparency
OLAP should be provided within the context of a true open systems architecture, allowing the analytical tool to be embedded anywhere the user-analyst desires, without adversely impacting the functionality of the host tool.

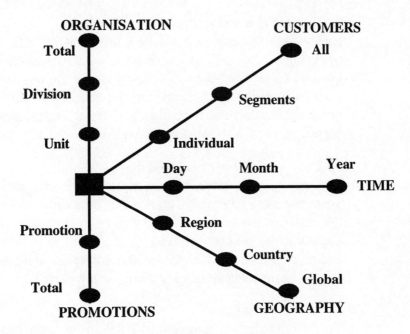

Figure 8.3 A typical OLAP multi-dimensional model

3. Accessibility
The OLAP system should access only the data actually required to perform the indicated analysis and should map its own logical schema to heterogeneous physical data stores, access the data, and perform any conversions necessary to present a single, coherent and consistent user view.

4. Consistent reporting performance
As the number of dimensions or the size of the database increases, the OLAP user-analyst should not perceive any significant degradation in reporting performance.

5. Client-server architecture
The server component of the OLAP tool should be sufficiently intelligent to enable various clients to be attached with a minimum of effort or integration programming.

6. Generic dimensionality

Every data dimension must be equivalent in both its structure and operational capabilities. Additional operational capabilities may be granted to selected dimensions, but since dimensions are symmetric, a given additional function may be granted to any dimension. The basic data structure, formulae and reporting formats should not be biased toward any one data dimension.

7. Dynamic sparse matrix handling

For any given sparse matrix, there exists one and only one optimum physical schema. If the OLAP tool cannot adjust according to the distribution of values of the data to be analyzed, models which appear to be practical, based on the number of consolidation paths and dimensions, or the size of the enterprise data source, may turn out to be needlessly large or hopelessly slow.

8. Multi-user support

To be regarded as strategic, OLAP tools must provide concurrent access (retrieval and update), integrity and security. The tool must support the requirement of end-users to work concurrently with either the same analytical model or to create different models from the same data.

9. Unrestricted cross-dimensional operations

The various roll-up levels within consolidation paths represent, in outline form, the majority of one-to-one, one-to-many and dependent relationships in an OLAP model. The OLAP tool should be sufficiently sophisticated to manage associated calculations among dimensions and the end-user should not be expected to explicitly define these inherent calculations. Such a language must allow calculation and data manipulation across any number of data dimensions and must not restrict or inhibit any relationship between data cells regardless of the number of common data attributes each cell contains.

10. Intuitive data manipulation

Consolidation path re-orientation, drilling down across columns or rows, zooming out and other manipulations inherent in the consolidation path outlines should be accommodated via direct action upon the cells of the analytic model, and should require neither the use of a menu nor multiple trips across the user interface.

11. Flexible reporting

Reporting must be capable of presenting data to be synthezised, or information resulting from animation of the OLAP model according to any possible orientation. All dimensions must be capable of being easily displayed including any sub-sets of the members of a dimension.

12. Unlimited dimensions and aggregation levels

An OLAP tool should be capable of accommodating at least fifteen and preferably twenty data dimensions within a common analytical model. Each of these generic dimensions should allow an essentially unlimited number of user-defined aggregation levels within any given consolidation path.

Because the essential multi-dimensionality of many queries is now recognized by the market, and because OLAP functionality is now regarded as an important aspect of any data exploitation strategy in data warehousing, the real issue relates to how this functionality is to be achieved. The market breaks down between tool vendors who offer multi-dimensional database products with associated OLAP tools and tool vendors who offer tools that create multidimensional views of the two-dimensional relational tables. These latter tools are called relational OLAP (ROLAP) and have, in most instances, been developed by the traditional SQL tool vendors in response to the OLAP onslaught in the data access market.

Before analyzing the relative merits of OLAP tools and ROLAP tools, it is necessary to first distinguish OLAP tools generally from traditional SQL query tools. SQL tools have traditionally been the only option available to data warehouse developers to empower end users with the means of interrogating the data warehouse. SQL has its drawbacks as a query tool, just as the relational database has its drawbacks as a platform for query-intensive processing. The downside of the relational database is that it is inherently two-dimensional while most queries that users wish to run are multi-dimensional. The most typical data warehouse query will include a number of dimensions like subject, time, geography or money (for example: 'how many London-based retail outlets exceeded their sales targets for product X by more than 20% in January 1996?'). This type of query is inherently more suited to a multi-dimensional cube of data that, typically, stores aggregated results and that can store or present computed dimensions such as "variance". Multi-dimensional databases optimize data storage by eliminating sparcity (the occurrence of null values in fields) and the multiple dimensions help to investigate patterns that are not revealed by long lists of tabular data. Most multidimensional databases and OLAP analysis tools use 'outlines' to illustrate the hierarchy of dimensions, where each dimension has a number of members (for example, the dimension 'time' would have members day, week, month, year). The physical organization of the data in a multi-dimensional database is typically a collection of arrays or matrices, and not tables as in a relational database.

Of course, not all queries are inherently multi-dimensional. Multi-dimensional databases are poorly equipped to deal with unrelated data (for example, where you have data about sales and data about operations) where there is no way of clearly relating the data. In addition, the multi-dimensional model fails if there is no inherent dimensionality in the data. Some data cannot be structured in the increasing levels of detail (for example, if the data cannot be decomposed from national sales to regional sales to retail outlet) demanded by the multidimensional 'cube'. Take, for example, the query: 'calculate the percentage of our top 1000 customers who purchase product X within six months of identifying Y fault in product Z'. This type of query would not be suitable to execute on a multi-dimensional database. It might even be impossible if the data exceeded 20 gigabytes, since conventional wisdom locates this as the upper threshold of data volumes that can be stored and manipulated in a multi-dimensional database.

The relational database is capable of being designed to optimize dimensional queries through specialized physical structures such as the star schema or snowflake schema, which seeks to create a central 'fact' table containing detailed transactional data and many smaller satellite tables containing dimensional data (about time, region, sales, budgets etc.). This approach has been perfected by Redbrick Software, who offer a relational database product which has been optimized for multi-dimensional analysis.

Most organizations now accept that there is a place for SQL and OLAP tools in their data warehouse architecture. The choice that is then presented is to (a) download some of the relational data onto a multi-dimensional data mart and interrogate this multi-dimensional data with an OLAP tool, or (b) use a ROLAP tool that will create static or dynamic hypercubes of multi-dimensional data on the existing relational database. And so the battle lines are drawn.

Every data management and data access vendor in the data warehouse marketplace has moved quickly to acquire dual SQL/OLAP functionality in order to cover both bases, but each offering now tends to belong in an OLAP or a ROLAP camp. The OLAP camp is more 'pure' in that they offer a multi-dimensional database management environment, while the ROLAP camp offer a 'virtual' multi-dimensional database stored on a relational database.

This conversion process does make demands on the system and many of these ROLAP tools require a datamart environment where the actual processing happens. Where the bulk of the processing load is located on the client (so-called 'fat' clients) there is always the danger that the pressure of frequently moving large volumes of data down to the client will create network bottlenecks. This potential danger with ROLAP tools needs to be analyzed carefully.

Looking into the medium and longer term, it is difficult to locate the multi-dimensional database within the overall evolution of hardware and software. Most of the existing products are EIS-type tools that have come from the past and were languishing in a stagnant market because of the perceived failure of EIS to deliver real benefits. EIS was a failure because, while the front-end tools were very pretty and reasonably function-rich, it was not always easy for the enterprise to inject into these products the operational data that was required. They now have a new lease of life with a rejuvenated DSS market driven by the data warehousing phenomenon, because cleansed and integrated data is available. The question that must now be posed is 'Is the multi-dimensional database the way forward for data warehousing or is it a temporary convenience to offer end-users a business-friendly presentation interface?'

The upside of the multi-dimensional database is fairly obvious. It is fast and it more accurately reflects the business view of corporate data and is therefore more attractive and usable for end users. But to look at the future one has also to consider the downside of the multi-dimensional database.

The most visible issue is that the multi-dimensional database (MDDB) doesn't scale and it is unclear that it will scale to the terabyte range in time for the market. Neither is the MDDB as resilient as the relational database. Then there is the fact that most products that are now available are proprietary which is distinctly unattractive. There is then the issue of distributing the data in the multi-dimensional database — this is not comprehensively supported at present by multi-dimensional database vendors and many DSS users want to have datasets distributed across LAN's and on notebook PCs. Then there is the problem of storage efficiency — multi-dimensional databases are exhaustively aggregated, redundantly storing information at every level of summarization. In addition, the MDDB is not flexible — it requires a dimensional structure to be constructed that is fairly static — the performance advantages evaporate rapidly if the developer gets the model wrong.

But it is the longer-term issues that present more fundamental questions about the multi-dimensional database. For instance, one has to consider where the multidimensional database fits into the future hardware directions. And then we come to an issue that gets very little airplay: where is the design rigor for the conceptual and logical design of a multi-dimensional database. Some would say that posing this question is absurd, as the multi-dimensional cube simply exists and it is the task of IS to inject the data into it, but this is surely a vacuous observation. Systems need to be modeled at a conceptual, logical and physical level and all of the tools and techniques that exist to do this assume that the end product is relational.

A tempting conclusion to reach would be that the relational database model will develop multi-dimensional extensions and that relational OLAP that is open, standard, flexible, resilient and scalable will emerge in the near future. Unfortunately, this is wishful thinking — the basic design assumptions underlying the relational and the multidimensional model are so different that a kernel that supports both views of the data is not a realizable short-term goal (some vendors, notably Oracle, are committed to a strategy that is essentially a hybrid solution using both a relational and multidimensional database).

All of the facts point to a simple reality: ROLAP compensates for the shortcomings of the relational database by augmenting its capabilities, while the multi-dimensional database does not have the same capacity to compensate for its intrinsic weaknesses. And that makes ROLAP a safer choice in most, but not all, circumstances.

DATABASE ABSTRACTION

The essential issue to consider in any tool selection, but especially with SQL tools, is the extent to which the tool provides database transparency, i.e. does the tool hide from the user the complex relational data schema that is implemented on the relational database? This feature of the software tool is likely to go by different names, such as repository, dictionary, universe, view, profile and catalog. What database abstraction means is that the user should be able to browse familiar business objects on the screen and formulate and construct a query without having to know how the database is constructed and without knowing the table and column names that were allocated by the database designers. Whatever it may be called by different vendors database transparency represents the highest priority, after ease-of-use, that needs to be considered by the prospective buyer.

One of the difficulties about database abstraction is that, in situations where the query tool environment is used to build multiple applications or multiple views of the data, each separate application may have to be populated with its own metadata.

Ideally, all applications should share the same metadata so that the data that is used by the different applications share the same precise definitions of the data and are synchronized with regard to the recency of the data. Otherwise, countless hours of wasted effort will be expended in discovering and explaining why different results are being generated by similar queries.

Managing metadata is one of the most challenging problems facing the data warehouse architect because of the need to devise a strategy, and support that strategy with appropriate tools, to ripple through the different layers of the data warehouse architecture the definitions of the data and any changes that occur to the data. Therefore metadata will be resident on the extraction and transformation tools, on the database and on the query tool suite that is being utilized by the end users. For some implementations the data warehouse implements its own database abstraction layer using a metadata management-type tool. In these circumstances the importance of the tool having its own database abstraction layer is replaced by the need to ensure that the suite of query tools being used are capable of importing and exchanging metadata with the metadata management tool that is employed by the data warehouse.

Whenever the transparency is implemented the database abstraction layer should protect the user by providing predefined joins, aggregated tables, filters, aliases and computed columns, and should present the user with familiar business objects. Most open metadata layers will be implemented as ODBC drivers so that front-end applications can access and use the metadata. Most abstraction layers will offer the choice of hiding some or all of the database physical schema. since some highly sophisticated users may wish to see the technical data structure of the database.

QUERY OPTIMIZATION

It will be necessary, even in the data warehouse environment, to impose some constraints on the user population. This need arises for the following three reasons:

User Error. Users will generate faulty queries which, because of faulty query construction, may attempt to read the entire database for no good purpose. It will be necessary to have a means of identifying and aborting such queries.

System Efficiency. Even in situations where users generate a correct query statement, their knowledge of the database (or the efficiency of the database abstraction layer) may be inadequate. Adding big tables to small tables is simply inefficient and some means of optimizing queries by re-parsing the select statements needs to be implemented.

Prioritization. Even where a dedicated decision-support engine exists to support knowledge workers in the enterprise, it is a fact of life that some users (and their queries) are more important than others.

Two utilities need to be examined in the context of implementing a managed query environment. One is a Query Optimizer which may be resident in the query tool or on the database or both. The purpose of optimization is to check that the query is being executed in the most efficient manner possible. The second is a Query Governor, which typically is resident on the database but the query tool may incorporate some governor features. The purpose of a governor is to identify and shut down runaway queries. Normally a governor is implemented by placing pre-defined limits on the numbers of rows returned in a result table but that is, in itself, inadequate to stop some queries from consuming vast amounts of machine resource. One common problem with implementing constraints is that organizations tend to want to impose different constraints on different users and some governors only apply universal constraints. It is important, in considering this aspect of a query tool, to probe at what level the required constraints are imposed. For example, if different constraints are applied to different groups of users, and if the constraints are implemented in the metadata layer, the solution may require the system administrator to maintain many different copies of the metadata dictionary. Here, the solution may be more dangerous than the problem. What is really needed is the capability to establish how much resource is required when the query is submitted but before it is executed. Some governors have the happy knack of identifying that the constraint parameters have been exceeded and shut down the query when it has almost run its course! This is, of course, worse than useless.

QUERY TOOL — EVALUATION CHECKLIST

Most query tools are capable of being examined from four functional perspectives. These are:

The *Data Browser*, where data sets are represented on the screen using standard GUI objects like drop-down boxes and lists.

The *Data Selector*, which enables the user to express the query that they wish to execute. Here what the prospective buyer should be examine is the degree to which the expression builder abstracts the database structure and permits he query to be constructed without having to specify joins.

The *Database Connectivity* function is an essential aspect of any query tool and most tools will offer a wide access to most of the database products that users are likely to query. Most tools will use ODBC drivers to access the database but some will also offer native connections to the database product. The key aspect of database connectivity that needs close examining is the efficacy of the client-server features of the tool — some are more elegant than others. It is also useful to establish whether the database connectivity software can utilize the database utilities such as the database governor or query optimizer which control the system resource.

The Information Catalog, allows the user to browse the metadata and enables the user to see the data definitions so that he/she can understand what the data means, the refresh/update schedule so that he/she knows the currency of the data and some information about the transformation rules that have been applied to the data. In addition, where a layer of database abstraction has been provided there should be information about aliases that have been employed to represent the relational tables and columns as familiar business objects.

The Presentation Interface, which may vary substantially from product to product, is the part of the product that users will either like or hate. The data should be capable of being presented as graphs and charts as well as textual reports and should be capable of being cut and pasted into the software products that users are familiar with using (spreadsheets, word-processing products and graphical display products).

The Administration Utility, which is not meant for end-users but which allows the system administrator to configure, maintain and manage the query tool environment. Ideally, the administrator should be able to configure the system so that queries are optimized and runaway queries are identified before they cause any serious system performance degradation. Some of these control functions are better implemented at the database layer rather in the query tool but the administrator must have the ability to interact with the database utilities.

CONCLUSION

Experience demonstrates that there are a number of key issues for the data warehouse architect to consider when deploying data access functionality to users. One overriding consideration is the separation of the data query logical layer from the application layer. As the data warehouse matures the volume of ad hoc queries is likely to diminish as a percentage of overall activity in the data warehouse and the scale of canned decision-support applications will increase.

The real test of the success of the data access layer of the data warehouse is that end users would be become independent of professional IT support to access and analyze corporate data. The existence of a data warehouse should eliminate the information backlog in the enterprise and, at the same time, increase dramatically the scope of information processing from that which exists in the era of legacy operational systems.

These will vary in importance depending on a number of factors including the following:

- The complexity of the data.
- User knowledge of the underlying physical schemas.
- The time constraints of the project timetable.
- The sophistication of end users.
- The anticipated query environment.
- The richness of the database environment.
- The quality of available metadata.
- The number of different tools that need to be deployed.

The 10 key issues to be borne in mind when architecting the data access layer of the data warehouse architecture are summarized in the following checklist:

1. Ensure that the query tool meets the end users' ease-of-use expectations.
2. Ensure that there is complete database transparency offered to the user.
3. Ensure that an information catalog that contains essential metadata is available to end users and that it can exchange metadata with other tool components in the data warehouse architecture.
4. Ensure that the range of different tools that are required by different users are offered (including where necessary SQL and OLAP tools) and that these different tools comply with the same metadata catalog.
5. Ensure that complex SQL operations can be handled by the tool.
6. Ensure that the tool can access and inter-operate with the necessary query management utilities on the database that will be used.
7. Ensure that the licensing arrangements are sensible and appropriate from the point of view of the individual data warehouse implementation.

8. Ensure that resource management is handled effectively by the tool or that the tool is compatible with any separate metadata layer that is implemented for this purpose.

9. Ensure that the tool can be effectively administered at a reasonable cost in terms of professional IT personnel.

10. Ensure that the tool is compatible with the desktop software standards (both operating system and application package) that are in force in the organization.

9

Data Mining

'Art is the imposing of a pattern on experience.'
— Alfred North

AN INTRODUCTION TO DATA MINING

Data mining is about finding hidden information — the golden nuggets of information that are disguised in the mass of data and that are unlikely to be uncovered by users with query tools, regardless of their degree of knowledge, creativity or intuition.

DATA MINING IN CONTEXT

Data mining techniques have been used extensively prior to the data warehousing phenomenon in specialised non-commercial applications such as geological research (searching for natural resources), military research (target pattern matching), and metreological research (weather forecasting). Now data mining is used by retail companies for customer profiling; by banks for risk and credit analysis, by insurance companies for fraud detection and cross-selling and by manufacturing companies to optimise work-load distribution. Data warehousing has allowed data mining techniques to move from the world of scientific analysis to the world of commercial analysis.

Because the data patterns that reflect behaviour can change in subtle ways, data mining is a valuable tool to detect and discover these trends at an early stage. In a dynamic world where preferences, risks, fashions and opportunities are constantly changing, there is a need to observe behaviour in a manner that allows for prediction and forecasting. Using conventional statistical analysis to model behaviour is reasonably accurate, but has drawbacks. For example, linear regression can be used to model behaviour by identifying the strength of the relationship between two variables (e.g. income and spending), but conventional statistical analysis becomes complex and unwieldy when there are a high number of variables and where the data includes a mixture of numerical and categorical data. Thus, while the conventional DSS analysis techniques are used to analyse relatively simple linear models, data mining is used to provide automated multi-variate analysis of data. With SQL and OLAP tools the data analysis is user-driven (i.e. the user needs to form a hypothesis that is then tested against the data). Data mining harnesses the power of artificial intelligence to analyse the data and the search is computer system-driven. The real value of the artificial intelligence techniques used in data mining is in the areas of pattern discovery, simulation modelling and predictive modelling.

In the following simple example, illustrated in Figure 9.1, there is a clear correlation between spending and income. What the scattergraph shows is not only that such a correlation exists but the strength of the relationship between the two variables. Such patterns, particularly ones that are counter-intuitive, are not always capable of being uncovered using standard query tools. The discovery of such patterns, using standard query tools, becomes more difficult where there are multiple variables (e.g. where age, sex, address, behaviour history and lifestyle data are included in addition to income). It is in this type of multi-variate analysis that data mining has the potential to be an extremely powerful adjunct to conventional tools for data analysis and exploitation.

The key distinction between data mining, as an activity, and ad hoc data analysis using SQL or OLAP tools is that the latter require the user to have a requirement or a hypothesis which

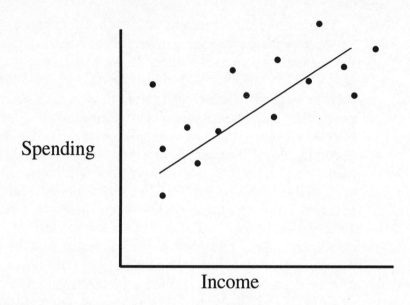

Spending

Income

Figure 9.1   A scattergraph with two variables

provides a clear and bounded focus to the activity of exploring the data. With data mining the power of artificial intelligence may be directed at finding a solution (or sets of solutions) to a problem that is less clearly defined — in essence, the data mining tool is targeted at data with a view to discovering trends and patterns that the user may never have envisaged.

As can be seen from these existing applications of data mining, the underlying principle is that large volumes of historical data can provide insights into future events or behavior. What is being sought by the user is an extrapolation of historical or current events to identify the likely direction of future events.

Different data mining algorithms are used for different purposes and there are clear strengths and weaknesses associated with the different techniques. In reality, what happens is that multiple techniques are brought to bear on a problem by using, for example, a clustering algorithm to identify a target group and then to use a predictive algorithm to forecast future behaviour. The following table identifies the different types of analysis that the different algorithms perform.

Table 9.1 The historical uses of data mining techniques

Data mining activities in the non-commercial sector	Description
1 Medical research	Data mining has been used to analyze empirical data regarding patient histories in order to identify correlations between specific diseases and lifestyle, age, sex, demographics, race, region and other patient characteristics.
2 Military research	Data mining has been used extensively by military users in the area of pattern matching which is used to aid target identification.
3 Astronomy research	Data mining has been used to predict and understand events occurring in the cosmos.
4 Geological research	Oil and mineral companies have used data mining techniques to help evaluate the propensity of a particular location having deposits of oil or other material.
5 Security analysis	Data mining has proved useful to police agencies in matching criminal events to criminal profiles.
6 Demographic research	Data mining tools have been used to analyze market surveys, census results, listenership figures for radio and TV and by academic researchers.

The need to create a representational model of the business under study may not be underestimated, and the skills required (especially for neural network modeling) are complex. A business model is a simplified representation or abstraction of a real business activity. A model that is over simplified may prove inaccurate or too general to be useful. A model that is too complex be not have a sufficiently manageable scope. Table 9.4 lists the most common problems that arise in the use of data mining technology.

Table 9.2 The use of data mining in commercial applications

Data mining activities in the commercial sector	Description
1 Market research	Predictive modeling using data mining tools have been used to forecast election results, customer propensity trends, lifestyle analysis and
2 Investment modelling	Data mining methods have been applied to the development of investment models used to anticipate stock market movements.
3 Fraud detection	Data mining is used to detect fraudulent activities by matching datasets.
4 Delinquency detection	Data mining is used to detect delinquent behavior by customers or suppliers (especially in cases where a party to a contract is exhibiting signs of defaulting).
5 Risk management	The insurance industry, in particular, is using data mining as a means of identifying risk by cross referencing economic and environmental data against exposure.
6 Market segmentation	Data mining offers a powerful means of clustering customers in segments where the customers share the same attributes or behavioral trends.
7 Supply-chain management	Matching demand with supply provides a useful applications for data mining technology and is used for this purpose by the retail sector.
8 Corporate planning	Data mining can be used to develop corporate models and scenarios with regard to workload management, cost control, revenue forecasting, competitor analysis and market analysis.

Table 9.3 Data mining algorithms

	Data Mining Technologies	Business Use
1	Neural networks	Prediction
2	Decision-tree algorithms	Comprehension
3	Genetic algorithms	Categorization
4	Fuzzy logic	Options
5	Association Rules	Association
6	k-nearest neighbor	Clustering

Table 9.4 Obstacles to successful data mining

Obstacles and Issues relating to the exploitation of data mining tools	Description
1 Data volumes	It is often difficult to determine how much data is necessary for a valid sample.
2 Data quality	Polluted data gives rise to the discovery of patterns that have no business significance and is time wasting.
3 Data availability	Sometimes the data to satisfy the needs of the model is not available.
4 User culture	Users may be wary of using advanced techniques for data analysis when they do not clearly understand the underlying logic.
5 IT architecture	The data mining server should be incorporated into the overall data warehouse architecture as a complementary mechanism for data analysis, but is often implemented as a separate stand-alone system.

STATISTICAL ANALYSIS TECHNIQUES

Statistical analysis is the precursor of data mining and statistical analysis techniques are generally divided into two categories. *Descriptive* statistics are used to describe the data and include diagrams, charts, tables and graphs. *Analytical* statistics seek to draw conclusions from the data which will guide the decision maker to the correct decision. The following is a brief description of the 10 most commonly used statistical techniques for data analysis.

1. Probability analysis
Probability analysis is concerned with establishing the probability of a given event. Probability is a forecast of a given event or condition which is measured on a scale from 0 to 1 where 0.5 represents a 50:50 probability of the event occurring.

2. Statistical inference
Statistical inference may be used to draw conclusions from a sample about a larger population. Statistical inference is used extensively in market research, political polls, quality assurance testing and consumer reaction testing.

3. Hypothesis testing
Hypothesis testing involves an assumption about what is referred to as a 'null hypothesis', which is the expected value and then to have an 'alternative hypothesis' which covers all other values.

4. Regression and correlation analysis
Regression analysis is a technique which allows the analyst to *describe* the relationship between two variables, and correlation analysis measures the *extent* of that relationship.

5. Composition analysis
Composition analysis is concerned with identifying the makeup of different objects which can be analyzed with a view to identifying changes in the composition of the object under analysis.

6. Value added analysis
Value added analysis is a useful technique for determining how much value is added to a product during different stages in the lifecycle of the product.

7. Time series analysis

An observation of data over time yields useful analysis potential since it is essentially an observation of the behavior of the data over time. This observation may identify a trend, or a pattern of over-laid trends.

8. Indices

Indices are normally used as a measure of performance and may be incorporated into a decision-support system as a useful statistical shorthand to describe the performance of a particular activity.

9. Impact analysis

Assesses the multiple impacts that a particular course of action in one part of the enterprise will have on other parts of the enterprise, or demonstrates the effects of slight or incremental changes to key objects in the business represented in the application model.

10. Proportion disparity analysis

This is the 80:20 rule familiar to everyone in business, where the disparity of proportions has long been observed as a common phenomenon.

USING DATA MINING TECHNIQUES

Data mining is the term that is now applied to the use of artificial intelligence in the discovery of valuable data patterns which provide insights into the behavior of the subject of the mining activity. Usually, the subject of data mining is the entity 'customer', which reflects the early use of this software in marketing/sales and cus-tomer care applications. Data mining has also found a ready market in the health care sector. Significant discoveries are being made about the causes of illness using correlation analysis tech-niques which identify the impact of environmental and genetic factors on the sample.

The use of artificial intelligence techniques to 'mine' the vast volumes of data in data warehouses has become an increasing feature of more mature data warehouse implementations. This level of interest in data mining tools is driven by the tangible business benefits that can be derived from identifying hidden correlations in data that unmask business opportunities directed at offering new services for hitherto unknown segments of the market. Because the term 'artificial intelligence' always tends to arouse technological mystique it is necessary to identify what it means in the context of data mining and data visualization tools. At a technological level, data mining may be defined as 'the application of advanced techniques of rule induction to large sets of data with a view to identifying patterns in the data'. At a business level, data mining may be defined as 'scanning large volumes of data to glean useful business information'.

When one is dealing with large volumes of data, there is always a problem associated with presenting the data in a manner that makes it easy to understand. This has led to the development of data visualization tools, which are tools designed to present the data that is being mined by the data mining tools. In fact, data mining tools are not fully optimized in the absence of data visualization software.

Applications will move from being designed in order to allow the user to interact with the data in response to a business event which has occurred in the external environment, to being designed to enable the system to identify patterns which trigger an event in the internal organization. This will represent the reduction of decision making to the status of an automated process and will mark a historic change in the nature of knowledge work.

Data mining is an adjunct to data warehousing, something all of the tool vendors agree on. But it is applicable in certain types of data warehousing environment. For example, data mining tools are only fully exploited when applied to transaction data and the warehouse may only have summary and aggregate data. In addition some data warehouses have only got a limited number of dimensions, often less than ten. Data mining becomes truly effective when it is applied to data which has many dimensions. In effect, the data mining project addresses the kind of data pattern recognition that is mot 'mind-sized' and is not accessible with ad hoc query tools. There is a clear implication that data mining is an activity that is most applicable to reasonably mature data warehouse sites where the warehouses comprise large volumes of clean and multi-dimensional data.

Because data mining tools can drill across dimensions, (like time, geography, subject, revenue, etc.), these dimensions can be included or excluded (or combined) for different passes through the data in a fashion that allows for levels of flexibility that would have required hundreds of thousands of lines of code in an older generation of computer system.

The most common way for data mining to be employed is for multi-step passes to be made through a data set in search of a target list. The first step is to use a cluster algorithm to find a control set. At each step the original data set reduces in size as potential targets are shed on the basis of successively refined criteria. Each pass through the data improves the quality of the list. The final list may be quite small and may justify a telesales campaign.

ARTIFICIAL INTELLIGENCE TECHNIQUES

For most of the data mining software in the data warehouse environment, one can read 'neural networks', which is an artificial intelligence technique that learns from experience. Compressed data can be represented as a cloud-like map of points where each point represent a datum in a database or an individual pixel of a video image. Any one point can be analyzed with reference to any other point presenting an almost limitless potential for pattern identification. Neural networks are not knowledge-based systems; all that they can achieve is pattern recognition in groups of numbers. Like a lot of technology innovation, the neural network has its origin in military applications and has been used to assemble sonar and radar images from data fragments. There are many variations of neural network but the most common is the multi-layer perceptron (MLP). The three layers of an MLP are the input layer (where neurons accept data), a hidden layer (which assigns a weight to the input) and the output layer (which outputs a result). The 'learning' aspect of the neural network occurs with the adjustment of the weights until the network is trained to identify the target pattern. (An alternative technique to the neural network involves the use of genetic algorithms, which consider a problem in terms of a string of characters, or chromosomes.)

As a general rule data mining software tends to be used when it is the business goal of the data warehouse to identify very complex individual trends in atomic level data where the volume of data is so great that the use of standard query tools by individuals would represent an unproductive use of time and system resource. Some enterprises, like holiday and mail order companies, may have 100 data fields for each customer record. Until the advent of the data warehouse there was no mainstream application for this type of artificial intelligence because there were no real world problems sufficiently complex to warrant the use of these tools and the pre-warehouse information systems were too fragmented to realize the potential that these tools offered. In addition, most data mining software assumes that the target database has available clean, integrated, consistent data about all of the dimensions that are being patterned. This might have seemed a reasonable assumption but reflects the fact that most artificial intelligence software originated in academia rather than in the real world. However, now that the target environment exists, the power of artificial intelligence can be unleashed in mainstream application domains, most especially in marketing and sales.

There should be no real constraints on the amount of data that can be accessed and analyzed by a data mining tool, other than the virtual memory constrains imposed by the host machine. The data mining tools now on the market can access data in all of the main relational database products on the market and allows user specified views to be accessed. Database access is normally via embedded SQL and should be able to work across networks using the TCP/IP protocol.

Individual data mining tools use a range of different algorithms to exploit the data and these will normally include neural networks and rule induction. Trained networks and induced rules can normally be stored (as icons in a graphical user interface palette). There are clear strengths and weaknesses associated with neural networks and rule induction. Generally speaking, neural networks are more accurate but are more difficult to train. Neural network outputs are often difficult to understand. Rule induction, on the other hand, is less precise but easier to construct and is particularly useful when targeting a sub-set of a large population.

It is normally a prerequisite of a data mining tool that it supports the full range of statistical techniques. The value of the data attributes under examination, and the relationships between them, should be capable of being represented by line graphs, histograms, pie charts, scatter diagrams and distribution curves.

THE BUSINESS CASE

The business case for using data mining tools is not normally made in isolation from the overall data warehouse project. Because it is not really feasible, for most enterprises, to use data mining techniques against their operational data, it is normally the case that the justification of the data warehouse investment is made by reference to (among other factors) the potential benefits that will accrue from the exploitation of the data patterns. Data mining tools are simply an advanced technique used as a data warehouse application tool after the organization has exhausted the possibilities offered by ad hoc SQL tools and OLAP multi-dimensional tools.

A common example of the type of applications which are being found for data mining tools include databased marketing applications which is focused on selecting suitable prospects from millions of potential customers for a specific direct marketing or telesales campaign. Because the traditional response rate to mass mailings is rarely more than 2%, even reasonably modest improvements in the quality of targeting can realize massive benefits. Data mining is also employed to study customer behavior for frequent user analysis by airlines, utilities, telephone companies and retail shopping companies. The use of neural networks, in particular, has made possible enormously complex analyses to be performed on buying patterns of individual customers and makes possible the monitoring of micro-segments of a company customer base that is simply not possible with conventional software tools.

The single most common application of data mining tools is the area of target marketing and that is likely to remain the case in the short to medium term. In the longer term, the use of data mining techniques will be applied to the production, quality assurance and financial subject-areas of the business as well as in meteorological and scientific applications.

Mail order companies have been amongst the earliest customers for data mining tools. Finding patterns in data and optimizing the expense of large-scale mailings is an obvious application of data mining techniques. Credit card companies have utilized data mining to discern detailed customer profiles to be used for target marketing. The level of sophistication achieved allows for mass mailings to be highly customized for different customer profiles, thereby resulting in high improvements in the yield ratio for this activity. Telecommunications companies have used data mining in order to achieve finer granularity in the level of segmentation that they can achieve. Airlines are using data mining techniques to better understand the behavior of their frequent fliers. The BBC has also utilise data mining in order to analyze viewing figures.

APPROACHING A DATA MINING PROJECT

A number of different factors have to be considered by prospective data mining users. The following list of points illustrate the issues which require consideration by the project manager.

- What competencies exist in the organization (or need to be developed) in order to fully exploit this technology?
- What kinds of data pattern represent the maximum potential business value to the enterprise?
- Where is the required data located in the enterprise?
- Is the data resident in a data warehouse environment (i.e. is all of the relevant corporate and external data integrated from

separate sources on one physical database which is fully available for decision support activities)?

- What other DSS application software is contending for the
  same system resource?
- Who are the decision makers who will sponsor this project?
- What is the quality of the data and will the data require
  cleansing before the data mining tool can be used?
- Are there up-to-date data models to reflect the semantic and
  syntactic meaning of the target data?
- Has the data mining initiative been located within an overall
  framework for exploiting data including SQL queries, OLAP
  queries, DSS applications, EIS applications and artificial intelligence?

TOOL CAPABILITY

A data mining tool can be evaluated by reference to 10 key
considerations. These are as follows:

1. Data access
The data mining tool must be capable of accessing the target data
and demonstrate good levels of performance against the target
database product. The tool should also allow for data to be
imported from the target environment into its own environment.
Careful consideration should be given to the different level of
performance that will be experienced in the proprietary tool
environment. Any constrains, with regard to data volumes that
apply to data being analyzed in the tool environment, and whether
the performance is linear at all data volumes, should be examined.
The impact of embedded SQL on the performance of the target
database should also receive some scrutiny.

2. Functional richness
The core of any data mining tool is the level of support offered for
the full range of algorithms that can be applied to pattern analysis.

These should include rule induction, decision trees, genetic algorithms and neural networks.

3. Data manipulation

The tool should be capable of selecting and merging the data according to complex criteria. It should be possible to derive new data and for existing data to be renamed or filtered out. The tool should have some dictionary/metadata capability to keep a record of any changes to the data.

4. Data visualization

In order to present the data under examination in a meaningful way, the tool should incorporate a data visualization assistant. The quality of the graphical displays of the different diagrams represents the key differentiator of this type of tool as well as the ability of the tool to support overlays and drill-downs of the different diagrams.

5. End-user programming

The tool should be capable of being used on a standard desktop PC or workstation without requiring the user to fully understand the data structures or any theoretical knowledge of the underlying algorithms. The human interface should be capable of providing the ability to develop customized applications that can be iteratively enhanced.

6. Extensible architecture

The tool should have the ability to integrate with the growing range of data management tools. It is desirable that the data mining toolset will evolve to interact with other data warehouse software including data extraction software products, data dictionary products, a metadata catalogue, database products, etc.

7. Library facilities

The tool should be capable of storing the output patterns of data as well as merged and derived data in a pattern library. The stored patterns stored should be capable of being time-stamped, overlaid, exported, contrasted and compared. The library should be supported by appropriate metadata and dictionary toolsets.

8. *Performance optimization*

The tool should be capable of exploiting the caching capability of databases so that immediate results can be stored. It should also be capable of aborting searches that are likely to become 'runaway' and utilize the SQL optimization facilities of database products when extracting data.

9. *Client Server architecture*

The data mining environment should be implemented according the principles of client server architecture. Ideally the data processing activities will occur on the server with the data visualization software resident on the client. The client machine would access the data warehouse directly or would access a data mining mart that contains data extracted from the data warehouse into the tool's own data management environment.

10. *Integration with desktop tools*

The patterns and data output from the data exploration should be capable of being loaded into standard desktop graphical display, word-processing, spreadsheet or database product.

PART 4

LOOKING TO THE FUTURE — NEXT GENERATION DATA WAREHOUSE

10

Future Directions in the First Generation of Data Warehousing

'The future is hidden, even from the men and women who make it.'
— Anatole France

This chapter is devoted to exploring the further developments that will occur in data warehousing during the first generation model of the data warehouse. The first generation of data warehousing is based on the principle of databases that are exclusively query-oriented. The next generation of data warehousing will challenge this assumption and we will see hybrid architectures that seek to re-integrate the decision-support activities in the enterprise with the operational processes.

During this current phase of improvement, (within the scope of the first generation of data warehousing), the core concept of the data warehouse — as a non-volatile store of data dedicated exclusively to decision-support — will remain the norm. Therefore all of the improvements that are forecast and anticipated in this chapter are predicated on the assumption that underlies all data warehousing at present; that there is a substantial logical and physical gulf between operational computing and decision-support computing. It will take some further time for this assumption

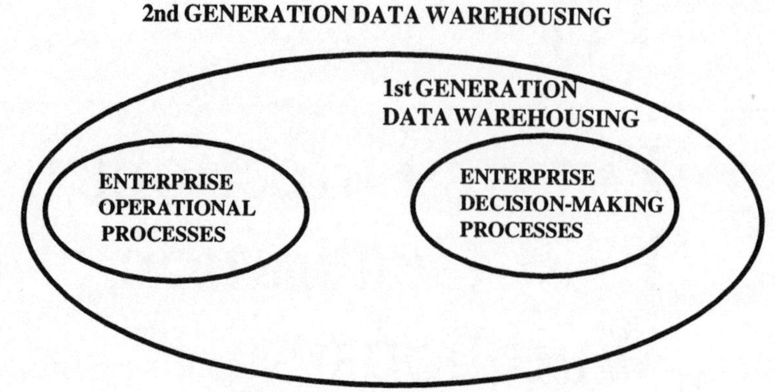

2nd GENERATION DATA WAREHOUSING

Figure 10.1   The progression in the scope of data warehousing

to be comprehensively challenged. When this does happen, the data warehouse architecture will change fundamentally and this second generation of data warehousing is the subject of the next chapter.

Some of the key contributors to altering or enhancing the first generation data warehouse architecture are contained in the following list. This chapter explores each of the following topics:.

- Syndicated data
- Data visualization
- Internets/Intranets
- Architecture
- Software agents
- Storage technology
- Artificial intelligence
- Security
- Metadata
- Multi-media
- Privacy
- Processing technology

SYNDICATED DATA

The unprecedented level of implementation of data warehouse systems is creating an expanded market for syndicated data suppliers. The use of data that is external to the enterprise has the effect of increasing the information content of the data in the data warehouse. The traditional suppliers of syndicated data (A.C. Nielsen and Information Resources Inc. For retail data; Dun & Bradstreet & Reuters for financial and economic data) are now being supplemented by many new suppliers offering demographic, psychographic and market research data. It is also the case that the information content of most products (bills, invoices, credit card statements) is increasing due to the demands of consumers and industry. This trend towards information being perceived as a product in its own right will be accelerated by the data warehouse phenomenon and will have the effect of considerably increasing the volumes of data being captured and manipulated within the enterprise.

The net effect of the increased availability, usefulness and sophistication of syndicated data will be to substantially increase the data volumes of corporate data warehouses.

DATA VISUALIZATION

Data visualization is clearly a key demand of a data warehouse user population that is rapidly becoming overwhelmed by the sheer scale of data and information that confronts them. One of the main reasons why the data is overwhelming is because data warehouse applications are 'visually challenged'. Huge potential exists to simplify the task of analyzing data by converting the data into graphical representations. More intelligence can be gleaned from analyzing a picture of the data than by analyzing rows and columns of text and figures.

Data visualization is most commonly associated with data mining for the obvious reason that the output of data mining — synthesis, correlations, trends, patterns, clusters and matches — is must better server by visual imagery than by tables of data. But data visualization extends beyond data mining to all forms of data interrogation and analysis. The concept of 'visual SQL' or 'visual OLAP' are just as valid as visual mining and are being developed as extensions to familiar data interrogation tools.

Data visualization allows the user to see an abstracted picture of a trend or pattern that can be viewed on its own or can be altered by changing the parameters of the query or search. Geographic maps that contain colour-coded information about regions (or other sub-divisions) that is dynamically linked to the data in the data warehouse remains the popular form of data visualization in use today. But increasingly, complex results can be illustrated as multi-layered three-dimensional bar charts, matrices, visual multi-dimensional cubes, contour maps, overlaid trend lines and scattergraphs.

Data visualization software will become the competitive battle-ground for all of the data exploitation tool vendors during the next few years. What users want is to reduce the time it takes to hypothesize the query and acquire the results and increase the time taken analyzing the discovered trend. This impetus will drive the data visualization market forward and will reward those vendors who respond to this need. The productivity advances that are possible with data visualisation are illustrated in Figure 10.2. The ongoing objective in data warehousing is to maximise the intellectual effort of knowledge workers and to minimize the technical and administrative effort that is required.

THE INTERNET AND INTRANETS

There is a strong trend emerging now for database developments to occur in conjunction with the Internet and to take into account the possibilities offered by the World Wide Web. The reason for the interest has to do with the advantage of Internet connectivity and the relative ease with which Web pages can be made available. The key factors which have contributed to the acceptance of the Web by business users include:

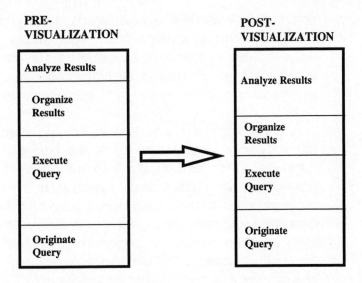

PRE-
VISUALIZATION

POST-
VISUALIZATION

Analyze Results

Organize
Results

Execute
Query

Originate
Query

Analyze Results

Organize
Results

Execute
Query

Originate
Query

Figure 10.2   The benefit of data vusualization

1. Simple acceptable design.
2. A standard existing infrastructure.
3. Cross-platform compatibility.
4. Instant deployment.
5. Global access.
6. Centralized maintenance and server-based control.
7. Low maintenance overhead.
8. Support for multi-media.

Most organizations have a need to disseminate information to the public, primarily for marketing and public relations purposes. But more and more organizations want to capture information from the public via simple applets available at their Web sites. The final stage in the first phase of internet usage will occur when business can be transacted on a widespread basis over the internet.

For most corporations it the intranet that offers most potential in the short to medium term. An intranet is a private corporate internet. The intranet is, for many organizations, replacing e-mail and groupware and is impacting to some extent on decision-support computing. What the intranet offers is a significant shift in intra-company communications and a potentially powerful means of disseminating corporate information. Early evidence suggests that much of the initial intranet developments are informal initiatives by groups of technology-aware business users in the larger corporations.

It is especially the case that technology companies, who have a more thorough understanding of the potential and application of intranets, have been to the fore in forging inter-personal, inter-group and inter-departmental intranets in order to optimize communications efficiency. Like most technology innovations (including data warehousing), the experience of corporate intranets is that the early informal initiatives develop in one of two ways. According to the malign scenario the early experiments are replicated by many user groups and tend to add small chunks of value throughout the organization. The strength of this organic growth is that the technology is adopted quickly by those who will actually use and exploit it. The weakness of this approach is that the intranets are exploited only at a low level for the exchange of reports, presentations and office memoranda. The linkage to corporate databases and the eventual integration of the range of intranets becomes a large headache for the central information technology function. The more benign scenario is that, after the early experiments, a strategic corporate implementation plan is effected which implements a standard intranet strategy. There is only sparse evidence that this formal strategic approach is being followed at this stage in the evolution of the intranet concept.

The single most attractive aspect of intranets is the ease of use. Because of the wide range and variation of desktop clients there has always been a problem of a common presentation interface and interoperability of applications. HTML (HyperText Markup Language) is the common publishing language for Intranets (and the Internet) and can be run on PCs, Unix workstations or Macs. Essentially the use of HTML and the use of Java applets solves the problem of having common clients, a common language and a common protocol. Indeed, strategies based on intranets have come to be referred to as 'server-centric' since all applications have to be written only once and placed on the server. These applications are then available to all clients at any location globally. It is for this reason that intranets have come to be of such interest of data warehouse architects. They offer the chance to genuinely achieve ubiquitous access to information.

In early intranet/data warehouse implementations the achievements have been fairly modest. Many users have simply saved output reports as HTML documents and made them available on an intranet server. In this example the intranet server simply becomes another subsidiary data mart within the overall architecture. Data access and reporting tools for accessing the data warehouse across the intranet are in their infancy but virtually every query tool vendor has delivered a version for intranet use. While there is some merit, from the point of view of fostering information, in allowing a measure of freedom in the early stages of intranet development, the benefits of exploiting centrally stored data will only be fully realized when a defined set of standards for intranet development tools (presentation, reporting and browsing tools) and user interfaces are determined for the enterprise.

The real value of the Web is that it has revolutionized the way that information is distributed. However, the challenge for data warehouse architects is to dynamically extract data from a database and present it in a desired format on a Web page. The Web is, essentially, a publishing medium. For those wishing to enhance their warehouse deployment strategy the Web offers a number of critical advantages. Publishing software is server-based and the client is easily downloadable to users' machines. There are no more worries about connectivity, differences in machine configuration, network structures or middleware. Ease of deployment and ease of maintenance make the Web an winning option for distributing corporate data.

Web users of the data warehouse can be broken down into the same categories as conventional data warehouse users ranging from active to passive. Passive users are described as users who spend most of their time 'digesting' pre-prepared reports and analyses to help them make informed strategic decisions. Generally the passive user has not the time to make detailed investigations into the data in the data warehouse. Investigative users of data warehouse information, on the other hand, do have the time for such activity — in fact, such activity makes up a significant part of their jobs. The passive user can be satisfied by the 'thin client' functionality of most web browsers, which facilitate the presentation of information, both textual and graphical. However, the investigative user needs to have 'fat client' functionality that will enable them to generate ad hoc queries. The challenge is to increase the power on the client side of the Web in order to improve the capability of the power user. This can be addressed in two ways. One is to improve the capability of the Web browser. The other is to incorporate Web access capabilities into traditional client server systems.

SAS Institute have adopted both of these approaches in the most cogent vendor effort to integrate the Web with their data warehouse product suite. SAS have clearly evaluated and considered alternative solutions to the problem of Web/data warehouse integration.[7] In each case SAS has delivered a solution based on the approach defined and these are outlined here:

Adding Value to Web Browsers

The first technique is to define helper applications that can be defined to process and render data which the browser itself is unable to handle. When such data is downloaded, the browser activates the required helper application, and passes it for further processing. A second technique is to use plugins, which are extensions to Web browsers which also enable the processing/ rendering of foreign data types. There is a much closer communication between the Web browser and the plugin than there is between a browser and a helper application. This technique allows a plugin to draw directly to an area of the browser window which makes operations much smoother from a user's perspective. Finally, the browser can be enhanced using the Java language from Javasoft (an operating company of Sun Microsystems) to

---

[7] For further information see the SAS White Paper, *The SAS System and Web Integration.*

provide the capability to download small applications, known as applets, from the Web server. These are then executed on the client. JDBC, the Javasoft database connectivity standard, provides an API to Java programmers with a uniform interface to a wide range of database systems.

Adding Value to the Traditional Client Server Systems

A number of approaches can be taken to extending the traditional client-server system to embrace the Web. These include converting reports to HTML so that the reports can be served by the Web. This usually occurs in static mode which means that the reports need to be regenerated if the data upon which they are based needs to be updated. The next logical step is to enable the HTML documents to be generated 'on the fly', in response to a query from a Web browser. This can be achieved through the use of gateway technology (using either CGI, the Common Gateway Interface standard or using an ODBC gateway). Another route is to initiate server processing in response to a Web client request. Finally, there is the possibility of accessing Web servers directly from client programs.

For the purposes of deploying decision-support functionality via the intranet, the following checklist of issues should be considered at the earliest possible stage:

1. Assess what datasets are best suited to intranet exploitation and define those datasets that can be exploited using text-search tools and those datasets that require manipulation using query tools.
2. Assess if the organization is capable of altering its structure to optimize the potential of intranets in order to devolve decision-making to the level of the workgroup.
3. Assess if the business processes that are supported by the subject-data in the data warehouse map on to the intranets that are seeking access to the data warehouse.

4. Assess the scalability of the toolsets being used to construct the intranets with regard to the long-term plans for the data warehouse data and architecture.

5. Assess if it is satisfactory, from the perspective of the business requirements, to publish corporate data in a static (i.e. HTML) format.

6. Assess if the requirements from the intranet workgroups would be better served by a dedicated document database.

7. Assess if the intranet workgroups have a requirement to load data from the web page into other software tools (i.e. spreadsheets, PC databases, OLAP databases, presentation software) and evaluate the requirement in the context of the standards that apply for direct data warehouse access.

8. Assess if live applications are to be deployed on the intranet and what development environment is appropriate to this task.

9. Assess what the security considerations are in relation to making data available on the intranet.

10. Assess if there is a requirement to make data available from the data warehouse on the internet for access by suppliers, customers, prospects or the general public. Apply a higher degree of rigor for these applications from the point of view of security, access standards and presentation standards.

DEVELOPMENTS IN DATA WAREHOUSE ARCHITECTURE

At present the data warehouse architecture comprises a number of layers (as discussed in Chapter 4) where various activities are performed in the process of converting and exploiting data. It is regarded, for the most part, as a holistic architecture that can be applied to the entire project. But experience has shown that the data warehouse project is, in reality, two separate projects, see Figure 10.3.

One project is concerned with corporate data standards, corporate information systems strategy and corporate information systems architecture. This is the part of the project that is

Legacy   Extraction Database Middleware Application

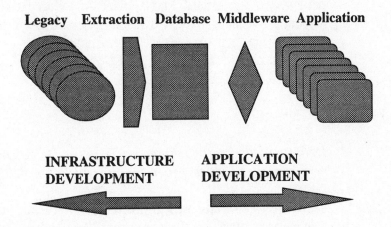

INFRASTRUCTURE   **APPLICATION**
DEVELOPMENT   **DEVELOPMENT**

Figure 10.3 The twin data warehouse projects

concerned with building the infrastructure to sustain decision-support computing. The second project is concerned with building the actual decision-support applications. Increasingly, enterprises are beginning to perceive this distinction. For most enterprises they will get only one chance to build the infrastructure and it is normally a finite project with a reasonably concrete deliverable. On the other hand, building new types of query and developing new applications to exploit the data is a continuous activity that will continue in an enterprise for so long as that enterprise continues to trade in the marketplace.

Focusing on architecture is the key to advancing the data warehouse concept. It is this authors contention that data warehousing as a concept will not remain static. It must either retreat or advance. In reality, some enterprises will downsize the concept into manageable chunks of business intelligence delivered via multiple data marts. Other enterprises will expand the boundaries of the data warehouse to include operational processing. History will determine which group will be more successful. Whichever route an enterprise follows the risk of having to re-orient the strategy is considerably assisted if the data exploitation layer (i.e. the applications that are resident on data marts) is separated from the infrastructure layer. In this way those who fail to invest in both projects to the extent that is necessary can have a conceptual and logical architecture that allows the maximum flexibility to orient their efforts more towards infrastructure or applications, as circumstances demand.

SOFTWARE AGENTS

Definition: A software agent is a program that is capable of performing repetitive programmable tasks on behalf of the user.

Software agents are becoming increasingly popular in a number of application areas. Software agents are, in a sense, a response to information overload. Web surfers, data warehouse users and syndicated data suppliers are all encountering the same difficulty — we are awash with data and are suffering from information overload. Users are demanding a tool that can distinguish useful data from junk data and they want a means of downloading what is useful when it becomes available without having to endure the tedium of engaging in long fruitless searches at intervals.

For example, software agents are being used extensively on the Internet for sorting and filtering e-mail according to rules defined by the user. Software agents are also being used to offer Internet users the possibility of more effective networking by identifying users at different locations who share the same interests or who are working on complementary research. Within the data warehouse, software agents are being used in conjunction with data mining tools and predictive modeling techniques. For example, users can configure software agents to identify (through changes in the pattern of data) a customer or customer segment that conforms to the profile of a cross-selling opportunity. The agent software can mark these customers and initiate a direct mailing process. The main short-term business driver of this technology will undoubtedly be the Internet community who are finding it increasingly frustrating as they wade through countless pages of dross in order to find a gem of information. The psychology of the Web surfer and the data warehouse surfer are identical in this regard. Too much time is being wasted in performing data analysis that is not proving useful. Much of the data trawling is inefficient and repetitive. While the architects and designers of data warehouses have to take some responsibility for this, it has to be accepted that the art of requirements gathering for decision-support applications is too immature to realize the dream of a fully comprehensive application architecture for the data warehouse. The answer lies in software agents.

Software agents are making an appearance in the data warehouse market because of the obvious applicability of this type of software to decision-support computing. The typical data warehouse user wishes to exploit data by means of identifying threat and opportunity conditions that can offer a clear business advantage to the enterprise. Some threat and opportunity conditions are only discovered after long periods of iterative analysis. Others are capable of being rigorously defined. Whenever a condition that has value to the business is discovered, it makes sense to describe the event to a program that will signal an alert every time that same condition is encountered in future. This is a very basic use of software agents and reflects the embryonic nature of this software.

Software agents will also be used in a quasi-operational manner by extending the life of legacy systems by using the data warehouse to identify alerts which are relayed to the operational transaction systems. For example, the data warehouse may be used to identify credit scores for customers and prospects, and when a change occurs in the credit rating of a customer, the software agent can identify this change and update the customer credit code on the operational system. Software agents are being used by retail companies to signal alerts to their suppliers when there is a run on a stock item, and are also being used extensively for fraud detection.

Research that is currently in progress promises to advance the present primitive agent tools and hold out the promise that agents can be used to fully automate operational processes such as purchasing. In this case, a purchase agent will attempt to find a match with a selling agent and a purchasing transaction is initiated. The scope for using agents in this manner is virtually limitless. They can be used to trigger events such as changes in product design, product launch, price adjustment, promotions, cross-selling, discounts, cost reduction, stock level adjustment, manning levels, credit ratings — virtually every conceivable event in the enterprise. Therefore, software agents represent one of the first components of the infrastructure that will bridge the world of decision-support computing to the world of operational transaction processing and will mark a significant change in the way that we will view the data warehouse in the future.

More sophisticated use will be made of this technology in the second generation of data warehouse architecture, which will incorporate process support for operational processes as well as decision-support for management processes. This next generation of data warehouse is explored in more detail in the next chapter.

DATA STORAGE

Significant economies are being made in the price of data storage and advances in optical storage technologies, in particular, have been significant in this regard. In 1995 IBM, in association with GTE, Kodak, Stanford University and Carnegie-Mellon University, initiated a 'holographic' data storage project. Holographic data storage uses laser technology to store bits of data holographically in an optical medium such as a crystal. Early results suggest that this technique is 12 times cheaper than conventional magnetic disk technology. More significantly, because laser technology is employed for both writing and reading the data, I/O throughput is estimated to be 10 times faster than magnetic disks. Already the researchers are talking about data rates of 1 gigabyte per second (1GB/sec). Equally exciting is the potential for using this technology for more efficient data retrieval.

PRIVACY AND DATA PROTECTION

As this author predicted in 1994 (in '*Data Warehousing — the Route to Mass Customisation*', John Wiley) the issue of data protection has reared its head, particularly in parts of Europe.

While there is no real evidence that national legislatures are coming to grips with the complexity that is inherent in data transformation, there is a growing public awareness concerning the close surveillance that is being exercised by industry on the consumer behavior of individual citizens. The issue of data protection is addressed in detail in the following four landmark documents:

Table 10.1   Data protection legislation

Origin	Document
European Community	Directive on the protection of individuals with regard to the processing of personal data and on the free movement of such data — adopted 1995
OECD	Guidelines on the protection and privacy of transborder flows of personal data
USA	Privacy Act 1974
UK	Data Protection Act 1984

The privacy issue is being voiced with considerably more force in Europe than in North America and a European Community directive on data protection comes into effect at the turn of the century. The title of this regulatory instrument is instructive — *'Protection of Individuals with regard to the Processing of Personal Data and on the Free Movement of Such Data'*. For the first time the guidelines go beyond the usual concerns such as data ownership, consent, accuracy and access to address issues such as the movement of the data, the source of the data and the logic involved in processing the data. However, the legislation fails to prescribe guidelines that might be applied to data warehousing since the legislators continue to be ignorant, it seems, concerning the complexities of transformed, integrated and derived information. The multiple sources of data for the warehouse are closely regulated but the information that is refined from this raw material remains a vague area of law and regulation.

In addition to the complexities of data integration the legal issues surrounding data sharing are unclear. Many enterprises now offer combination promotions (for example, air mile credits for credit card usage) and these promotions gather intelligence about customer behavior which can then be shared by the sponsoring companies and merged with existing data. In the retail sector multiple retailers are combining to offer loyalty schemes where all those who are party to the loyalty promotion share data about the customer.

The Internet also provides a rich source of customer behavior data with the possibility to identify user preferences by monitoring the sites normally accessed by users. While the entire area of consumer behavior analysis presents a difficulty challenge for legislators, it must be anticipated that, in the future, some form of regulation will be applied to the use of data in these circumstances.

THE DATA WAREHOUSE MARKET

Various estimates have been made of the size of the data warehouse market and the growth projections for data warehousing. The general consensus by market analysts is that investment in data warehousing will peak in 1998/1999 in the USA and in 1999/2000 in Europe and that the total value of the data warehouse market when it peaks will be in the region of $8 billions. However, extreme caution must be exercised when considering estimates of the size of the data warehouse market because of difficulties in defining the boundaries of the market. For example, some market predictions are based on the premise that data warehousing is synonymous with all types of decision-support systems. In addition, in the rush by vendors to be positioned in this burgeoning market, many software products that have long occupied niches of the market have been re-labeled as 'data warehouse' products. In addition, may user organizations have re-categorized many of their existing databases as data warehouses. To make the picture even more complicated, the cost of a data warehouse infrastructure includes all of the desktop software and communications networks which may have been deployed by the enterprise, regardless of the data warehouse project.

Therefore, the critical issue that remains obscure is: 'What precisely is a data warehouse?' For the purposes of analyzing the market it is probably wise to distinguish two distinct markets. One market is that for corporate data warehouse strategies where there is a conscious strategy to integrate data with a view to transforming the enterprise. This may be referred to as the market for strategic data warehouses. The second market is more diffuse and includes small point-solution data marts, business intelligence systems, executive information systems, database marketing systems and a range of specialized decision-support systems. This latter market is likely to be considerably larger, in terms of the value of global sales, than the market for strategic corporate solutions. Of course, the strategic implementations will, in most instances, incorporate subsidiary data marts and decision-support systems as well as the base warehouse infrastructure — so the distinction is not very real from the perspective of the user organization. But from the perspective of the market the distinction is real enough and each of the two distinct markets is dominated by different vendors and these leaders of the respective markets rarely compete head-on with each other. Table 10.2 outlines the distinguishing features of the two markets:

Table 10.2 The two markets for data warehousing

Issue	Strategic Data Warehouse Market	Tactical Data Warehouse Market
Dominant vendors	This market is dominated by high-end hardware vendors who normally fulfil the role of systems integrator.	This market is dominated by software vendors with a background in EIS and business intelligence systems.
Products	Strategic projects tend to be focused on architectural components.	Tactical projects tend to be focused on application software.
Cost	The cost of a strategic data warehouse solution is generally not less than $1 millions.	The cost of tactical data warehouse solutions begins at $30,000.
Market Size	The strategic market is likely to account for no more than 25% of the total data warehouse market.	The tactical data warehouse market is likely to account for 75% of the overall market size.

The data warehouse market will diverge to an even greater extent with reference to the goals of the projects that are labeled 'strategic' and 'tactical'. The market for tactical data warehouse solutions will become much less homogeneous over time. Distinct applications will be bundled with these data warehouse solutions and these will be directed at specific vertical industry sectors and specific types of applications. Thus, information technology solutions for the retail industry will become specialized as vendors develop specialized applications for basket analysis. Likewise, in the insurance and banking sectors specialized decision-support applications for cross selling and up-selling will be perfected.

In the case of common data warehouse applications such as customer-segmentation, supply chain integration and customized billing, it is likely that generic applications will be developed for the market. The overall prognosis for this segment of the market is that it will become increasingly specialized and that the products will eventually become 'shrink-wrapped' with the application solution available from a single vendor. For the most part, the customers for these packaged solutions will be small and medium-sized enterprises which do not have the capability to wrestle with complex systems integration projects — and which, in most cases, do not suffer from the degree of data fragmentation that is common in large enterprises.

In the case of the strategic implementations, the focus will remain fixed on generating the corporate capacity to develop bespoke applications that deliver competitive differentiation. These strategic projects will, in the main, be sponsored by larger corporations and will continue to require more significant architectural input by specialists. The breakdown of the data warehouse market for strategic systems is likely to be facilitated more and more by consultants with the specialist expertise that can facilitate higher levels of innovation. While the goal of organizations deploying tactical data warehouses is to maintain competitiveness with their peers in a situation where everyone is investing in this type of technology; the goal of those deploying strategic solutions is to establish competitive dominance in the marketplace.

Table 10.3 outlines the past, current and future split of the data

Table 10.3 Breakdown of data warehouse costs

Year	1996	1997	1998
Hardware	40%	30%	25%
Database/Access tools	25%	25%	25%
Copy management tools	17%	19%	20%
Systems integration/Consultancy	18%	26%	30%
Total	100%	100%	100%

Source: Data Warehouse Network.

warehouse market for strategic systems with reference to the four principal product categories.

By 1997 there were a total of 150 different vendors offering data warehouse products with the greatest concentration of vendors in the data access and exploitation end of the spectrum. The number of vendors with a comprehensive vision for enterprise decision-support computing is a small fraction of that number. What can be predicted with confidence is that, over the next two years, the market will consolidate significantly. This will occur by reason of the natural dynamic of an expanding market but will also be driven by the need for more integrated solutions.

DATA WAREHOUSING AND BUSINESS PROCESS REDESIGN (BPR)

Investment in IT now represents 70% of all capital investment and the benefits of that investment are often questionable. This implies that the potential of IT has forged far ahead of the ability of organizations to use that technology to transform their business processes. The objective of the workshop will be to identify and exploit the synergies which exist between IT and BPR.

Most companies now have some kind of standard information technology architecture or information systems planning process. Systems analysts have been capturing the different processes in the enterprise for decades in order to divide the processes into sub-processes to computerize. The complex interconnected web of business processes which comprise the total enterprise are often detailed in process models of the enterprise used by the data processing department. There will also be data models of the enterprise or a single corporate data model which constitutes the foundation stone of any corporate IT architecture. Therefore, the foundation skills for BPR are to be found in most IT departments. IT personnel are also the most conscious of the discontinuities which occur in business processes. And IT has been identified, in every study in the subject, as the key enabler in the BPR intervention.

11

The Second Generation of Data Warehouse— Reintegration with the Operational Systems

'All great truths begin as blasphemies.'
— *George Bernard Shaw*

THE CONCEPT OF SECOND GENERATION DATA WAREHOUSING

As more and more improvements are made in the way that we design, build and maintain first generation data warehouses, the next milestone to be encountered is the second generation data warehouse concept. It is entirely unclear, at this stage, what precise shape this second generation of data warehouses will take. The best guide to a fundamental paradigm shift is to be found primarily, in the opinion of this author, in the dynamic of the business environment rather than the dynamic of technological development. Ongoing technological innovation in data warehousing is directed primarily at improving the functional richness of the dedicated decision-support data warehouse.

But businesses are facing an increasing challenge to innovate and improve customer service using the information that is harvested by the first generation data warehouse. Ultimately, this can only be achieved through a synthesis of the decision-support domain and the operational domain of the business. In the first generation of the data warehouse concept the focus of attention has been in converting data into usable information. This activity may be referred to as data exploitation. The second generation of data warehouse will be more concerned with using the informational trends and patterns to automatically alert the operational processes in the enterprise to threat and opportunity conditions that have been identified and taking appropriate action. This activity occurs, at present, through managerial intervention to initiate the appropriate response by the business to the intelligence that is gleaned from data exploitation. For the purposes of clarity we may refer to this separate activity as information exploitation. Bridging the link between data exploitation and information exploitation now presents the next challenge to data warehouse architects and will form the basis for an entirely new layer in the existing data warehouse architecture. It is inevitable that this loop between the operational systems and the decision-support systems will be closed in order to fully optimize the corporate information technology infrastructure.

The difference between the business demands that drive first generation data warehousing and second generation data warehousing is illustrated in Table 11.1.

What distinguishes first generation from second generation data warehouse requirements is that first generation users are concerned with discovery and second generation users are concerned with action. It is a crucially important distinction. First generation data warehouses offer the business the potential to realize business benefits and second generation data warehouses are concerned with actually realizing those benefits. When considering the second generation of data warehouse it may not be appropriate to use the term data warehouse at all, since the data warehouse simply becomes part of an overall holistic information technology architecture which comprises both the domain of decision-support applications and the domain of operational processing.

Table 11.1 First and second generation applications

	1st Generation data warehousing requirements	2nd Generation data warehousing requirements
Retail industry	Identify slow moving items by outlet, region and country.	Redirect slow moving items to outlets demonstrating higher levels of demand.
Utility industry	Identify customer behavior by value and segment.	Apply discount factors to specific segments according to value of business.
Banking industry	Identify delinquency pattern of behavior by customers in specific business segments that are under-performing.	Adjust the credit rating ofcustomers who exhibit certain characteristics of delinquency behavior.
Insurance industry	Identify opportunities for cross-selling insurance products with reference to customer profile and segment.	Offer combination products, with variable discounts, to customers who exhibit a propensity for expanded insurance cover.
Health industry	Match the characteristics of a particular illness to the lifestyle and other characteristics of those suffering the illness.	Alert all patients exhibiting a propensity to contract a particular illness and identify the preventative and/or remedial treatment required.

Charting the progression of data exploitation commences with the pre-warehouse enterprise which is dependent on fragmented reporting systems for business intelligence. This type of enterprise we may refer to as 'primitive'. The first generation of data warehouse increases the value of the data and permits data discovery and data mining to occur, thereby improving considerably the ability of the enterprise to amass business intelligence. But, at this stage, the enterprise is still reactive, in the sense that the enterprise is becoming more informed but not necessarily becoming more adaptable. This type of enterprise we may refer to as 'intelligent'. The second generation of data warehouse architecture, comprising

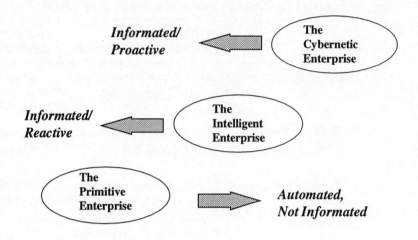

Figure 11.1   The progression of data warehousing

the link between discovering and doing, is capable of dynamically linking the actions of the enterprise to the information that is discovered in the data warehouse. This type of enterprise may be referred to as 'cybernetic', in the sense that there is a feedback loop from the systems that determine what is happening in the market-place (the traditional data warehouse) to the systems that support the business processes that interact with the marketplace (the traditional and new forms of operational system). In effect, this new manifestation of a fully integrated information technology architecture becomes a holistic control mechanism for the enterprise organism. The progress towards this new concept is based on successively increasing the value that is achieved. This progression is illustrated in the Figure 11.1.

THE SECOND GENERATION ARCHITECTURE

While some measure of agreement exists among analysts and commentators that this is the likely evolution path for data ware-housing, considerable disagreement exists concerning the manner in which information technology architects will respond to this challenge. Despite the paucity of research and reticence of industry analysts generally to commit to a vision of the future, there are, at least, four competing options being considered. These are included in Table 11.2:

Table 11.2 Second generation concepts

	Concept	Description	Originator
1	Enterprise Information Factory	An integrated decision-support and operational environment based on a co-operative database environment which actually uses multiple databases — one for operational functions and one for informational functions — working together.	NCR Corp.
2	Operational Data Store	An integrated decision-support and operational computing architecture based on two physical implementations — one of the data warehouse and the other is the operational data store which represents a copy of the data warehouse schema and which is used for the operational processing.	W.H. Inmon
3	Enterprise Server	A single physical implementation of a database which supports both transaction-intensive and query-intensive processes.	Various
4	Hybrid Enterprise Architecture	An architected approach to delivering operational functional enhancement comprising a data warehouse, software agents and operational marts.	Data Warehouse Network

THE WEAKNESSES OF FIRST GENERATION DATA WAREHOUSING

Obviously, the core concept of the data warehouse is not flawed in itself: data warehousing is the only response that can be applied to the challenge of data exploitation at the time of writing. But it is not, in itself, a solution that has been fully optimized and we can expect to see a number of significant advances made in both the tools and techniques used to build data warehouses.

It is clear that data warehousing is a growing and unstoppable phenomenon. It is equally clear that the concept of the data warehouse is not static and will, inevitably, mature and mutate in the near future. We will now explore what is going to happen next.

First, it necessary to explore why the existing data warehouse paradigm is going to be relatively short-lived. In a nutshell, data warehousing is an accident of history — it is an aberration in the continuum of technological evolution. This may seem to be a radical assertion, particularly, coming as it does, from someone who specializes in data warehousing. The essential distinction which needs to be made is between the What (exploiting data for competitive advantage) and the How (the data warehouse). The What is enduring and will always be pursued. The How is temporal and will always be subject to change.

Let us indulge for a moment in some retrospective What If? Analysis.

1. What if the CASE initiative in the 1980s had been a success and if every corporation had implemented all of their operational systems according to a single model of the corporate data and maintained a common repository of metadata for these operational systems? Well clearly the degree of data fragmentation that is evident today — and which is a major driver of data warehousing — would not be as severe.

2. What if the cost of computer processing and storage had dropped at an earlier stage (say, in the 1980s) and had enabled companies to maintain image copies of the data for analysis?

Well clearly this route would have been followed by companies who were intent on raising the decision-support capabilities of their companies.

3. What if the conventional systems development methodologies had anticipated the need to integrate and exploit corporate data and had incorporated a higher degree of decision-support capability into the operational systems in the first instance? Clearly, this would have obviated the need to make significant investments in data warehousing now.

4. What if data quality and consistency had been higher on the corporate agenda? Then clearly the data warehouse project would be considerably less complex and the impulse to construct data warehouses would be less compelling.

We can only conclude from such analysis that the data warehouse is made necessary in order to clean up the sins of the past. To this extent, it may be said that data warehousing is an accident of history: it is not, an any sense, a natural solution that will be permanent. Data warehousing is a response to a physical problem which has to do with the constrains of the existing technology, rather than the actual requirements of the business. And because the data warehouse architecture is rooted in a physical framework, it is conceptually weak.

It seems as if the information technology strategies of corporations are always in full pursuit of the short-term agenda and will forever be storing up trouble for the future. So too it will be, unless we are very careful, with data warehousing. The data warehouse is a historical necessity because it is, with available technology, the only way that we can integrate data in any meaningful way to support the business. But it is also antithetical to the business because it disintegrates the business process into those parts that are deemed to be operational and those parts that inform and support decision-making. At an abstract level this is obviously synthetic and, in the long run, dangerous for the business.

At some stage there will have to be an attempt to integrate the data warehouse architecture within an overall framework for information systems in the enterprise. Business processes cannot be supported in an optimized fashion by separating the strategic and the operational. To be truly effective an enterprise needs to have the strategic and operational elements of the business process closely coupled. In short, the data warehouse will have to have an operational role if the business patterns that are discerned in the data are to be fully exploited by the business.

This aspect — the combining of the operational and decision support frameworks — is the key to envisioning the future evolution of data warehousing.

Corporate organizations have seen a number of initiatives which attempted to transform the enterprise and seen the majority of them failed or abandoned. In this category of corporate fads that experienced limited success and then fizzled out, we can locate Total Quality Management (TQM) and Business Process Re-engineering (BPR). Neither of these particular concepts is flawed in any respect but neither have achieved anything like the potential that they promise. Therefore, we must conclude that the inherent danger of any pan-corporate initiative lies in the potentially crippling lack of vision and wholehearted sponsorship that is required for genuine transformation. Total information management is also a pan-corporate initiative that requires the complete attention of the enterprise to be fully successful. The popularity of point-solution data marts is further evidence that data warehousing, in common with the experience of other pan-corporate projects, is degenerating into pockets of achievement rather than enterprise transformation.

But the problem with disjointed data integration initiatives is that they cannot be introduced in an isolated part of the enterprise. The simple truth is that few organizations have the vision, or the courage or the energy for total enterprise transformation. And so these strategic initiatives are often perceived as less than completely successful and often as expensive failures. Data warehousing is an activity that falls into this category of potentially fragile pan-corporate initiatives.

There is a real danger that the concept of the point solution data mart will gain wide acceptance because of its ease of implementation but will encounter severe criticism when the limited success of this approach becomes more apparent to hard pressed users. On the other hand, the enterprise data warehouse concept may decline in popularity because of the considerable cost and complexity that is associated with this approach. It is a kind of catch-22 where the project may be damned if it takes an ambitious route and damned if it doesn't. The solution, as almost always, lies in the enterprise having a coherent vision of where it is going. In reality, the uncertainty engendered by this central dilemma normally has to be absorbed by the data warehouse architect, who must attempt to ensure that whatever approach is followed is not an architectural cul-de-sac.

Therefore, the choice is between retreating to a scaled-down vision of data warehousing or advancing the existing vision to encompass a more ambitious vision. Current estimates indicate that many enterprises will opt for the low-risk scaled-down project focused where the business pain is most acute — i.e. multiple tactical solutions. Of course, taking this route does not prevent the development of ancillary operational functionality and may, in certain circumstances, simplify the task by confining the scope of the project to a dedicated area of the enterprise and addressing both the decision-support and operational aspects of the business process under examination. On balance, however, it is more likely that rich new operational functionality will result only from a situation where fully integrated corporate data has already been achieved because the potential for new applications is enabled by the richness of the fully integrated environment.

THE NEW OPERATIONAL APPLICATIONS

Traditionally, on-line transaction processing applications were characterized by a high volume of relatively simple transactions and data warehousing is characterized by a relatively small number of complex transactions. The evolving computing environment, based on the requirements now being voiced by users, is rapidly moving towards an environment of ubiquitous complex trans-actions. As events occur that trap data, that data is fed into the data warehouse for analysis and the resultant intelligence is fed to a new operational application or is fed back to the operational system that interfaced with the original event. Therefore, real world operational events are informed by the pattern analysis that occurs in the data warehouse environment, and the loop between the operational domain and the decision-support domain of the business is closed.

It is also worth remembering the considerably different types of decision support work. Special studies or marketing campaign planning can usually be done 'off-line' and separate from operational databases. So can detailed segmentation analysis or fraud analysis. However, operational management control queries, such as 'How many Christmas trees did we sell before lunch in Newcastle?' clearly have to be bridged to the operational applications and integrated with the business process. But often these are relatively simple queries or summary totals that can easily be run alongside OLTP transactions (for example, an MVS query is now supported by new functions in DB2 such as uncommitted reads).

Other functional requirements point more clearly to the need for a hybrid environment comprising both the data warehouse and operational systems. For example, in a telephone sales environment, where an enterprise is responding to a flood of calls following a national TV commercial, they will want to do 'instant' analysis of leads, proposals, prices and acceptance rates. . . and perhaps change the product prices 'on the fly'. This environment requires the capability to deliver continuous availability, and dynamic prioritization of workload for such business-critical applications.

Because the legacy operational systems now in use will not be quickly discarded and because it is not technologically feasible, in the short term, to provide concurrent access to data for both transactions and queries on the same database, the way forward is likely to require an architected solution with multiple layers of data processing, integrated using metadata.

The operational applications that are beginning to happen fall into two categories. There are those where the DSS applications enhance the functionality of the legacy operational systems (by, for

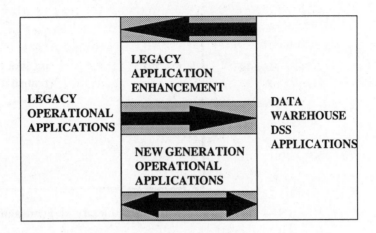

(Source: Data Warehouse Network)

Figure 11.2 The hybrid enterprise architecture

example, sending encapsulated objects back to the legacy operational system to trigger events). And there are new operational applications that are developed on subsidiary marts (Opmarts) which physically reside within the overall architecture of the data warehouse but which logically belong to the operational systems architecture. This hybrid architecture is outlined in Figure 11.2.

Traditional online transaction systems are characterized by a high volume of relatively simple transactions. First generation data warehouse systems are characterised by a relatively small number of highly complex queries.The effect of this new type of architecture is to create an environment of high-volume high-complexity transactions. This tendency is illustrated in Figure 11.3.

BUSINESS TRENDS IN THE GLOBAL ECONOMY

A number of distinct trends are now becoming visible in the global economy which have implications for the data warehouse project. The general thrust of these trends is to increase the importance of information as a weapon for competitive survival in the course

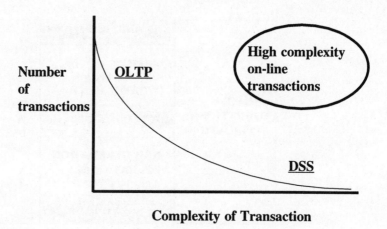

Figure 11.3

of the next decade. The key trends that are likely to impact on data warehousing are presented here:

1. The information content of services is continually increasing due to consumer demands for information and the competitive pressure to respond to this demand.
2. Information is increasingly being viewed as the single most important corporate asset available to the enterprise and will exceed in importance more traditional corporate assets such as financial, intellectual, channels to market, corporate identity and fixed assets.
3. Organizations are continuing the tendency to be leaner, flatter with a growing tendency to outsource, franchise and sub-contract the operational aspects of the business. In this climate the control and co-ordination of the enterprise will be dominated by information.
4. Regulatory demands of legislatures and industry agencies are placing increasing demands on corporations to supply detailed information about their activities, products, recruitment profiles, risk and exposure as well as information on cost structures designed to regulate the incidence of cross-subsidization and monopoly practices.

5. The marketing of goods and services is moving rapidly from a model of mass production to a model of mass customization. This transition brings with it a requirement for more and more detailed and complex data about the behavior of different customer segments.

6. There is an increasing requirement for enterprises to become more adaptable to change in an increasingly competitive and turbulent global marketplace. This requirement demand that enterprises pay more attention to technological infrastructure as the means of re-orientating applications at short notice.

7. The trend towards utilizing the Internet and the World Wide Web for sales and marketing purposes is placing severe demands on companies to provide more sophisticated and timely information delivery services to customers and prospects.

8. The dangers of making disastrous strategic decisions about technology choices and market forecasts are increasing all the time. This is leading to a return to strategic planing and positioning activities inside corporations which will have to be supported by information systems which provide a pan-corporate perspective of the corporations activities.

9. The tendency, especially among larger corporations, to grow their business through mergers and take-overs will continue. The challenge of data integration presents the greatest challenge to realizing the synergies that can be realized through such mergers.

10. There will be an explosion in the volume of data being made available by government agencies, third-party information brokers and market intelligence companies which will be required to be fully integrated in corporate databases. The increasing availability of demographic, psychograpic, and econometric data will fuel the growth in the size of corporate databases.

All of these trends re-inforce the need for data integration, data access and adaptability at the enterprise level.

Enhancing Core Competencies in the Enterprise

Data warehousing, as a technology framework, presents real opportunities to the enterprise to enhance and enrich the core competencies of the organisation. The idea of an enterprise having distinctive competencies — a set of activities at which it excels — is driving a good deal of current strategic corporate planning. As more and more organisations adopt competence-based corporate planning strategies, attention will increasingly focus on information as a key ingredient in any strategy to exploit existing competencies or develop new ones. Competencies within an enterprise tend to be viewed as either assets (including technology) and capabilities (including the skills of knowledge workers). Data warehousing practice tends to suggest that gaining competitive advantage through data warehousing is influenced as much by organisational and cultural issues than by technology. Organizations that have the capacity to fully appreciate the potential of information as a means of enhancing customer-care, devising new products, identifying new niche markets and streamlining existing processes are the ones which succeed in generating significant value from data. Therefore, the data warehouse impacts on the core competencies of the organization since it is both an important asset in itself as well as a means of leveraging the specialized skills of the organisation. For many enterprises the core competence of the organization will, more and more, be located exclusively in the management of information. Such enterprises will tend to shed (through outsourcing and sub-contracting) more and more of the non-core activities of the enterprise in order to focus exclusively on the management and exploitation of information. Thus, companies who excel at information management will have a tendency to become virtual enterprises exclusively focused on identifying and anticipating customer requirements, responding to changes in customer behaviour and managing the customer relationship. In such cases, (and they will become increasingly common), information management will become *the* critical competency in the enterprise and the critical infrastructure required to support this competency will be the data warehouse.

Trends in Corporate Strategic Planning

After a long period in the wilderness while enterprises grappled with the imperative to downsize, re-engineer and restructure, strategic planning is making a comeback in the boardroom. But it is back with a difference. The reason strategic planning got such a bad name in the 1980s was that it was seen to be too divorced from the day-to-day business; it was, in many instances, a sterile, academic activity. But now there are clear signs in the USA that it is making a comeback, with companies like IBM, Hewlett Packard, Sears and United Parcel Services re-introducing it as a formal strategic planning process within the corporation. The reason why it is back in fashion has largely to do with technology. Because of the need to truly understand the technological options that are available to enterprises and because it is so critical to choose the winning options, companies are spending more time evaluating, comparing and debating the information technology strategies that they intend to pursue. Much of this renewed enthusiasm is based on the realization that technology has the capacity to transform the position of players in the marketplace. Every year, established companies which have been blind to technology innovation have found themselves facing new nimble competitors who are capable of transforming a niche market situation into a dominant market position. The fear of being blindsided to new technology opportunities is at the heart of much of the strategic planning that is now happening in corporate USA and Europe.

The new model of strategic corporate planning is based on the idea of strategy as a process rather than an endeavor carried out by a separate corporate planning department. Key to the success of this model is the notion that strategy is closely coupled to the business and its processes and, critically, its customers. An important implication of this thinking is that business intelligence systems to support corporate planning that are based on older models of corporate planning (modeling key financial and economic indicators) are not valid in this new era. The new strategic methodologies are based on assessing the customer base of the entire enterprise and applying the core competencies of the enterprise to better serving those customers. The enterprise data warehouse architectures that exist now must evolve to realize the vision of coupling the process of identifying strategic opportunities and acting on those opportunities.

A surprisingly high number of the technology-enabled market breakthroughs that have been witnessed in the past five years have been closely associated with data warehousing. Examples abound of enterprises which have come from nowhere with information-intensive strategies, as well as established companies which have successfully defended their positions by exploiting their corporate data. One example from the UK is the Tesco retail chain, which introduced a loyalty card scheme well ahead of Sainsbury's, its main competitor, and established a significant lead in customer behavior analysis.

There are also, it has to be said, a large number of enterprises which have pursued a data warehouse strategy unsuccessfully. The majority of these failures have to do with a failure to understand the need to align corporate business strategy to take advantage of the possibilities offered by data warehousing. Simply integrating the corporate data is never enough. It is not even sufficient to construct business applications to exploit the data unless there is a clear corporate vision of how the business is going to apply the knowledge that is gleaned from these sophisticated decision-enabling technologies. The clear lesson here is that the business must understand how to exploit the information content of products and services for competitive advantage. To do this successfully requires a close coupling of the information technology strategy and the business strategy.

One of the achievements of data warehousing is to enable the enterprise to gain more revenues from existing customers. Strategies based on micro-segmentation of the market have managed to create new wealth from existing markets by customizing services, identifying latent demand, identifying cross-selling and up-selling opportunities and by creating completely new products by identifying segments that are not being served by existing products. In the decade from 1985 to 1995 it is reported that $163 billion of stock market value has been created in the US retail industry. In the forefront of this achievement is one of pioneers of data warehousing — Wal Mart

Stores Inc. A US retailer that did not participate in that growth was Sears and the Arthur C. Martinez, CEO at Sears, conceded frankly in 1996 that "There was a hole in our strategy. We did not know who we wanted to serve". The difference between success and failure in the next decade is going to be determined largely by the ability of the enterprise to be able to anticipate customer behavior. In order to do this successfully enterprises are going to have to capture more data about customer behavior and integrate that data with data about suppliers, staff and costs in order to be able to respond in a meaningful way to the conscious or unconscious demands of the market. The information technology enabler to achieve this today is what we now call a data warehouse.

The Concept of Value Exchange

Businesses are now beginning to get some idea of the value of data in diversifying the product range of the enterprise or even entering new businesses. The most visible sign of this phenomenon is the speed with which the retail sector has realized that the data that they hold on their customers can be used to sell more than conventional retail products. This is an evolving trend but some early examples can be seen in the following sectors:

- The early signs indicate that large **retail chains** are rapidly moving into the financial services business and are already brokering insurance services through their retail outlets. Taken together with in-store credit cards and the advent of new smart card technology, the retail sector is better placed than many conservative banking institutions to reap the benefits of data pattern analysis for financial services products.

- Some **postal organizations** throughout the world are looking for a new business as the existing surface postal system contracts and some are set to become data providers of household and neighborhood data. Brokering demographic and psychographic data is likely to be big business in the future and represents an excellent utilisation of an existing infrastructure.

- **Credit card** companies have now amassed vast volumes of data about the purchasing habits of their customers and are beginning to offer customized cards for different customer segments. In addition they have begun to liase with the airline and hotel industries in order to optimize their marketing strategies. In fact, some credit card companies and airlines have launched common advertising campaigns which offer air miles credits in respect of hotel and credit card usage.

The underlying strategy that is driving much of this marketing innovation is to be found in a new theory for growing corporate revenue. This new model is based on the assumption that there are only three ways in which a company can increase its revenue. It can:

1. *Acquire new customers who then consume the existing products and services of the company and therefore grow the revenue stream that accrues from the existing product lines.* This has always been seen as the primary method of growing the business. By and large this method is enabled through advertising and promotions rather than by technology.
2. *Enhance the profitability of existing customers in order to maximize the revenue that is generated by those customers.* This method is only now beginning to be used as companies realize that there is a lot of latent demand in the marketplace. It is aided by data warehouse technology since it is based on a strategy of customer behavior analysis which requires significant technology support.
3. *Extend the duration of customer loyalty and thereby maintain a level of enhanced consumption over a longer period of time.* This method is relatively immature since few organizations in the mass market were really aware of the rate of customer turnover since individual customer behavior was never analyzed. This method is fundamentally enabled by data warehouse-type technology and is based on forging close customized links with each and every customer.

It has been suggested that methods 2 and 3 are only now on the marketing agenda because of advances made in data warehouse technology and data exploitation awareness in the business. Once companies began to study the behavior patterns of customers, it was inevitable that the potential to the business of ensuring customer loyalty over long periods would dramatically enhance profitability. It is in the level of detail that companies are now analyzing customer behavior that offers the opportunity to exploit the latent value of these customers.

The name that has been given to this new concept is *value exchange* and the purpose of the strategy is to optimize the value exchange that a company achieves. What is meant by the term 'value exchange' is that there is a relationship between the *investment* that a company makes in a given customer relationship and the *return* that the customers generate to the company by consuming its products and services.

The following passage is from the *Harvard Business Review* (September/October 1995), and is worth quoting in full:

> 'Companies embracing the principles of value exchange are operating on an entirely new playing field. These organizations don't evaluate their performance based on comparisons with last year's figures or with their competitors. They don't focus their time and money on abstract metrics such as market share, quality indices or customer satisfaction. And they don't use the power of information technology to turbocharge their marketing functions. Instead they define their target customer base, quantify the current and full-potential value of these relationships, and commit the entire company to closing the gap between the two.'

For most enterprises the gap between the full potential value of their customer base and the existing realized value is enormous. It offers the real opportunity for sustained growth in markets that are highly competitive, highly saturated and where existing levels of products differentiation between competitors is primitive. In one example of value exchange analysis that has been documented, a Canadian grocery chain concluded that, given the fixed cost structure of a grocery store, each additional dollar spent by a customer can earn ten times the store's net profit margin. Findings such as this are exciting and point to new era of marketing which will be based on a new model for achieving enhanced profitability and which will be based on applications that require, as a prerequisite, that a data warehouse infrastructure is in place.

Like most recent innovations in corporate strategy the key enabler for this new way of doing business lies with information technology. Some commentators simply observe that the data warehouse is the key technology enabler of this new style of marketing. Others assert that it was the data warehouse that made possible the vision for this new kind of business strategy. While both of these observations are true, it is too simplistic to conclude that the data warehouse, as we know it, is the only technological ingredient for successful value exchange. The real discussion that should now be occupying the time and attention of IT planners and architects is the degree to which the concept of value exchange is going to couple more closely the planning activity of analyzing customer behavior and the operational activities of serving those customers needs. For the concept of value exchange to truly work we will need to know, not just the different behavioral patterns of customers but also the means of interfacing with those customers in a way that is customized to that individual customer. The conventional data warehouse may have the power to demonstrate the benefits and potential of optimizing the customer relationship. But it is an entirely different challenge to lever the core competencies of the enterprise to respond to the individual requirements of customers. This will, in part, signal a new phase of data warehousing, which will comprise operational enablement in addition to decision-support capabilities.

Valuemetrics

The concept of value-exchange creates a challenge for information technology which the traditional model of the data warehouse can address through the measurement of customer value — a process which may be referred to as valuemetrics. Valuemetrics represents a calculation of customer value measured in terms of the expected lifetime value of a customer. The measurement requires a knowledge of the consumption levels and patterns of the customer, the costs associated with the provision of that service and an estimation of whether the future consumption by the customer is expected to grow or decline. Ultimately, valumetrics will be used by most enterprises as the main ingredient of customer segmentation. Customer segmentation will, in turn, become the boilerplate for all decision-support applications which are developed to support corporate strategies for defending and growing the business.

The following example in Table 11.3 outlines a typical template for measuring the valumetrics in respect of customers of a cellular telephone operator.

Table 11.3 A sample valuemetric table

Customer	Present value		Latent value	Credit history	Future value	Churn
Level	Outgoing calls (monthly) $	Incoming calls (monthly) $	Failed calls/value added	Range 1–5	Increase/ decrease	No
1	1000	1000	High	1	Increase	0
2	1000	1000	Low	1	Increase	0
3	500	3000	High	2	Increase	1
4	700	2000	Low	3	Increase	1
5	500	500	Low	4	Decrease	2
6	300	600	High	5	Increase	5
7	200	500	Low	3	Decrease	3
8	100	200	Low	3	Decrease	4
9	50	100	Low	4	Decrease	4
10	50	70	Low	5	Decrease	6

The Table illustrates that a number of factors impact on the calculation of value (and only some of the key factors have been included in the table), and that revenue per se is not always the overriding factor in determining value. Issues such as the latent demand that may exist in respect of a customer and the estimated future value of the customer are key inputs. For example, a customer with a high value, but with saturated usage in a declining industry, might represent a lower real value to the operator than a customer which is generating less revenue now, but is in a burgeoning industry sector. Likewise, the propensity of a customer to churn is a key factor in assessing value, since the cost of re-acquiring a cellular customer (who has transferred to a competitor and back again) is estimated at $400 and this has a marked influence on the profitability of a customer when taken into account. Value analysis, when studied in the context of other criteria (such as geo-demographics and psychographics) offers valuable insights into the types of customer who generate value and the types of customer who do not. These factors may be influenced by a variety of other factors which are captured at a more detailed level in the segmentation grid and will provide opportunities to design marketing and sales strategies for customer acquisition, retention, stimulation and the identification of emerging niche markets.

CONCLUSION

Because information technology is now a key enabler of corporate strategy, the link between business strategy and decision-support stytems will grow stronger in terms of synergies and crossover influences. Any attempt to locate data warehousing as an exclusively technological development divorced from the wider business strategy is to fail to understand the nature of data warehousing and the potential which it offers. Future trends in business strategy will increasingly be based on innovative ways of exploiting information and new information exploitation technologies.

Web Sites

The following Web Sites are recommended to readers for further information on data warehousing.

Data Warehouse Network [http://www.dwn.com/dwn]
The Data Warehouse Network is Europe's centre of excellence in data warehousing practice and provides information on a wide range of subjects including market assessments, vendor evaluations, technology reviews, methodology and design. Services include consultancy, publications, events, and research. Corporate, vendor and personal membership schemes are available.

The Data Warehousing Institute [http://www.dw-institute.com/]
The Data Warehousing Institute is dedicated to helping organizations increase their understanding and use of business intelligence by educating decision makers and I/S professionals on the proper deployment of data warehouse strategies and technologies. Services include events, publications and training.

The Data Warehousing Information Center
[http://pwp.starnetinc.com/larryg/]
This site is maintained by Larry Greenfield, LGI Systems Inc., and contains the most comprehensive directory of links to data warehouse vendors, publications, asociations and other sources of information. Discussion papers on different aspects of data warehousing are also available.

The International Data Warehousing Association
[http://www/dwa.org]
The International Data Warehousing Association is an independent non-profit organization dedicated to advancing the knowledge, theory and application of data warehousing and is open to all qualified professionals.

Vendors

The following list of vendors and their products offers a broad overview of the shape and scale of the data warehouse marketplace. It is an not a complete list, but does attempt to cover all of the major players. The nature of a rapidly growing and innovating market is that there will be a high incidence of consolidation. Take-overs, mergers and new entrants that will have the effect of changing the shape of the market until such time as the market matures.

ANDYNE SOFTWARE
(http://www.andyne.com)
Kingston, Ontario, Canada.
Andyne offer the *GQL* (Graphical Query Language) query tool which enjoys a large market share with 50,000 licences at 2,500 sites. Andyne also market the *Pablo* development environment for multi-dimensional analysis.

ANGOSS SOFTWARE LIMITED
(http://www.angoss.com)
Guildford, Surrey, UK.
Angoss market the *KnowledgeSEEKER* data analysis tool for statistical and multidimensional analysis.

APERTUS TECHNOLOGIES INC.
(http://www.apertus.com)
Eden Prarie, Minnesota, USA.
Apertus offer the *Enterprise/Integrator* tool for developing and maintaining programs that transform, cleanse, merge and synchronize data from heterogeneous databases.

ARBOR SOFTWARE
(http://www.arborsoft.com)
Sunnyvale, California, USA.
Arbor markets the highly successful *Essbase Analysis Server* multi-dimensional database which provides a spreadsheet-like interface for OLAP users.

BRANN SOFTWARE
(http://www.brannsoftware.co.uk)
Gloucestershire, UK.
Brann Software offer a range of marketing-oriented solutions for vertical industry sectors. Tools include *BrannViper* for query, *BrannAsp* for data extraction and *BrannAdder* for data analysis.

BRIO TECHNOLOGY
(http://www.brio.com)
Palo Alto, California, USA.
Brio Technology offers *BrioQueryEnterprise*, which supports integrated query, OLAP and interactive charting and reporting. Brio also have brio.web.warehouse for web-enabled querying.

BUSINESS OBJECTS INC.
(http://www.businessobjects.com)
Cupertino, California, USA.
Founded in France, Business Objects now enjoy a large share of the US and European market for end-user query tools, supporting both SQL and OLAP, with 110,000 users at 2,000 sites..

CARLETON CORPORATION
(http://www.carleton.com)
Burlington, Massachusetts, USA.
Carleton was one of the earliest vendors in the copy management segment of the data warehouse market. *Passport* is the data extraction tool on offer and it incorporates a metadata directory as well as facilities for warehouse administration and end-user browsing.

COGNOS CORPORATION
(http://www.cognos.com)
Burlington, Massachusetts, USA.
Cognos offer data access software for the data warehouse in the form of the *PowerPlay* multidimensional database server, the *Impromptu* reporting tool and *Axiant*, a GUI application development environment.

COMPUTER ASSOCIATES
(http://www.cai.com)
New York, USA.
The main interest of CA in the data warehouse market lies in the promotion of the *CA/Ingres* relational database and gateway products.

COMSHARE INC.
(http://comshare.com)
Ann Arbor, Michigan, USA.
Comshare market the *Commander* query tool and development environment for DSS applications and *Commander ADL* for multidimensional analysis.

DATAMIND CORP.
(http://www.datamindcorp.com)
Redwood, California, USA.
This vendor offers server and client based business oriented data mining tools.

DIGITAL COMPUTER CORPORATION
(http://www.digital.com)
Maynard, Massachusetts, USA.
DEC have not made any spirited foray into the data warehouse market but the VAX series of mid-range systems and the powerful 64-bit ALPHA processor is commonly used as a hardware platform for data warehousing. DEC's data distributor is also used as a data replication tool.

DIMENSIONAL INSIGHT, INC.
(http://www.dimins.com)
Burlington, Massachusetts, USA.
The *CrossTarget* data analysis tool from Dimensional Insight offers robust analysis functionality and is a popular tool for marketing and sales applications.

D2K
(http://www.d2k.com)
San Jose, California.
This vendor offers the *Tapestry* data transformation tool for end-to-end knowledge distribution in a multi-tiered data warehouse environment.

EVOLUTIONARY TECHNOLOGIES INC.
(http://www.evtech.com)
Austin, Texas, USA.
ETI offer a comprehensive copy management tool suite *called ETI Extract* which is used for data transformation and data extraction.

HEWLETT-PACKARD COMPANY
(http://www.hp.com)
Palo Alto, California, USA.
HP's strategy for data warehousing is based on the *HP Intelligent Warehouse* which is both a concept and a suite of software designed to middleware, administration and end-user functionality. HP are focused on managing as well as building the data warehouse and the component software includes *IW Hub* which manages the mapping of the virtual warehouse view to the physical schema, *IW Advisor* which is a tool used to identify usage patterns, *IW Administrator* which is a DBA tool and *IW Guide* which is an information catalogue for end-users.

IBM CORPORATION
(http://www.ibm.com)
San Jose, California, USA.
IBM are leaders in the data warehousing market and developed the Information Warehouse framework in 1991. IBM offers a variety

of hardware platforms for data warehousing including S/390, mid-range solutions (*RS6000and AS400*) and a massively parallel solution (*SP2*). The IBM database products for data warehousing are *DB2* and *DB2-PE*. *Visualiser* is the data access tool on offer from IBM. A full (even crowded) range of software tools are available from IBM to facilitate copy management, data propagation and middleware management.

ICL HIGH PERFORMANCE SYSTEMS
(http://www.icl.com)
West Gorton, Manchester, UK.
ICL's data warehouse solution is based on the *Goldrush MegaSERVER* massively parallel computer system. ICL has a comprehensive data warehouse associates program to support the software and consultancy components of their data warehouse strategy.

INFORMATICA CORPORATION
(http://www.informatica.com)
Menlo Park, California, USA.
Informatica provide a tightly integrated data mart solution, the PowerMart suite, which includes data migration and administration functions.

INFORMATION ADVANTAGE
(http://www.infoadvan.com)
Eding, Minnesota, USA.
Information Advantage, founded in 1990, offers *DecisionSuite* which includes query, analysis and alert software and a workbench for customised applications.

INFORMATION BUILDERS, INC.
(http://www.ibi.com)
Broadway, New York, USA.
Information Builders have been serving the decision support user community for a long time and offer a strategy for data warehousing based on a virtual warehouse as well as the *Fusion* OLAP database. *EDA/SQL* middleware offers transparent access to more

than 60 database types, the *FOCUS* reporting tool, *Enterprise Copy Manger* for data extraction and transformation, *SiteAnalyser* for analyzing usage patterns and *SmartMode* for governing the system resource.

INFORMIX SOFTWARE INC.
(http://www.informix.com)
Menlo Park, California, USA

Informix have made an aggressive bid to be leaders in data warehousing through their *Online Extended Parallel Server (Online XPS)* database and have evolved a data warehouse strategy based on partnerships.

INNOVATIVE SYSTEMS INC.
(http://www.innovgrp.com)
Pittsburg, Pennsylvania, USA.

Innovative Systems offer a range of data cleansing and conversion tools based on the *Innovative Warehouse Solution* suite of products.

INTEGRAL SOLUTIONS LTD.
(http://www.isl.co.uk)
Basingstoke, Hampshire, UK.

Integral Solutions offer the *Clementine* data mining tool which is one of the longest established tools utilising neural network software.

INTELLIDEX SYSTEMS
(http://www.intellidex.com)
Boston, Massachusetts, USA.

Intellidex have developed *ControlCenter*, an integrated metadata management software suite to support an active information catalogue for the entire data warehouse architecture.

KENAN TECHNOLOGIES
(http://www.kenan.com)
Cambridge, Massachusetts, USA.

Founded in 1989, Kenan Technologies offers a development environment called *Accumate* for customised applications for OLAP decision support as well as *Acutrieve*, an end-user query tool.

MANAGER SOFTWARE PRODUCTS INC.
(http://www.mspusa.com)
Lexington, Massachusetts, USA.
MSP offer the *METHODMANAGER* repository product that is used in many legacy environments and is sometimes used as the software platform for metadata management.

MEIKO LTD.
(http://www.meiko.com)
Aztec West, Bristol, UK.
Meiko offer a powerful massively parallel computer for data warehousing based on transputer technology.

MICROSOFT CORP
(http://www.microsoft.com)
Seattle, washington, USA.
Microsoft's participation in the data warehouse market has generally been confined to the use of *NT Server* platforms and the *SQLServer* database for data marts, but Microsofts participation can be expected to intensify.

MICROSTRATEGY
(http://www.strategy.com)
Vienna, Virginia, USA.
DSS Agent is the OLAP tool for relational databases offered by Microstrategy. It comprises a query tool, an EIS toolkit and a GUI development environment.

NCR
(http://www.ncr.com)
Dayton, Ohio, USA.
Formerly AT&T GIS, this company had a clear head-start in the data warehousing market through its ownership of the Teradata technologies acquired through the purchase of the Teradata Corporation. While this lead has been squandered AT&T still have a formidable offering including the *Teradata Database System*, the powerful *System 3600* massively parallel computer and the mid to high range *WorldMark 5100* server for symmetric multiprocessing.

ORACLE CORPORATION
(http://www.oracle.com)
Redwood Shores, California, USA.
Oracle is the largest database vendor in the software market and is rapidly, if belatedly, moving into the data warehouse market. On offer is the Oracle relational database and the *Oracle Express* multidimensional database. Oracle offer the *Parallel Query Option* with release 7.1 of Oracle and also offer *Oracle Replicator* for data replication.

PLATINUM TECHNOLOGY
(http://www.platinum.com)
Arlington, Virginia, USA.
Platinum offers the widest range of data warehouse software tools that are available from a single vendor and has grown through aggressive acquisition. These tools include *InfoPump* which is middleware software for routing, integrating and synchronizing dissimilar data, *InforRefiner* for data transformation and movement, *Platinum Repository* for managing metadata, *InfoTransport* for enterprise-wide data distribution, *InfoSession* for read/write access to legacy data, *InfoHub* for access to host-based legacy systems, *DataShopper* for providing an information catalog function to end users and the *Forest & Trees* reporting tool.

PILOT SOFTWARE
(http://www.pilotsw.com)
Cambridge, Massachusetts, USA.
Founded in 1984, Pilot Software Inc., spearheaded the birth of the EIS industry with one of the first EIS commercial systems. A company of the Dun & Bradstreet corporation, Pilot Software offers its *Lightship OLAP Server* and *Lightship Professional* GUI development environment.

PLANNING SCIENCES
(http://www.gentia.com)
Dual headquarters at London and Boston.
Gentia is the data access tool made available by Planning Sciences

and it combines ad hoc SQL query capability as well as an OLAP database.

PRAXIS INTERNATIONAL INC.
(http://www.praxisint.com)
Cambridge, Massachusetts, USA.
Praxis provides the *OmniReplicator* data replication software for bi-directional data replication in the data warehouse and incorporates a scheduling utility that offers run-time functionality.

PRISM SOFTWARE, INC.
(http://www.prismsolutions.com)
Sunnyvale, California, USA.
Prism is closely associated with Bill Inmon, the 'father of data warehousing'. The tools offered by Prism include *Prism Warehouse Manager* which generates programs to extract data from source databases, *Prism Directory Manager* which provides metadata management capability and *Inmon Generic Models* which offer high-level models to guide the corporate modelling process.

PYRAMID TECHNOLOGIES CORPORATION
(http://www.pyramid.com)
San Jose, California, USA.
Pyramid Technology is a Siemens-Nixdorf company and is a high-end open systems hardware vendor. They offer the *Nile* series of symmetric multi-processing systems and the *Reliant* massively parallel computer. Pyramid have a data warehouse framework called the *Smart Start* program which encourages users to validate their cost-benefit assumptions at low cost (and risk) based on a pilot system strategy.

REDBRICK SYSTEMS
(http:/www.redbrick.com)
Los Gatos, California, USA.
Redbrick developed one of the very few database products dedicated to supporting a query-intensive environment. The *Redbrick* database utilizes a *STARindex* system to optimize query performance.

SAS INSTITUTE INC.
(http://www.sas.com)
Cary, North Carolina, USA.
SAS is a well established decision-support systems vendor that can offer a number of the data warehouse components. These include *SAS/ACCESS* for data capture, *SAS Metabase* for metadata management, *SAS Information Database* for data management, *SAS/ASSIST* for ad hoc reporting, *SAS 4GL* for application development and a range of *SAS System* tools for data analysis.

SEAGATE SOFTWARE
(http://www.seagatesoftware.com)
Bellingham, Washington, USA.
Seagate Software offer *CrystalInfo*, a three-tier cliant-server reporting package and the *Holos* OLAP database product.

SEQUENT COMPUTER SYSTEMS INC.
(http://www.sequent.com)
Beaverton, Oregon, USA.
Sequent offer a range of high-end open systems hardware platforms for the data warehouse. Sequent's strategy for data warehousing is based on its *DecisionPoint* methodology for building decision support systems.

SILICON GRAPHICS COMPUTER SYSTEMS
(http://www.sgi.com)
Mountain View, California, USA.
Silicon Graphics have located themselves within the data warehouse market as the vendors of choice for hardware platforms supporting high resolution graphics display for data visualization and data mining software using the range of *CHALLENGE* servers.

SOFTWARE AG
(http://www.sagus.com)
Darmstad, Germany.
Software AG has made significant inroads into the data warehouse market with a comprehensive set of tools and a credible strategy for

partnering with other vendors. The product offerings are the *ADABAS D* database product, *SourcePoint* for copy management, *ENTIRE* for middleware and the excellent *Esperant* query tool.

SPSS
(http://wwwspss.com)
Chicago, Illinois, USA.
SPSS is a statistical analysis/data mining solution vendor. *SPSS Diamond* tracks relationships in multivariate data and *NeuralConnect* is a neural network mining tool.

SQL GROUP LIMITED
(http://www.sqlgroup.com)
London & Redwood, California.
The SQL Group offers data migration services and the *Information Junction* software tool provides extraction and transformation functionality.

STERLING SOFTWARE INC.
(http://www.clear.sterling.com)
Dallas, Texas, USA.
Sterling offer the *Clear Access* suite of decision support software for query and reporting.

SUN MICROSYSTEMS INC.
(http://www.sun.com)
Mountain View, Virginia, USA.
Sun's *Decision Warehouse* scalable warehouse architecture expands from a single system to a cluster of SMP nodes. Sun's *SPARC* servers and *Solaris* operating environment provide the base technology environment for Sun's data warehouse strategy.

SYBASE, INC.
(http://www.sybase.com)
Emeryville, California, USA.
Sybase offer the *Sybase SQL Server* relational database that came to prominence with the trend towards client-server computing.

Sybase have a data warehouse strategy called *Sybase Warehouse Works*. this is, essentially, a partnership program that includes most of the key players in the data extraction, transformation and access activities. Sybase also offer *Sybase Enterprise CONNECT* which is an interoperability architecture which provides transparent access to over 20 data sources.

SYLLOGIC BV
(http://syllogic.nl)
Houten, Amsterdam, The Netherlands.
Syllogic offer the *Syllogic* data mining tool which incorporates neural networks, genetic algorithms and statistical analysis.

TANDEM COMPUTERS INC.
(http://www.tandem.com)
Cupertino, California, USA.
Tandem offer a scalable hardware solution for the large data warehouse based on their massively parallel *NonStop SQL/MP* server technology.

UNISYS CORPORATION
(http://www.unisys.com)
Blue Bell, Pennsylvania, USA.
Unisys offers the *Open Parallel Unisys Server (OPUS)* parallel procesing system for data warehousing at the high-end and the *U6000/500 Series* of mid-range symmetric multiprocessing systems.

VALITY TECHNOLOGY INC.
(http://www.vality.com)
Boston, Massachusetts, USA.
Vality offer the Vality data cleansing tool to tackle problems of data conditioning and data integrity.

VERTICAL INTEGRATION TECHNOLOGY INC.
(http://www.vit.com)
Cupertino, California, USA.
VIT offers software and consultancy assistance to data warehouse developers. Products include *Meta Warehouse* for repository

management, *DataMapper* for capturing source-to-target mappings, *InfoNav* for browsing information held in the Meta Warehouse.

VMARK INC.
(http://www.vmark.com)
Westboro, Massachusetts, USA.
Vmark offer the *UniVerse* database product with enhanced relational capabilities as well as the *DataStorage* product for data marts.

WHITECROSS SYSTEMS
(http://wcs.co.uk)
Bracknell, Berkshire, UK.
Whitecross Systems offers a scalable parallel processing hardware designed to be used as a large database server for query-intensive databases.

Glossary

All new areas of endeavor are plagued by the confusion created by language — its unconscious abuse by uninformed commentators, its conscious abuse by vendors, the awkwardness of some of the ideas that we are attempting to communicate — and, sometimes, by the happenstance that the same concept (or very similar concepts) are often originated by different people within the same timeframes and are labeled differently.

The following is a list of definitions that has been compiled by this author from the many variations that exist. It is not intended to be either fully comprehensive or fully definitive since it is the nature of many of the developments that are now occurring in data warehousing that concepts evolve and mutate almost as soon as they have been named.

Agent — Software agents are now much in vogue as a result of data warehousing and are much confused with triggers and alerts. An agent is a piece of software that is trained to identify a certain pre-defined condition and to take a corresponding pre-defined action in response to the condition. For example, a software agent might be trained (using pattern recognition or rule induction) to identify a certain type of customer behavior that is known to reflect a pattern of behavior that indicates fraud.

ASCII — The American Standard Code for Information Interchange — the format for encoding data that is stored on databases (also refer to EBCDIC).

B-Tree — A method for structuring data so that it can be accessed more efficiently.

Batch Processing — Uninterruptable computer programs that run for a defined period in respect of a specific objective. Most batch processing in an operational environment occurs overnight and typical batch processes would include payroll, billing as well as crude decision support reports.

Bit — This is an abbreviation of 'binary digit', i.e. 0 or 1.

Bitmapped Indexing — This an advanced form of indexation whereby almost all of the operations that are required to be run on the database can do so by accessing the indices only, without having to scan the actual data.

BLOB — Binary Large Object — this is the technical description of the way in which multimedia objects (like video or sound) are stored. Some relational databases can store limited BLOBS.

Byte — A byte represents eight bits and data storage capacity is measured in bytes, megabytes (MB), gigabytes (GB) and terabytes (TB).

Business Events — The essential activities of the oganisation that management wants to control, plan, monitor and evaluate in order to achieve its business objectives

CASE — Computer-Aided Software Engineering — This refers to tools (and associated methodologies) designed to help to automate the task of designing, describing and building software. In data warehouse projects, CASE tools may be used to capture data definitions, build the data models, and capture the mappings from the source systems to the target warehouse.

CIO — Chief Information Officer — a term used to describe the most senior IT executive. Normally only applies as a title where that executive reports directly to the Chief Executive Officer (CEO).

COBOL — Common Business Oriented Language — One of the two most common business systems programming language used in legacy operational systems. (the other is PL/1). Software engineers who understand the COBOL application code in the legacy environment should be highly valued by the data warehouse project manager.

Crash — What may happen when a complex query is introduced into an operational application environment with many on-line users. Most operational system crashes are attributed to bugs (IT blames vendors) or runaway queries (IT blames users).

Data — Stored numbers and text that may or may not have any real meaning or context (see Information).

Data Conditioning — The process of cleaning data that is inconsistently entered on legacy systems. For example, a name field might contain the prefix 'Mr' as the first word or a First name or a Company Name. This data, while not invalid, needs to be conditioned to be useful for decision-support applications.

Data Dictionary — A description of the different types of data that is contained in the database, the format of the data and (sometimes) a definition of what the data represents.

Data Dimension — A conceptual categorization of data, normally intended in the context of multi-dimensionality where a dimension (e.g. time) has many members (e.g. day, month, year).

Data Element — A combination of one or more data items to form a unit of data such as a number in a date field.

Data Mining — The non-trivial extraction of implicit, previously unknown and potentially useful knowledge from data. A term that encompasses advanced techniques for discovering data patterns including neural networks, genetic algorithms, decision trees and association rules.

Data Model — A model of the data in the enterprise or in a subject-area of the enterprise which contains standard semantic and syntactic standard definitions of the data and the relationship between the different data entities. Usually expressed in an entity-relationship diagram. Real people who have built real data models within reasonable timescales are the heroes of the information revolution — without them there would be no blueprint.

Database — A structured means of storing computerized data. Database technologies include relational, network, hierarchical and object databases.

Data Mart — Sometimes used to refer to a small data warehouse. Sometimes used to refer to multiple isolated point-solution decision-support systems. Sometimes used to refer to local application-specific servers that are populated by a central warehouse (better called subsidiary data marts).

Data Validation — The process of correcting incorrect data that occurs in the legacy databases.

Data Visualisation — Software that allows the user to 'see' the data patterns in a manner that is more readily comprehended. Normally this means that the data is presented pictorially in three-dimensional visual images.

Data Warehouse — A subject-oriented, non-volatile, time-variant store of integrated corporate data (Inmon). An enterprise architecture for pan-corporate data exploitation comprising standards, policies and an infrastructure which provide the basis for all decision-support applications (Kelly).

DBMS — Data Base Management System — See Database.

Decision Support System — Any computerised system which is designed to enhance the quality of decision making. More recently, it has come to be applied to the application layer of the data warehouse architecture that uses a variety of different means to exploit the data in the data warehouse.

Derived Data — Derived data is data that has been derived from base data in the data warehouse as a result of operations to calculate or otherwise pre-process the data in order to improve the performance of the system so that the calculation did not have to be rerun every time that a query requiring that calculation was executed.

Disk — A medium for the storage of data. Magnetic disks are the most common and use a magnetic coating that contains the representations of the data that is stored. A slower disk type is the optical disk which uses a laser to read a reflective coating that contains the representations of the data.

Download — To move data from a large server (data warehouse) to a smaller server (data mart) or directly to a client PC.

EBCDIC — Enhanced Binary Code Decimal Interchange Code — the IBM mainframe standard for coding and compressing textual data.

Entity — A person, place, thing, concept or event of interest to the enterprise about which data is stored.

Entity Normalisation — A technique used for ensuring that attributes have been allocated to the correct entity type and that no additional entities are needed.

Entity Relationship Diagram — A representation of the data entities and their relationships comprehended by a computer system within any given subject-area. For example the entity 'Customer' might have a relationship with the entity 'Product' that would be described in the ER diagram. The ER diagram is normally the basis of the logical design stage for the data warehouse which precedes the physical design stage.

FDDI — Fibre Distributed Data Interchange — A high bandwidth fibre optic cable that can transmit data at the rate of 100 megabits per second. Sometimes used to link mainframe source systems to the data warehouse platform.

File Server — Normally a high specification PC on a local area network that stores the data and applications to be shared by the PC's on the LAN. Some data warehouse applications might reside on the file server.

Firewall — Most data warehouse implementations construct a security firewall between the database server containing the data and the external world through the use of passwords and other restrictions.

Flat File — This is the format that you will always want to receive the data in, but never want to read the data in. It is a format with minimal structure which is why data is normally reduced to this state while in transit between databases.

Genetic Algorithm — One of the newer artificial intelligence algorithms that is widely used to select optimum outcomes from a variety of data patterns. Like real genetics, the genetic algorithm breeds the most efficient pattern through iterative cycles. The pattern in question might be a pattern to detect fraud, or a pattern to select prospective customers, etc.

Gigabyte — Colloquially, a billion bytes. Actually, 1,173,741,824 bytes. Most data warehouses are measured in gigabytes.

GIGO — Garbage In, Garbage Out — An ancient proverb, still true.

Groupware — Software that is used to share information between knowledgeworkers that need to co-operate in doing their work. Most common groupware product is Lotus Notes.

GUI — Graphical User Interface — An intuitive interface comprising windows, icons, pull-down menus and mouse pointing device. It replaced the Character User Interface (CUI). Invented by Xerox, perfected by Apple, exploited by Microsoft.

Heuristic — A much used term in data warehousing circles, particularly with reference to the iterative nature of queries. Heuristic comes from the Greek, to estimate, and refers to the use of knowledge, wisdom and experience to solve a problem as opposed to a clinically mathematical calculation of the result.

Hierarchical Database — The pre-relational generation of database technology was largely hierarchical and consists of a hierarchy of data that is notoriously inefficient for ad hoc query purposes. A customer database might have customers divided into categories by reference to the products that they purchase. This is fine if you want to know the how many customers who purchase product X spend more than Y amount. If, however, you want to select all customers of any product with purchases greater than Z, then see Runaway Query.

Homonyms — A homonym is a term used (normally in the data modeling activity) to describe two data elements in the source systems which have the same name but which have different semantic meanings (see also Synonyms).

Hypertext — A method of storing (and presenting) text so that it can be exited, re-entered and linked to other text in the document. An ideal Help environment and widely used as an Information Catalog environment.

Index — A table that can be created in a relational database to facilitate fast access to records in those tables that are indexed. Indexed tables retard the speed at which additional data can be inserted in the tables.

Information — Data that has a context that provides a basis for action.

Information Catalog — A file that contains the metadata (the data about the data) that an end-user would be interested in accessing. It might contain data about the semantic meaning of the data, when it was last refreshed, what the source is, etc.

Information Superhighway — Term applied to the international broadband network, most notably the Internet, that offers an apparently endless source of data.

Index — A table that can be created in a relational database to facilitate fast access to records in those tables that are indexed.

I/O — Abbreviation for input/output. Some data warehouse implementations are sometimes referred to as 'I/O bound' which means that the query programmes require a large number of input/output operations which results in inefficient CPU wait time (most query-intensive systems create I/O stresses).

Iterative — The process of proceeding with tactical increments of the data warehouse.

Join — The connecting together of two relational tables of data so that a result may be obtained. For example, a query designed to identify high-value customers might join a table containing customer names with a table containing a record of purchases. Obviously, to be joined the two tables must share an index.

LAN — Local Area Network — the data communications network that links computers together. Based on different technologies and topologies, most notably Ethernet and Token Ring.

KDD — Knowledge Discovery in Data — An overall term that describes the activity of extracting knowledge from data.

Legacy Systems — Term applied to the source systems for the data warehouse data. Normally operational systems that cannot be redesigned or scrapped (like billing systems), the data warehouse is the only way to leverage advantage from the data generated by legacy systems. It should not be (but sometimes is) used pejoratively since legacy systems usually perform what they were intended to perform quite well.

Mainframe — Introduced first in 1952, the mainframe was the reliable workhorse of corporate computing and represents the most common platform for legacy systems. The most recent S/390 soluion now offers the scalability (as well as robustness) for data warehousing.

Managed Query Environment (MQE) — A term originally coined by Andyne which has now come to refer to the ability to construct a coherent environment for different types of users who wish to interrogate data.

Megabyte — Colloquially, 1 million bytes. Correctly, 1,048,576 bytes.

Metadata — Data about data, indicating the source, use, value or function of the data.

Methodology — A structured system for performing tasks, especially project management and systems design and construction tasks. Designed to manage the risk inherent in software engineering by providing tasklists that anticipate every likely contingency and to routemap every likely implementation path.

MIMD — Multiple Instruction, Multiple Data — A parallel processing architecture which allows each separate processor to execute a different query on different data. Generally, more appropriate for large volumes of different queries. See also SIMD.

MIPS — Millions of Instructions per Second — Measured by reference to the number of Assembler-language instructions executed in a second. Often used by the unwary as a measure of the horsepower of a computer. It is a bad measure for two reasons. First, CPU bottlenecks are much less common than I/O bottlenecks in data warehouse implementations. Second, not all microprocessors handle the instructions in the same way and MIPS cannot be used to compare different microprocessors. If in doubt, do a benchmark.

MPP — Massively Parallel Computing — A loosely coupled, multinode architecture based on very high speed interconnects and distributed memory.

Neural Network — This is a form of artificial intelligence that presents exciting possibilities for data warehousing. A neural net comprises a number of nodes connected together which can identify complex patterns by adjusting the strength between the nodes. The neural nets can be trained to identify particular patterns by successively demonstrating to the net examples of right and wrong answers.

Object Database — Likely to be the post-relational model of data management, the object database can manage simple objects like data as well as complex objects like video and sound.

OLAP — Online Analytical Processing — The term that is applied to multi-dimensional analysis and database products.

OLE — Object Linking and Embedding — A Microsoft standard for the updating of an object in one application by data in another. For example, a word-processing document could have graphs that could be updated by calculations on a spreadsheet package.

OLTP — Online Transaction Processing — The term that is applied to the operational systems in the enterprise that are updated online.

Power User — A skilled user of complex business-critical applications.

Query — A noun denoting a request to a database, usually by way of an SQL SELECT STATEMENT.

RAID — Array of Inexpensive Disks — This concept utilizes relatively cheap disks with redundant capacity (in case an individual disk fails) in order to store and access large volumes of data at a low cost.

Relational Database — The relational database remains the standard for large data warehouse implementations. Originated by Ted Codd in the early 1970s the relational database organizes data in tabular rows and columns.

Replication — The process of copying data from one server to another. Normally associated with the movement of data sets from the warehouse to data marts.

Repository — A location where data definitions that are relevant to current software applications are stored. Terms such as repository, dictionary, directory, catalog and encyclopedia have all begun to be used with abandon by data warehouse practitioners to describe the location where metadata is stored.

SCSI — Small Computer Systems Interface — A technical standard that is used to provide connectivity for disk drives and other peripherals to a computer.

Semantic (Error) — Semantics is the relationship between symbols and their meaning. A semantic error is a logical nonsense. For example, a query requesting the value of historical sales from prospective customers does not make sense. However, computers will execute semantically incorrect queries as long as the syntax is correct. People have even been known to make key decisions on the basis of such nonsense. Such is life!

SMP — Shared Memory Architecture — Where all of the processors in a multinode system share the same memory

Shared Nothing Architecture — Where each node in a multinode system has its own memory and I/O (Normally associated with MPP systems)

SMP — Symmetric Multi Processing Computer — A shared memory parallel processing technology which employs a single copy of the operating system. (Normally associated with SMP systems).

Snowflake Schema — This term refers to an extension of the Star Schema where additional tables radiate out from the dimensional tables. The Snowflake Schema can be used to implement a higher level of normalisation (see also Star Schema) at the expense of performance.

SIMD — Single Instruction, Multiple Data — A parallel processing architecture which allows each separate processor to be engaged on the same query. Generally, more appropriate for small numbers of complex queries (see also MIMD).

Slice and dice — This colloquial term refers to the analysis by users of multi-dimensional data where users can cut across dimensions and across subsets of dimensions.

Sparsity — A sparse matrix refers to a matrix where not every cell in the matrix contains data. A non-sparse matrix, such as a multi-dimensional database, will have all of the dimensions populated with data.

Star Schema — Refers to a physical schema which is commonly employed in data warehousing which comprises a central fact table containing numerical data about the subject which is qualified by dimensional data which is held on satellite tables (because, when illustrated, the dimensional tables radiate out from the central fact table, the schema resembles a star).

Synchronisation — The activity of ensuring that all data held on the data warehouse (or within the entire data warehouse architecture, including subsidiary data marts) is the same consistent version.

Syndicated Data — This refers to data that is available from commercial sources external to the enterprise (e.g. Standard & Poors, Dun & Bradstreet).

Synonyms — This term is used to describe two (or more) different data elements which have the same name (see also Homonyms).

Syntactic (Error) — Where the syntax is incorrectly expressed. Unlike a semantic error you will immediately know when you encounter a syntactic error — it will not compute.

SQL — Structured Query Language — The computer language used to interrogate the relational database. Originally developed by IBM, its greatest contribution to decision support computing is not its functional richness but the fact that it is one of the few real standards in the DSS environment. It should be noted, however, that most vendors offer proprietary extensions to the ANSI standard SQL.

Tape (Drive) — Data that is backed up or archived is normally written to tape cartridges which normally hold 150 megabytes of data.

Terabyte — Colloquially 1 trillion bytes. More accurately, 1,099,511,627,767 bytes.

Unix — An operating system, developed originally by AT&T, and associated with the open systems movement. Many variants of Unix now exist, but its potential to emerge as a interoperability standard for database server technology remains high.

Upload — To send data from a smaller platform (a data mart) to a larger platform (the enterprise warehouse).

Von Neumann Architecture — Now more commonly referred to as the Von Neumann bottleneck. John von Neumann laid down the first designs for computers in the 1950s and the key characteristic of the architecture is that instructions are handled sequentially. This architecture is now being replaced by parallel processing computers.

Waterfall Model — The traditional systems development model which moves sequentially from planning to design to construction to testing etc. This is not the recommended model for data warehouse development which is more suited to rapid application development techniques.

Windows — The Microsoft GUI product that provides the platform for most data warehouse applications. Windows is the most common client environment for data warehouse servers and is upgradable to Windows '95.

WORM — Write Once, Read Many — A data storage format for optical disks that are read only and not updatable. Increasingly used for data warehouse data that does not require the rapid response times offered by magnetic disks.

Index

Index compiled by Geoffrey Jones